A Woman of Quality

A Woman of Quality

by Stella K. Hershan

Crown Publishers, Inc.   New York

For Larry and Sheryl

CONTENTS

	Preface	ix
1	A VISITOR	11
2	THE WILTWYCK SCHOOL	20
3	THE REFUGEES	33
4	THE NEW YORK CABDRIVERS	48
5	FANNIE HURST	53
6	THE REPORTERS	63
7	FALA AND OTHERS	74
8	PEOPLE FROM OTHER LANDS	79
9	THE HANDICAPPED	90
10	CHILDREN AND SCHOOLS	104
11	BRANDEIS UNIVERSITY	114
12	THE JEWISH PEOPLE	123
13	THE ENTERTAINMENT WORLD	138
14	THE NEGROES	155
15	THE DEPRESSION	168
16	THE LABOR UNIONS	176
17	HER CRITICS	185
18	SOME PEOPLE WHO WORKED FOR HER	194
19	HER FRIENDS IN HYDE PARK	201
20	STRANGERS IN ALL PLACES EVERYWHERE	227
21	THE UNITED NATIONS AND HUMAN RIGHTS	247
	Epilogue	249
	Index	251

ACKNOWLEDGMENTS

I WOULD LIKE TO EXPRESS MY GRATITUDE for the unique experience this project has given me. Trying to trace only a few of Mrs. Eleanor Roosevelt's steps has taught me what it means to be a human being. It has opened the doors and the windows of the world to me. I could not have done it alone. Not without the hundreds of people who wrote to me, the many who permitted me to interview them. I could not have done it without the Human Relations Center of The New School and its two directors, Alice Rice Cook, who started the Center and Ruth Van Doren, who continues it. I could not have done it without all the teachers at the Center from whom I learned not to focus on myself but on the world around me. I could not have done it without Professor Walter James Miller, who helped me to get the story of my own visit with Eleanor Roosevelt into print. Certainly I could not have done this book without the deep interest, endless patience, and creative editing of Professor Warren E. Bower of New York University.

And finally I want to express my gratitude to the only country in the world where it is possible for someone like me to write a book like this, the United States of America.

PREFACE

THIS STARTED AS A BOOK about Eleanor Roosevelt. As it progressed, a curious thing began to take place. It was as if Mrs. Roosevelt was quietly stepping into the background. No matter how hard I tried, I could not impel her to move from this position. "I am not important," she seemed to be saying. "These other people are the ones whose courage, vitality, and striving to make the world a better place to live in should be known." And so it became a book about the lives she touched and by her touch transformed. The people who wrote and the people whom I interviewed—many of them world-famous personalities—became exciting components of the story. In numerous cases, even the way in which the interview was obtained gave an inside glimpse of the character of a movie star or political figure and illuminated the power and the magic of the name—Eleanor Roosevelt.

Chapter One

A Visitor

"WHAT PERSON IN PUBLIC LIFE do you admire most?" Dr. Daniel
I. Malamud asked his adult students in a psychology class at New
York University.

"Eleanor Roosevelt!" I called out instantly. I was not alone in
my choice. To be sure, there were three votes for Abraham
Lincoln, two for George Washington, one for Marilyn Monroe.
But Mrs. Roosevelt won by a landslide.

The next question was: "Why do you admire her?"

Everyone started talking at once. "Her courage and honesty!"
"Her humane way of thinking!" "Her interest in what is happening in every corner of the world!" "Her compassion!" "Her determination to rise above an unhappy childhood!" "Her hu-
mility!"

A cold voice cut through the tumult. "I think the woman is a
fraud," a young man stated flatly. "I don't really believe she cares
for people. All she wants is to be in the limelight."

"That isn't true!" A young Negro had jumped from his seat.
"I have met her and . . ." He faltered when he realized that all eyes
were directed at him.

"Tell us about it," Dr. Malamud said.

"I wrote Mrs. Roosevelt a letter," the student started diffidently.

"Don't ask me why, I don't know myself. But it was important for me to do it. I suppose I wanted someone to like me. She invited me to her apartment and she talked to me for half an hour. She wasn't rushed and she concentrated all her attention on me. She didn't say anything about herself; she only wanted to know about me. It was the biggest experience of my life. She gave me courage to go on."

Later, I could not get the young man's voice out of my mind. "I wanted someone to like me." What a wonderful thing it was, I kept thinking, to be able to give someone the courage to go on. What a pity it was that Mrs. Roosevelt did not know about this. The thought would not let me rest until I sat down and wrote her a letter telling her of the incident. I addressed it to *The New York Post,* in which her column, "My Day," appeared. I did not really believe that it would come to her attention. Surely it would be submerged in an avalanche of mail.

But a few days later, I found a simple white envelope in my mailbox. On the back it said—"Mrs. Franklin D. Roosevelt."

"It was heartwarming to get your letter and I want to thank you warmly for your thought in writing," she said. "Your report makes up for much time that I thought wasted."

Time wasted! Eleanor Roosevelt? I could not believe my eyes. Like the young man in my psychology class, I suddenly felt that I too had to meet her. I wrote another letter, asking for an appointment.

The next white envelope looked familiar. "I would love to meet you," wrote Mrs. Roosevelt. "But I am sorry that I cannot manage an appointment until a month from now. Would it be possible for you to come here then at 4:30 P.M.? With my good wishes . . ."

A month! I crossed the days off my calendar. When there was only one week left I became apprehensive. It occurred to me that I had been quite forward. What was I going to say to Mrs. Roosevelt? Then, just a few days before the appointment a devastating notice appeared in the newspapers. Eleanor Roosevelt had had an accident. A car had backed into her, she had fallen and had torn a ligament in her leg. She was laid up at home, and all her appointments had been cancelled.

But the following day this statement was qualified. Mrs. Roosevelt felt better. The cancellations pertained only to her outside appointments. She would keep the ones she had at her home.

I arrived near her apartment on East Seventy-fourth Street an hour before the given time. I stopped at a florist on Madison Avenue, and asked whether they knew Mrs. Roosevelt's favorite flower.

Holding a small bouquet of freesia, I finally entered a quiet brownstone house. I climbed up a carpeted staircase. An elderly maid opened the door. "I have an appointment with Mrs. Roosevelt," I managed to say.

"Come right in."

Then I stood in the small vestibule. The door to the living room was ajar. I could hear the famous voice quite distinctly. I also heard the beat of my own heart.

"Your next appointment is here, Mrs. Roosevelt," the maid said inside.

"Tell her to come in," Mrs. Roosevelt replied.

Eleanor Roosevelt was seated in a comfortable chair in the center of the large room. Her leg was bandaged and rested on a stool before her. Sitting next to her was a young woman reporter.

The lively eyes of Mrs. Roosevelt focused on my face. I walked toward her. She took my hand with both of her own. "I am sorry that I cannot get up," she said. "Do sit down for a moment over there. I shall be with you in a little while."

Friends asked me afterward how the room looked, how it was furnished. I tried to remember details but I couldn't. All I knew was that it was a large, friendly room. There were a desk, many books, many photographs. I did not recognize all the persons in the pictures. Everything seemed blurred except the woman with the bandaged leg. I always had been under the impression that Eleanor Roosevelt was tall and stately. But now she seemed fragile, a little tired. She talked to the reporter about unemployment in West Virginia.

"They have got to think in terms of attracting new industries," she said. Her voice was concerned and insistent.

"Please, Mrs. Roosevelt, take care of yourself now," the young lady said as she rose to leave. "Don't do anything against the doctor's orders." She sounded as if she were admonishing a beloved grandmother.

Mrs. Roosevelt beckoned me to come to her. "Now we shall have our chat." She patted the chair next to hers. I gave her the flowers, she took the paper off and sniffed them. "Oh, how lovely!" She glanced around helplessly.

I took the paper and the flowers; we searched for a vase. The maid came in and rescued me.

"I am so sorry about your leg," I said as I sat down.

"It is nothing," Mrs. Roosevelt said quickly. "It was entirely my fault. I am old enough to look both ways when crossing a street."

(Several years later I was told that the accident had happened in front of her hairdresser's, François, in Greenwich Village. The young man who had hit her with his station wagon was a Puerto Rican. He did not know that the injured lady was Mrs. Roosevelt. But she, aware that he would get into trouble, told him to leave quickly.)

"At least that leg forces you to rest for a while, Mrs. Roosevelt," I said.

"Not at all." She laughed as if this were a big joke. "All the people with whom I had outside appointments now come here to see me. The doorbell has been ringing all day. This morning I saw a delegation of Negroes about Civil Rights. Just now I had a group of Democrats with photographers and newspaper re- porters." She chuckled, shaking her head. Her eyes did not shift from my face for a moment. "What specifically is it you want to talk to me about? In what way can I assist you?"

I stared at her. My mouth felt very dry. "I . . . I don't really want anything," I stuttered. "I just wanted so very much to meet you."

"Oh."

Detecting a faint flicker of impatience on her face, I fought down a wave of embarrassment. "Do you mean to say that all the people who come here want something from you, Mrs. Roosevelt?"

"But of course." Eleanor Roosevelt laughed, the flicker of impatience gone, her eyes sparkling.

My embarrassment vanished. "But what do they want?" I in- quired.

"Connections mostly, jobs, sometimes money, political favors.

There is little that I can do for them in that last respect these days. Ever since Mr. Eisenhower has been President, I have to tell them to go to a Republican instead for help."

We laughed. Mrs. Roosevelt became serious again.

"I become so discouraged when I actually cannot help. Lately, every now and then I get the feeling that all those appointments are time wasted." She sighed heavily, the sparkle in her eyes had vanished.

"Your time can never be wasted, Mrs. Roosevelt!"

"Well . . ." she said thoughtfully, "the other day I heard a story that a young man who came to see me and for whom I could do absolutely nothing, still felt encouraged by just talking to me. Wait a moment," she exclaimed and her eyes that had never left my face became quite intense, "wasn't it you who told me about this?"

I could not trust my voice so I just nodded.

"Perhaps—" Mrs. Roosevelt said in that same thoughtful tone, "perhaps by just talking to those people I do help a little after all. Even without accomplishing something concrete. What do you think?"

"Mrs. Roosevelt," I said, "you do so much by just being you. Because of you, the world is a better place to live in."

Her face brightened. "How long have you lived in this country?" she asked.

"Twenty years. Unfortunately I have not managed to lose my accent," I added.

"Have you found it difficult to adjust?"

I smiled. "I don't think there is another country on earth in which it is as easy to adjust as in the United States."

"Yet," Mrs. Roosevelt said earnestly, "democracy is the most difficult type of government there is."

"Difficult?"

"Of course. Democracy imposes a great deal of responsibility on the individual." Mrs. Roosevelt's eyes were grave now. "We must learn what our institutions are and how they function. We must not be indifferent. We must not only vote but we must vote intelligently . . ."

The doorbell rang. "Oh dear," Mrs. Roosevelt said, "this must be my next appointment. It is a rabbi and without thinking I let him come late on a Friday afternoon. I must not make him wait and spoil his holiday."

I quickly got up from my chair.

"Thank you so very much for seeing me," I said. "I hope your leg will be better soon." We shook hands. "Good-bye, Mrs. Roosevelt . . ."

"How was it?" my family asked when I got home. "How did she look? What did you talk about?"

"It was very nice," I said slowly. "Mrs. Roosevelt looks more fragile in person than she does on television. One can see that she is seventy-six years old. She was very friendly, very warm. We did not talk about anything in particular."

"You seem disappointed," said my daughter.

"No!" I protested too quickly. "I am not disappointed at all."

And yet . . . I did not know what I had expected. Perhaps I had thought that meeting Mrs. Roosevelt would be an awe-inspiring event. It would be like going to a church and suddenly being overcome by the bright light of revelation. A blinding truth, a deeper meaning of life for which I had been searching. Something that would change me. But I had to admit that I was still the same, unchanged by my meeting with this kind, friendly, somewhat harassed lady.

It took me about a year before I began to understand what did happen to me through meeting Mrs. Roosevelt.

One day, for no conscious reason, I joined the League of Women Voters. At the first meeting, the chairlady explained that the purpose of the nonpartisan League was to acquaint people with politics, give them the facts about the persons running for election, explain bills to be vetoed or passed. "I wish the new members would tell us how they happened to join," the president of the group said.

When it came my turn, I suddenly recalled sitting in Mrs. Roosevelt's living room. "Democracy imposes a great deal of responsibility on the individual," I heard myself saying. "I realized this only a short time ago."

Several months later I volunteered some of my free time at a clinic for mental health.

"We need help so much," the social worker in charge told me. "We are so grateful you came. What made you do it?"

Again I remembered the room in the brownstone house on East Seventy-fourth Street. "I met a very busy lady," I explained. "She convinced me that more people should try to help others."

My visit with Mrs. Roosevelt was beginning to change me after all. Whatever it had been that she said to me, that little seed had taken root and commenced to grow. It was growing into something that made life much more meaningful to me than before.

I wrote an article about the entire experience which was published in a New York University magazine called *Pleasures in Learning*. I sent the very first copy to Mrs. Roosevelt. Her reply came at once.

"I was very moved by your article and am happy to know that you feel our talk was helpful in some way."

That year, on November 7, 1962, in New York, Eleanor Roosevelt died.

Strangers wrote to me. "I was very touched by your article on Mrs. Roosevelt," they said. "I too met Mrs. Roosevelt once." "How fortunate you are to have spoken with her."

One day I was having lunch in the cafeteria of The New School for Social Research in New York. Selma Fromkin, another student in a writing course, came to join me with her tray. "I like your writing," she said. "Did you ever have anything published?"

I gave her my Eleanor Roosevelt article which I just "happened" to have along. She read it at once.

"This reminds me of another story," she said as she returned the magazine to me. "A young woman I know lived in the same building with Mrs. Roosevelt on Washington Square. She had a baby and one day when she was invited to a wedding, her maid had to leave in an emergency. The substitute, too, phoned at the last moment that she was ill. My friend remembered that her maid knew Mrs. Roosevelt's maid and, hoping that she would be able to recommend someone, she went to the Roosevelt apartment. When she rang the bell, Mrs. Roosevelt herself opened the door. Quite flustered, the young woman explained her predicament. Mrs. Roosevelt said that she was sorry but it was her maid's day off. She must have seen how distressed the young mother was for she added, 'But if you like, I shall be happy to baby-sit for you myself.'

" 'Oh no!' the girl protested. 'I could never accept this from you, Mrs. Roosevelt!'

" 'Nonsense,' Eleanor Roosevelt said. 'I am only working on my daily column and I can do that just as well in your apartment as in my own. And you don't have to worry either,' she added with her wide smile. 'I am a very experienced baby-sitter from having stayed with my own grandchildren.' She gathered up her notes and proceeded to the young stranger's apartment.

"When the girl returned from the wedding, where she had asked everyone to guess the identity of her baby-sitter, Mrs. Roosevelt gave her a complete report. She said that she had changed the baby once and also fed it. In the kitchen on the sink stood the rinsed bottle, and the nipple was soaking in a jar with water."

For a while, Selma Fromkin and I sat silent in the noisy cafeteria of The New School.

"You are going to write a book about Mrs. Roosevelt, aren't you?" my classmate asked then. It really was more a statement than a question.

I rejected the idea at once. "At least a dozen books have been written about her," I said. "I could not possibly contribute anything that is not already known about Mrs. Roosevelt."

"You could assemble a collection of anecdotes like the one I just told you," Selma persisted.

A collection of anecdotes! The idea took hold of me. I discussed it with several professional people. Everyone agreed that the idea was intriguing. But they also agreed that it would be impossible. There would be no way to gather the material.

I wrote a letter to James Wechsler of the *New York Post,* telling him what I planned to do, and asking him how to go about it.

"If you put your request into a brief, concise form," Mr. Wechsler replied, "I will try to publish it among my 'Letters to the Editor.' "

He did, and soon the responses began to arrive. Excited strangers told me of their own experience with Mrs. Roosevelt. The "Letters to the Editor" were the answer to my problem, I realized, and I wrote to as many newspapers and magazines as I could.

In the following months, my appeal for stories, anecdotes, and memories of Mrs. Roosevelt appeared in many publications in the United States, England, Canada, and Israel. I was soon buried under an avalanche of letters. People wrote to me as though to a friend: housewives and movie producers, cabdrivers and politicians, old people who remembered the days of the Great Depression, young reporters whom Mrs. Roosevelt helped get started. I got letters from Frank Sinatra and Jack Benny, a phone call from Cary Grant. I interviewed business people in their offices and sat with Charlie Curnan, caretaker of Mrs. Roosevelt's home, in the kitchen of his house in Val-Kill. It became an everyday experience to meet strangers who, with moist eyes over a coffee cup, recalled their own special, vivid, and deeply personal memories of Mrs. Roosevelt.

Getting the material was no longer a problem; to cope with letters that kept coming had become one.

"I am going to help you," declared my daughter. She got herself a typewriter and while her two young children slept, she copied hundreds of those letters for me. My husband claimed that it had become impossible to live with me. All that I was talking about was Mrs. Roosevelt. Yet every night when he came home he would look at me inquiringly: "Any new stories?" And when I had recounted to him the new things I had learned about Mrs. Roosevelt, he would turn his head away so that I would not see the tears in his eyes.

Here, then, are the fruits of what had started out as an impossible project: the stories of people whose lives were touched by Eleanor Roosevelt.

Chapter Two

The Wiltwyck School

WHEN A PROJECT ESPECIALLY CLOSE to Mrs. Roosevelt's heart was in financial trouble, it was only natural for her to turn to her friend Harry Brandt.

Mr. Brandt is the president of the Brandt movie theater chain. After I read an article about him in a newspaper, I wrote him a letter explaining what I was doing and asking if he would talk to me about Mrs. Roosevelt. His reply came at once. "Since I am in Florida," he wrote, "I cannot make an appointment with you at the present time. However, anyone who loves Eleanor Roosevelt is someone whom I would want to help. I will be back in New York at the end of April; if you will call my secretary then, she will make an appointment for you."

In the beginning of May, I went to West Forty-second Street in New York where, above one of his movie houses, Harry Brandt has his office. A tiny elevator took me up to the second floor. I looked around the foyer. The first thing I saw was a bust of Eleanor Roosevelt above a bronze plaque that read: "To Harry Brandt for his Work on Behalf of the Eleanor Roosevelt Cancer Fund." There were more plaques and certificates of appreciation. In fact, the walls were covered with them. "To Harry Brandt for his services to—" they all started. And then I read the names of the

many distinguished and worthy causes to which Mr. Brandt had
contributed: the Salk Vaccine, the March of Dimes, the Einstein
College of Medicine, the Wiltwyck School for Boys in Apprecia-
tion to its Godfather, the National Conference of Christians and
Jews, the Red Cross, the Cerebral Palsy Fund, the Boy Scouts of
America . . .

Before I could finish reading all the many other awards, Harry
Brandt arrived. He was Florida tanned, his bright blue eyes
twinkled. "Here," he said and gave me a handful of candies,
"that's for having to wait for me."

He took me into his office. On the walls were many photographs: he and Eleanor Roosevelt smiling broadly, Franklin D.
Roosevelt in his famous cape. On the other walls were pictures of
Fiorello La Guardia, Harry S Truman, John F. Kennedy and
many more.

Mr. Brandt asked me to sit down and took his place behind
a huge desk in an enormous dark red carved chair.

"How can I help you?" he asked.

"Tell me about your friendship with Mrs. Roosevelt. How did
it begin?"

"Begin?" His face became pensive. "It began a long time ago.
I was always interested in the Democratic party. FDR once called
me and asked me to help raise money for his Warm Springs
Foundation. I was pretty good at raising funds."

"I gathered that from all the awards outside," I said.

"I like to help," he said wtih a grin. "My father did too. He
came from Vienna and he raised seven kids on seven dollars a
week. Yet he could never walk past anyone in distress without
offering to help. Anyway, after I helped FDR raise some money for
the Warm Springs Foundation, a close friendship developed between him, his wife, and me."

"Is there any particular memory you have of Mrs. Roosevelt?"
I asked.

The twinkle returned to his eyes. "I think that it was in 1942,
when Mrs. Roosevelt asked me to visit her in Hyde Park. When
I arrived she took me to her small quite old Ford car and informed me that we were going for a ride. When I asked where to,
she just laughed and declared that this was to be a surprise. She
got into the driver's seat and I took my place beside her somewhat

reluctantly, since I had driven with her before. Mrs. Roosevelt was a casual driver. I held on to my seat with both hands. We came to a tree-covered meadow, where black and white little boys came running from all directions. They laughed and shouted and waved at us. Mrs. Roosevelt waved back. With both hands! I asked her what we were to do there. But all that really concerned me at that moment was that her hands return to the steering wheel.

" 'This is Wiltwyck,' Mrs. Roosevelt explained as she slowed down. 'It is the only home these children have. Some have been found on doorsteps, others have psychotic mothers, many of their parents are not married. We have no money to keep the school running. If you don't help us to raise the necessary funds, we might have to close the school down.'

"I remembered my own youth on the lower East Side, when my first job was to fill paprika cans after school for twenty cents an afternoon. I promised that I would help the Wiltwyck School for the rest of my life. She rewarded me with one of her broad smiles and put her hands back on the wheel."

We both laughed as I rose, thanked Mr. Brandt for his time, and said good-bye.

The thought of the Wiltwyck School haunted me. I wanted to find out more about it. The office of Wiltwyck is on Park Avenue South in New York. When I went there, another bronze bust of Mrs. Roosevelt greeted me in the foyer. Mr. Sterling, who is the head of the publicity department, was sympathetic when I told him what I was doing and asked him for more information about the school.

He gave me a pamphlet to read:

> In 1936, a shaking little ten-year-old stood before the Court, charged with habitual delinquency. "There is nothing to do, Your Honor," the probation officer told the judge, "until he is twelve years old. Then he can be sent to the State Training School." Judge Justine Wise Polier, daughter of Rabbi Stephen S. Wise, collected twenty such cases and presented them to the Mayor of the City of New York. Thus started an experimental summer camp on the Wiltwyck estate for delinquent and pre-delinquent Negro boys. By fall those engaged in this program could not tolerate the thought of closing its doors to children who had responded so quickly to a healthy, happy summer of

activity and friendly guidance. The Altman Foundation provided a heating plant and Wiltwyck began operation as an all-year school for delinquent children. In 1939, the interest of Marshall Field was enlisted. He provided funds for a gymnasium, the remodeling of the school building, and the recruitment of the staff needed to provide case-work services and psychiatric consultation. In 1942 the school was in financial difficulties and could not continue its program. The property was transferred to a group of interested persons who undertook to carry on the work. Wiltwyck School was incorporated and the charter stated its objectives: "To administer for neglected and abandoned children without discrimination to race and color, a constructive program of moral and spiritual enlightenment, character development, correction of behavior problems, education for good citizenship, and to conduct a home for such children." Reorganized, Wiltwyck School was administered by an interracial and non-sectarian Board of Directors. This reorganization was conducted under the leadership of Mrs. Eleanor Roosevelt. Wiltwyck remained close to Mrs. Roosevelt's heart from the first Board service to the last weeks of her life.

I asked Mr. Sterling whether it would be possible to contact some of the former boys. They might have some personal memories of Mrs. Roosevelt.

He shook his head regretfully. This was against the regulations. Then he slapped his forehead. "I have an idea for you," he exclaimed. "Call Dr. Ernst Papanek. He was director of the school from 1949 until 1958. He will be able to tell you much more than I can."

The next morning I called Dr. Papanek. He was most interested in my project and we made an appointment to meet in his office at Queens College, where he is Professor of Education. It was the first of many meetings and the beginning of a long friendship.

Dr. Ernst Papanek studied at the Medical School and Faculty of Philosophy of the University of Vienna. He held various posts with the Child Welfare Department there and later became a prominent member of the City Council, deeply involved in the educational reform work done in Austria. In 1934, due to the political turmoil in Europe, he had to leave his native country abruptly. From 1938 on, Dr. Papanek directed homes in France for displaced refugee children smuggled out of Germany by l'Organisation de Santé, a private Jewish group.

Ernst Papanek still remembers Emil, a boy of about thirteen, whom he found early one morning in front of the door of the main home, about ten miles north of Paris. The child somehow had got there from his native Saarbrücken, which had fallen under Nazi rule. When they began their assaults upon the Jewish population, the storm troopers burst into Emil's home one day and dragged his father off to a concentration camp. A few weeks later they returned to deliver to his mother an urn containing the ashes of his father. The mother threw herself upon the men, screaming that they were fiends and murderers. So the storm troopers carried her off to a concentration camp also. Emil was warned by the rabbi of Saarbrücken that he had better get out of town before the troopers came back for him.

Through Dr. Papanek and other people who shared his dedication, thousands of prospective victims like Emil were saved from Nazi concentration camps and certain extermination. When France fell, Ernst Papanek himself was in danger of losing his life. At first he refused to leave his children. The American visa which had been obtained for him became invalid while he kept postponing his departure.

His friends pleaded with him to save himself. "How can I leave sixteen hundred children?" he asked. "They have no one but me." His friends in the underground said that he would not be able to do anything for the children if the Nazis killed him. But once he was in America he could send for them. Ernst Papanek put the question before the children themselves. "Go!" they said. "Go! It's our only chance."

And so, Ernst Papanek gave in. One night he was led through the woods and over the border.

"Some of the children I was able to save," Dr. Papanek told me. "Many of them perished. Those I feel I have deserted." His child-like and trusting eyes spilled over.

In the United States, Ernst Papanek first worked with the Children's Aid Society and became director of the Child and Youth Project Department of the Unitarian Service Committee. Later he was Executive Director of the American Youth for World

Youth, a project involving more than three thousand schools in America, with millions of students participating in the creation of international understanding, goodwill, and providing help to children in war-torn countries. The chairman of that board was the prominent educator Dr. William H. Kilpatrick.

After his work with the American Youth for World Youth, Ernst Papanek became Director of the Brooklyn Training School for girls. Finally, in 1949, he came to Wiltwyck; the acquaintanceship between Dr. Papanek and Mrs. Roosevelt grew into friendship.

Wiltwyck was the converted servants' quarters of an old estate near Hyde Park. The doors had heavy locks, the dormitories had unconcealed toilets, the windows were barred. It housed about one hundred rejected, disturbed, delinquent, and neglected boys from eight to twelve years old. One afternoon the children were told to assemble in the auditorium to meet their new director. The counselors usually had a lot of trouble getting everybody to the auditorium for anything other than a movie.

"But that day we all were curious," Claude Brown, a former Wiltwyck boy said in his book, *Manchild in the Promised Land.**
"We wanted to know what this cat looked like, if he was big or small, colored or white, young or old, mean like the outgoing director who never smiled and was quick to take off his belt and beat your ass. Most of us still were looking for the new cat when he started talking and said, 'I am Ernst Papanek.' He wasn't tall or short, and he was real straight, with a bald head and a kindly face. He didn't look real bold, but he seemed to have a whole lot of confidence, as if he knew he could handle Wiltwyck. He was slick, real slick. Papanek was so slick that he didn't even have to be mean."

The first thing the boys were told by Dr. Papanek was that, from now on, no one would ever be hit. Then he removed the bars from the windows, unlocked the doors and built enclosures around the toilets. "You must understand that these children had been punished enough before they came to Wiltwyck," Dr. Papanek told me earnestly. "David, for instance, was nine when he was sent to us for pushing a little girl of five from a tenement roof. We found out that his mother kept him tied to a bedpost all day while she was out working. If he had soiled himself by the time she got home, she whipped him. The Judge sent Nate to us because he had set fire to the tenement in which he lived. He told us that his home was a single room which he shared with his mother. She worked there as a prostitute. One of the men gave her a silk scarf and Nate tried to burn it in the closet. Jake arrived with his face completely scarred. The glassful of lye which his father wanted to throw at his mother landed on him when he tried to defend her. Do you think these children need more punishment?"

"No," I said, "I suppose not. But how can you teach a child what is right without punishment?"

"We tried to reeducate them," he said. "For instance, when Danny came to Wiltwyck he was ten. The first day he broke several windows. He was brought to me and I told him that he would have to pay for them. The boy shouted that he was told there was no punishment at Wiltwyck. I said that this was true but wouldn't he agree that the windows had to be replaced? He admitted that this was so. Wasn't it also true then, I asked him, that the person who broke the windows was the one who had to pay for them? This logic seemed to penetrate. But after a few moments of silence he argued that he had no money. I explained that at Wiltwyck the boys received an allowance of one dollar a month. We would deduct one fourth of this dollar until the windows were paid for. The amount did not mean anything to Danny and so we sat down and figured out together how many bottles of Coca-Cola this amount would buy. Slowly our boys began to realize that bad deeds always brought on bad consequences. Coca-Cola bottles became a wonderful tool to learn almost anything. It is amazing how quickly a child will learn almost anything if he has a reason for it.

"Mrs. Roosevelt was deeply interested in the treatment of our boys," said Dr. Papanek. "Just because she, the First Lady, was there so much, everyone felt a little worthier." To Eleanor Roosevelt, as she said in her autobiography, *duty* was the motivating force of her life. She kept reminding Dr. Papanek that the boys first of all had to learn a sense of responsibility. Dr. Papanek, however, felt that they could not learn this before they realized the meaning of love. "They must come to realize that we at Wiltwyck are their friends and want to help them," he would say. "Punishing only teaches a child how to punish; scolding only teaches him how to scold. But by showing him that we understand him, we teach him understanding; by cooperating, we teach him how to cooperate."

Eleanor Roosevelt did not argue with this concept. What she wanted the boys to learn was a sense of responsibility based on love and respect for the other person.

It was usually in June that Mrs. Roosevelt invited the entire Wiltwyck School for a picnic to Hyde Park.

"One hundred children, eight to fourteen, accompanied by a host of staff members would descend upon the estate at eleven o'clock in the morning," reported Herb Rosen who used to be on the Wiltwyck staff. "The kids were dressed in clean sport clothes and were primed for days in advance to behave themselves. The veterans among the children would describe to the neophytes how mountains of food, hot dogs, and ice cream would be laid out on long tables for them to devour.

"Mrs. Roosevelt would be waiting for us at the entrance to the estate, smiling broadly," Herb Rosen remembered. "There was something about her relaxed presence and accepting nature that set the tone of the day. Some of the children referred to her as 'Mrs. Rosebell.' Some had a vague idea that she had something to do with the White House. Once she was asked: 'Mrs. Rosebell, did you know George Washington and Abraham Lincoln?'"

On the lawn was a huge fireplace. Mrs. Roosevelt herself, in a plain white dress, with her gray hair drooping over her perspiring face, was broiling the hot dogs, the yellow ears of corn and buttering the hundreds of rolls before placing them on the grill. Dr. Papanek pleaded with her not to work so much and assured her that the boys would eat the rolls even without butter. Mrs. Roosevelt gave him an indignant look. "When the King and Queen of England had hot dogs here we buttered the rolls. Why should we do less for the boys from Wiltwyck?"

The importance of teaching the boys a sense of responsibility must have been on her mind, considering the way she called the children together when the food was ready.

"I wish you a very good appetite, boys," she would say cheerfully. "Enjoy yourselves and eat as much as you want. But I would like you to know that I have two hundred forks and two hundred knives and I want all of them back after you have eaten!"

From someone else these boys might have taken the warning

as an insult. But Eleanor Roosevelt's voice was so kind and her face so good-natured that not for a moment did the children seem to take offense. Perhaps they realized that it would have been easy for Mrs. Roosevelt to serve them with plastic forks and knives and that she wanted rather to honor them with her trust.

"Sure," the boys replied in chorus as they grinned, "sure, Roosevelt"—some of them expressed their feeling of ease by leaving out the Mrs.—"we'll see to it that you get every one of them back!" They would line up at the tables cafeteria style and have their plates personally stacked by Mrs. Roosevelt. And instead of forks and knives they stuffed ears of corn dripping with butter into their pants pockets for the ride home.

After the boys had eaten their ice cream, Mrs. Roosevelt again called them together. Holding several volumes of Rudyard Kipling which were almost falling apart, she placed herself on a tree trunk. "Which will it be, boys?" she asked. " 'Rikki-Tikki-Tavi,' 'How the Elephant Got His Trunk,' or 'The Butterfly That Stamped'?"

In response to a letter I had written to her, asking her for memories about Mrs. Roosevelt, Margaret Mead replied that she had been present once at one of the picnics for the Wiltwyck boys. She remembered Mrs. Roosevelt reading Kipling to them. "I thought that for once Mrs. Roosevelt had made a mistake," wrote Dr. Mead. "These boys seemed too old for those stories. But they were not restless and they listened raptly. I later found out that they were much younger than their faces looked and realized this was because of the terrible deprivations they had suffered until they came to Wiltwyck."

Mrs. Roosevelt herself reported in one of her columns, "My Day," that once, instead of reading the Kipling stories to the boys, she had a magician perform for the Wiltwyck children. Although the children greatly enjoyed and took part in all the tricks, some of them came up to Mrs. Roosevelt and complained that they missed "the story." So she promised them that she would come over to the school later that month, read them the Kipling story, and provide ice cream and cake for a second party.

Once after a picnic the grounds were covered with half-eaten rolls, hot dogs, bare ears of corn, and crushed paper cups. Dr. Papanek told the children to clean it all up.

They were just starting to do so when Mrs. Roosevelt came

rushing up to Dr. Papanek and protested, "No, no! You must not let them do this!"

"But why not?" Dr. Papanek asked puzzled. "You are the one who always insists that the boys must learn a sense of responsibility. They made this mess and it is only right that they clean it up again."

"But you know that my grandchildren were the hosts for your boys," Mrs. Roosevelt explained. "They must learn responsibility too. I promised I would pay each one twenty-five cents for cleaning up. If they have no work left, I could not possibly give them the money and they would be so disappointed!"

One of the boys once came up to Mrs. Roosevelt and asked her, "Do you remember me?"

"Yes," she said, "of course. You were here at the picnic last year."

"That's not what I meant," the boy said as he clutched her hand and anxiously looked at her face. "Do you remember my name?"

Mrs. Roosevelt shook her head. "I am getting old," she explained, "and I forget names. Sometimes even those of my best friends. You must forgive me."

"Well, my name is John Owen," the boy said, then ran away. A few moments later he came back. "Now do you remember my name, Mrs. Roosevelt?"

"Of course I do," she said and smiled. "You are John Owen."

He nodded and ran away again.

Half an hour later he returned a third time.

"You still know my name?"

"John Owen," Mrs. Roosevelt said promptly.

"Okay," he said and brightened. "Now you have repeated it three times. I guess from now on you'll know who I am."

This incident impressed Mrs. Roosevelt deeply. She often told it to friends and repeated it in her book *You Learn by Living.* "There is a desperate need for identification and recognition as an individual all through life to people who, because of circumstances or some limitations in themselves, have not learned to feel they have developed as individuals or have been so accepted," she said.

Before these boys came to Wiltwyck, stealing had been a way of life for them. Mrs. Roosevelt and their visits to Hyde Park had awakened their sense of honor. Because *she* was interested in them, the children felt they couldn't be so bad. Because *she* was interested in them, they all had to be a little better. After one of the trips to Hyde Park, it was brought to Dr. Papanek's attention that one of the boys had stolen a silver dollar. The boy was not punished but he had to send the silver dollar back to Mrs. Roosevelt with an accompanying letter of apology. She replied at once, saying that she was so glad to have it back for it belonged to one of her sons who had gotten it from his father for a good report card.

One of the most famous of the former Wiltwyck boys is Floyd Patterson, one-time heavyweight champion of the world. Floyd Patterson was sent to Wiltwyck and Dr. Ernst Papanek recognized a spark of gentleness and decency in the husky young boy. He channeled Floyd's explosive energy into a more socially acceptable outlet. Boxing, however, was not the career Dr. Papanek had imagined for him. "I really felt that he shouldn't be a boxer," Dr. Papanek said recently, "because he is a very gentle man. When he began his career I was against it, but he managed to find a way to box without being violent or a killer."

It was reported that during an important fight in Chicago, when Floyd was on his way to the top, his opponent lost his mouthpiece. According to the rules of boxing, the fight is continued anyway. But Floyd found his opponent's mouthpiece and gave it to him. The fight started again and in a few seconds Floyd knocked his opponent out.

"When I returned from the Olympics in 1952," Floyd Patterson said in a newspaper interview in 1962, "Dr. Papanek said to me, 'If you want it forgotten that you were ever at Wiltwyck, it is forgotten.' I made it clear to him that I never wanted to forget and that I wanted to help Wiltwyck because it had helped me. I can't withhold my love and respect for the fine people there who helped to straighten me out. They taught me to read and to write, they gave me a sense of belonging. I learned how to make friends there, how to live with myself and others. Once I even trained at Wiltwyck for a fight. . .

"For a boy like me, a Negro, for whom there had been a growing awareness of what a difference in color meant, the interracial activities, whites being treated the same as the colored with no preference at all, this was a tremendous awakening. All religions were represented among the boys, but none was treated better or worse than any of the others. That's what helped to bring me out of the shell in which I had been living and what helped me to make friends finally."

Floyd Patterson often visits Wiltwyck and supports it in many ways. The boys once asked him whether he had ever lost a fight. Floyd Patterson replied that it is important to keep your head up in defeat; it's easy to have your head up in victory. Floyd Patterson has donated the money for a town house which is named after him. It provides a rehabilitation center and readjustment home for the boys. "Floyd is a tremendous person," Dr. Papanek said to me, "even though he can crush both of my hands in one of his own." Among the flood of telegrams from well-wishers that come to Floyd Patterson's dressing room before a fight, there is always one from his friend Ernst Papanek. Mrs. Roosevelt, too, developed a warm friendship with Floyd Patterson and she often was photographed with him. This friendship contributed a great deal to Floyd Patterson's gentle and kind personality, rather rare among boxers. From Mrs. Roosevelt he had also learned to give and help others who needed him.

On Mrs. Roosevelt's seventieth birthday, Dr. Papanek and some of his boys paid her a surprise visit. They serenaded her with her favorite song "Beautiful Dreamer" and brought her presents which every single one of the Wiltwyck boys had made for her.

That night at the official dinner given for her at the Waldorf-Astoria Hotel in New York, Mrs. Roosevelt announced that she had just received one hundred pot holders and anyone who needed some should just ask for them. Later, when several people did come up to the dais for the pot holders, Eleanor Roosevelt laughed and said that she had changed her mind. These boys, after all, had made them for *her*, and she would rather keep them herself.

It was fortunate that she *had* changed her mind. For a moment after her announcement, four of Dr. Papanek's boys marched in, carrying an enormous birthday card which all the boys at Wiltwyck had helped to make and had signed.

Eleanor Roosevelt's trust and devotion to the Wiltwyck School for Boys proved justified in the years that followed. Only twenty percent of the "Alumni" got into further trouble with the law. The school made a deep impression on its students, and many returned for visits long after they had "graduated." Every Christmas, forty-five boys who were receiving Wiltwyck aftercare, were invited to return for the Christmas dinners. To everyone's surprise, twenty-five of the eligible boys accepted the invitation—something unheard of in the history of correctional institutions. Even those who left with poor prospects sometimes turned out extremely well.

One boy was picked up as a narcotic user almost immediately after he left and soon afterward was shot during an attempted burglary. But he kept coming back in search of help and even went to Dr. Papanek's New York apartment several times to talk about his problems. For Dr. Ernst Papanek and his wife Helene, a noted psychiatrist, no hour of the day or night is inconvenient when someone in trouble is asking for help. At last this boy decided that what he needed was an education. While working as an elevator operator, then as a messenger for a jeweler who hired him in spite of his record, he went through night school and worked his way through high school. Then he went on to college and became a prelaw student. In spite of his work and his studies, this young man somehow found the time and the drive to write a book. Its title was *Manchild in the Promised Land*. It became a national bestseller.

Its author, Claude Brown, dedicated his book "To the Late ELEANOR ROOSEVELT, who founded the Wiltwyck School for boys. And to the Wiltwyck School, which still is finding Claude Browns." *

---

* Claude Brown, *Manchild in the Promised Land*. New York: The Macmillan Company, 1965.

Chapter Three

The Refugees

IT WAS ON A MONDAY, January 30, 1933, that the man with the Charlie Chaplin moustache, who in his youth had been an out-and-out tramp in Vienna, was pronounced Chancellor of the German Reich. In that same year on March 4, a new First Lady, Mrs. Franklin D. Roosevelt, moved into the White House in Washington.

While President Roosevelt grappled with the gigantic task of pulling the United States out of the Depression, the world became aware almost at once that the person to approach when it concerned help for the downtrodden was his wife.

In Germany, Hitler began to persecute the Jews, and in Washington Mrs. Roosevelt began to help the first trickle of refugees. As the years went on, that trickle became a stream. Country after country fell under the Nazi boot and the bigger the task of helping grew, the more energetic became America's First Lady. She never seemed too busy to pay attention to each individual who appealed to her for assistance.

I myself found a haven in the United States in 1939, one year after Hitler and his storm troopers invaded Austria, my native country. Therefore, I was especially interested in the stories of emigrants who were helped to come to America by Eleanor

Roosevelt. My appeal for personal memories appeared in the German-language weekly paper *Aufbau (Reconstruction)*, and the letters which began to arrive told of men, women, and children who had been trapped in the Nazi holocaust and to whom every door of escape seemed irrevocably closed.

At 6 A.M. on March 5, 1939, German troops marched into Czechoslovakia. The Jews and all other people who were threatened by the invasion desperately tried to flee the country.

"My parents were alone in Prague at that time," wrote Mr. Robert Eisner. "My mother was eighty and my father ninety years old. I, my two brothers, and our families had managed to get to the United States. It took us two years to obtain affidavits and passage money for our parents. It was useless. No United States consulate in Central Europe was issuing visas . . ."

The reason for this was that on May 27, 1941, President Roosevelt declared a national emergency. After German U-boats had sunk or attacked a number of American ships, cumulative evidence showed that the German consuls were the key men in Nazi espionage and propaganda; the State Department also demanded that all German consulates in the United States be closed. As a result, American consuls were also ordered out of Germany, thus ending all chances for Jews in Germany, Austria, and Czechoslovakia to come to the United States. The only possibility was to obtain entry permits to countries like Cuba, which still had consular representation in German-held territory, and try for admission to the United States from there.

In Prague, Mrs. Eisner declared, "So we'll go to Cuba!"

But it was not to be as simple as that. The immigration visa for Cuba could only be obtained in Vienna. Such a small matter did not deter this woman of eighty. Somehow or other the aged couple managed to travel on crowded trains to Austria, a journey that took several days and nights. Since the Cuban visa had been prepared for them through their sons in the United States, they had no difficulty getting it. However, in order to board a ship in Bilbao, Mr. and Mrs. Eisner needed a transit visa through Spain. This could be obtained only in Berlin. And so they traveled from Vienna to Berlin. During this journey, their age and determination alone saved them from imprisonment and eventual extermination in a death camp. They got their visas to go through Spain.

In those years, as a refugee from any German-occupied country, one could only obtain a visa to another country if one had one visa; the authorities had to be certain that these people without a homeland would not remain indefinitely in their country. After Berlin, the Eisners had to return to Prague for their exit permit which, miraculously, was granted by the Gestapo. At long last, Mr. and Mrs. Eisner happily left the country where they had been born almost a century before.

They arrived in Havana and went immediately to the United States consulate. Their papers, the Eisners were told, were in order. But after Pearl Harbor, there were new regulations. As of July 1, 1941, a few days before Mr. and Mrs. Eisner's arrival in Cuba, in order to set up a "sieve of screen, excluding persons who might be sent into the United States in the guise of refugees," a new bill had been signed in Washington. It designated the Visa Division of the State Department as the sole agency authorized to issue visas. The papers of Mr. and Mrs. Eisner had to be sent to Washington for thorough investigation.

"How long will this take?" Mrs. Eisner asked anxiously.

The official shrugged. "A week perhaps. It could be several months, might even take a year. We just don't know."

On hearing this news, the ninety-year-old Mr. Eisner collapsed. Somehow his wife got him back to the small room they had rented. A week passed, a month, two months. There were no visas for anyone Mrs. Eisner was told at her weekly trips to the consulate. The line of applicants grew longer and longer.

Finally, without telling her husband, Mrs. Eisner sat down to write a letter.

"Dear Mrs. Roosevelt," she wrote, "as one grandmother to another, I am asking your help. Here we sit idle, a short distance away from our six grandchildren. Our days are numbered and every hour counts. My husband is ninety, and I am eighty years old. What possible danger can we be to the United States? Why not let us spend our few remaining years, perhaps only months, with our family?"

Five days later, a telegram arrived from the United States Embassy in Havana. It said: "Will you please call us for an appointment at this office? Approval of your entry has been received from the Department of State."

The receptionist greeted Mr. and Mrs. Eisner with a warm smile, the secretary winked, the doctor laughed and the vice consul stood up. "As a father to a grandmother," he said as he shook hands, "I hope I'll be talking to you one day as a grandfather to a great-grandmother. Here is your visa to America."

"My parents never forgot what Mrs. Roosevelt had done for them," wrote the younger Mr. Eisner. "No prayer was said without including her name. Her photograph dominated their living room in Forest Hills, New York. And when my mother's eighty-fifth birthday came around and I asked her what she would like to have, she said she had only one wish: to meet Mrs. Roosevelt face to face and to have the opportunity to say thank you to her."

Another letter was written to Mrs. Roosevelt, this time by the son who explained the entire situation.

"Mrs. Roosevelt will be delighted to meet your parents at any time at all," Mrs. Roosevelt's secretary replied instantly. "Considering their age she would like to make this meeting as easy as possible for them and has three suggestions. Mrs. Roosevelt will be giving a lecture at Forest Hills High School which is in their neighborhood, and she would be happy to talk with them there, either before or after the lecture. If this should be too strenuous for them she would be glad to visit them in their apartment that evening. Or, if they prefer, she would be delighted to have them for tea in her own apartment on Washington Square the following Saturday afternoon."

Mrs. Eisner was beside herself with excitement. She would not dream of putting Mrs. Roosevelt to so much trouble as to visit *them* in Forest Hills. "We are not that old," she declared. "Of course we will visit Mrs. Roosevelt in *her* apartment on Washington Square!"

"My mother prepared a long speech to express her gratitude," Mr. Robert Eisner wrote. "But when Mrs. Roosevelt herself opened the door to her apartment, held out her hand and said, 'So here you are at last, Mr. and Mrs. Eisner, nice to see you! Come right in . . .' my mother just sat down and cried. It was the first and only time in all of my life that I saw her speechless!"

Mrs. Miriam X too came from Cuba during those terrible years and she also was helped by Mrs. Roosevelt to remain in the

United States. "I was born in Poland," Miriam told me over the telephone, "and I spent three years of my childhood in a Displaced Persons Camp. When I was nine years old I went to join my father in Cuba and became a Cuban citizen. Later, when I grew up, I met an American fellow who became my husband. With him I went to the United States. It was some time later, after our son had been born that, because of some new immigration laws that had come into effect, the U.S. Government wanted to deport me to Cuba. We appealed to Congressmen and Senators, it all was to no avail. While this was going on I had to report twice a week to Ellis Island. Finally, as a last resort, we wrote a letter to Mrs. Roosevelt. I never thought it actually would get her attention. 'Such a big lady,' I said, 'the President's wife! Why should she bother about me?'

"Very shortly after we had sent the letter, we received some communication from the Immigration Department in Washington, and I was permitted to stay. We have been married for fifteen years now and have two wonderful children who, thanks to Mrs. Roosevelt, had the good fortune to grow up in America."

Mrs. Julia Rosenstein was a young girl when she fled Nazi-occupied Vienna in 1938. On a domestic permit she went to England, where she stayed for two years. In March 1940, her brother-in-law made it possible for her to join him and her sister in the United States. But Julia's mother was still in Vienna. Her brother-in-law now sent the mother the necessary affidavits and the boat tickets to come to America. However, the mother was born in Czechoslovakia and she cabled her family in the United States that the Czech quota was filled, no more visas could be issued and they should cancel her reservation on the boat.

"Thank God, we did not do that," Julia Rosenstein wrote. She was deeply concerned and depressed about her mother's delayed departure and she tried to think of some way to remedy that unhappy situation. "Mrs. Eleanor Roosevelt was my ideal," Julia Rosenstein said, and so, on Mother's Day 1941, she sat down and wrote a letter to the White House. "I was so desperate," she said, "that I didn't even reread the letter before mailing it. A week later I received a letter from the State Department telling me that Mrs. Roosevelt had turned my letter over to them and that they would check into the case. If there was nothing against the Constitution, my mother would get the visa. Shortly afterward we received another cable from my mother. She was on the boat, on her way to the United States.

"My mother loved to tell the story of how she received a telegram from the American Consulate, telling her that the Consul wanted to talk to her, and how he received her personally to tell her that there still was one place open and available for her. She was so proud of this and thought it was all her personality. We never had the heart to disillusion her. She later died of cancer.

"Shortly before Mrs. Roosevelt's death, in September 1962, I was fortunate enough to meet and talk with her personally. It was at the Assembly of The United Nations Association in the Waldorf-Astoria Hotel. Mrs. Roosevelt was chairman of the board. In the crowded elevator, Eleanor Roosevelt was squeezed in the rear. No one noticed her." Julia Rosenstein thought that this was because no one could possibly believe that Mrs. Roosevelt could be there, mixed with all the crowd. When she recognized Mrs. Roosevelt and looked at her, Eleanor Roosevelt smiled.

"As we were getting out of the elevator," said Julia Rosenstein, "I finally had the opportunity to thank Mrs. Roosevelt in person for her great kindness in helping my mother so many years before. I still and always will remember her friendly and kind words in response," Julia Rosenstein said. When she later heard that Mrs. Roosevelt was very ill in the hospital, she sent her flowers and, in response, received a note from Mrs. Roosevelt saying, "My best wishes to you."

Every year at Christmas, Julia Rosenstein sells UNICEF cards and her ten percent discount she turns over to the Eleanor Roosevelt Foundation.

"My name is Simone," said a young woman who called me on the telephone. "I would like to tell you what Eleanor Roosevelt did for me. But it would take too long over the telephone. Couldn't we meet someplace?"

We made a date in the cafeteria of The New School. Somehow we recognized each other at once. Simone was a pretty, dark-haired woman about forty; she spoke with an accent.

"I was born in Poland and grew up in Belgium," she told me as we sat down at one of the tables. "I was fifteen when, on May tenth, 1940, German bombs began to fall on our country. Belgium was neutral and most people were convinced that the Nazi army would not succeed in occupying our country. But my father was very pessimistic about the situation. Especially so, because we were Jewish. He abruptly decided that we were to leave the country. We hastily packed some clothes and drove out of Belgium with our car."

While Simone and her parents were on the road, a great Anglo-French army rushed to the main Belgian defense line east of Brussels. On May 15, 1940, French Premier Reynaud called Winston Churchill to tell him, "We are defeated."

In the meantime, Simone and her family had safely arrived in France. But on June 14, 1940, the swastika was hoisted on the Eiffel Tower. Simone's father had driven with his family out of France the day before. An endless odyssey then began for them. Their next stop was Spain. Simone's father was financially comfortable but even his money could not buy him permission from the Spanish government to remain there longer than a few days. So they went on to Portugal. It was the same story there. Their visa to remain in the country was running out and there was no other country to run to. Stretching before them was the vastness of the Atlantic Ocean. Across this ocean, of course, there was a country—America. But the borders of that country were closed to Simone because her father had been born in Poland. The American quota for Polish and Russian immigrants had been exhausted long before.

Lisbon was teeming with European refugees. The most prominent among them were the Duke and Duchess of Windsor who, it was rumored, were in danger of being kidnapped by the Germans. People endlessly congregated in the hotels and cafés of Lisbon, debating what to do. It began to seem that the only solution left was for everyone of the refugees to drown himself in the Atlantic Ocean. But Simone's father decided against this final solution. About one hundred Jewish families attempted to hire a steamship, which would take them out of the country. Even though the amount of money these people were offering to pay was considerable, they were turned down by captain after captain. At long last they found *The Quanza*, a 16,000-ton boat of the Compania Portuguesa de Navigacion whose regular run was to the African Colonies.

Some of the individuals had obtained Mexican visas in Perpignan from an honorary Mexican Consul who was a French citizen. Others had gotten visas through the Mexican Consulate in Brussels on the strength of a letter from the Mexican government that stated that consideration was being given to their applications. Some people had visas for America. But the majority of the passengers had obtained their Mexican visas illegally.

When the refugees finally boarded *The Quanza,* they found some uncongenial companions—swarms of cockroaches. They were everywhere: in the bunks, in the food, soon in the clothes of the immigrants. It did not matter. At least they were not Hitler's storm troopers.

The Quanza steamed into New York harbor to let the few fortunate people in possession of American visas debark. Immigration officials swiftly came aboard. The people without visas pleaded with them to let them come ashore too. "Impossible," said the officials. "No one can step onto American soil without the proper papers." Through an interpreter, the fathers of the families pleaded and begged. They explained that they had relatives in various cities of the United States, money in American banks. "Have mercy," they implored. The officers shook their heads. There was nothing within their power to do. They had no authority whatsoever. In order for these people to enter the United States without a visa, Congress would have to pass an act. The President would have to propose it. Even if he did, with the world situation what it was, he almost certainly would be turned down. There was nothing that could be done. Nothing

And so, with about eighty families left, *The Quanza* sailed on to Veracruz. The Mexican authorities came aboard. They took one look at those visas that had been obtained in Lisbon illegally and declared them worthless scraps of paper. The ship was ordered to return to Europe. Complete despair overwhelmed the passengers. Europe to them was a German concentration camp.

On the return trip, with its holds empty, the captain decided to load up in Norfolk, Virginia, with coal, which was practically nonexistent in Portugal.

While *The Quanza* was docked there, officials and lawyers from various Jewish organizations came aboard. They wired the State Department and tried to work through lawyers. Relatives of the passengers, settled in the United States, declared themselves willing to issue guarantees for them. Secretary of State Cordell Hull said he had to obey the immigration laws of his country. There was nothing that could be done. Nothing. Finally, the mothers on the ship decided to make a last attempt for survival, at least for their children. Through lawyers of Jewish organizations they appealed to Mrs. Eleanor Roosevelt in Washington for help. They told her that they had resigned themselves to their fate of having to return to Germany, where they were certain to die. But, they pleaded, don't make us take our children with us. They have relatives in the United States, bank accounts in American banks. They will not be a burden to the country. Mrs. Roosevelt's reply arrived swiftly. "We Americans do not believe in separating families," she cabled. "I could not possibly do what you are asking. But please have a little patience. I am trying to work something out to help you."

Somehow, the departure of *The Quanza* was delayed. A few days later, the passengers were permitted to disembark on American soil. They had been invited as political refugees under the auspices of Mrs. Roosevelt.

"Mrs. Roosevelt saved my life in September 1940," Simone said to me as she ended her story.

Dr. Sophia M. Robison is an eminent sociologist who was on the Technical Fact-finding Staff of the Mid-Century White House Conference during the early forties.

"As more and more refugees were arriving in the United States during those years," she told me, "Mrs. Roosevelt found herself bombarded with hundreds of letters of complaint by American citizens.

"People wrote that 'those refugees constitute a threat to American security. . . . Our country, still in the throes of a great depression, is now immersed in a war overseas,' they said. 'As though this were not enough, the foreigners take away jobs from Americans.'"

"After December seventh, the day of Japan's attack on Pearl Harbor, the letters increased in quantity to such an extent," Dr.

Robison remembered, "that Mrs. Roosevelt asked Clarence E. Pickett of the American Friends Service Committee to head the Committee for Selected Social Studies to investigate the validity of the accusations. We worked under the auspices of a technical volunteer advisory committee and I compiled our findings."

Dr. Robison gave me the book.* Mrs. Roosevelt had written this Preface:

The study on refugees was undertaken by the Committee for Selected Social Studies at my request, in the hope that the findings would serve to answer the countless inquiries that were made of me concerning the refugee, and whether he did or did not constitute the threat to American security—economic and other—that many feared him to be.

It was my desire to secure completely unbiased sponsorship. The American Friends Service Committee was asked to sponsor the study, and it was arranged that the Committee would work under the auspices of Columbia University.

The study in New York showed a considerable group who had transplanted skills to America and, instead of displacing Americans, were employing them in new trades. There, also, proved to be groups who were employed in necessary jobs in the service industries but at very nominal wages, so that family incomes were no larger than those of their American neighbors, although there were sometimes as many as three or four wage earners in the family.

Among the refugee group there was no evidence of any lackadaisical attitude. They were found willing to do anything that needed to be done, and to accept the situation in which they found themselves. They have, in a sense, been so long in the presence of a war situation that their attitude is one that might often serve as an example for our own conduct now that we are ourselves at war.

I hope that this study will be widely read so that it may allay the fears of those who are now making it more difficult for the refugees to make a real contribution to their new homes, through fear of competition when there may be a new lag in employment.

It seems more and more evident to me that this group will be

---

* Sophia M. Robison, editor. *Refugees at Work.* New York: King's Crown Press, 1942.

helping us to revise our economic system and to find new ways of keeping people employed at a high level.

We are fortunate indeed to have some of the best trained minds of Europe among us now as citizens and we should welcome them and use them to the limit.

In the study it also is explained that the people immigrating to the United States did so legally and within the limit of their national quota which before had only been used to a very small extent.

The only emergency visas issued were in August 1944. A letter from Mrs. Lily Ernst, in Springfield, Massachusetts, explained how these emergency visas were granted.

"My husband was interned in a camp in Southern Italy during the war years. In July of 1944 a representative of the United States Government visited the various camps and explained that President Roosevelt got a bill passed in Congress which permitted one thousand refugees to come to the United States until such a time when they would be able to return to their countries of origin. They were transported by army trucks, sailed on troop ships, and arrived in New York on August 4, 1944. From there they were taken by train to Fort Ontario, an abandoned army camp in Oswego, New York.

"They were taken care of in a wonderful way, had food, clothes and all kinds of medical attention. Mrs. Roosevelt visited the camp, welcomed the people and ordered curtains for the barracks. Although the refugees were extremely grateful and happy to be there, the camp with all its advantages felt, after a few months, like another internment. Children went to school in Oswego, but adults needed special permission to go downtown, and there was a curfew. Those restrictions were later relaxed. They could have visitors, who, of course, stayed at Oswego hotels. My husband, who had been editor of a Viennese newspaper, founded a camp newspaper. He also wrote a letter to Mrs. Roosevelt thanking her for her visit and also explaining how hard it was to still have to be separated from families and friends. Mrs. Roosevelt replied that she realized and understood the position of the people in Oswego. However, she added, only Congress could make a change and the President could not ask for it because this might prevent his being able to induce Congress to let other people into the country on a similar agreement and might mean there would be no chance to save the lives of other refugees.

"At Christmas 1945, President Truman was able to have a law passed that permitted all those who desired to, to immigrate; the people were taken by buses to Canada and allowed to enter legally."

A letter which further explained Mrs. Rooosevelt's feelings about the refugees came to me from Mrs. Janet Neuman of Washington, D.C.

"During the period of the Hitler madness in Europe," Mrs. Neuman wrote, "many people, especially Jews, were forced to leave their homelands. Quite a few came to Washington. To them it was a new and strange city. Their pasts were behind them and their futures uncertain. To ease the difficult transition, various social-orientation groups were formed. The one I helped to organize met twice a month, giving the newcomers an opportunity to meet sympathetic Americans, to learn about various facets of life in the United States and to have fun and relaxation. A variety of programs were arranged to fill these needs. "Why not invite Mrs. Roosevelt to address the group?' someone suggested one day. It seemed unlikely that our busy First Lady could even add one more activity to her overcrowded schedule. However, nothing could be lost by asking her, I thought. So I wrote a note explaining what we were doing and asking whether she perhaps could talk to us some evening. Her acceptance arrived almost by return mail.

On the given date, Mrs. Roosevelt arrived, prompt to the minute. Her handsome, simply styled dress seemed carefully chosen to make this an Important Occasion. As she welcomed the exiles, many of them wept. But the sorrow left their lined faces as they listened to the conclusion of Eleanor Roosevelt's speech:

" 'We Americans,' the famous voice said, 'are well aware that this is not a one-sided relationship. We are offering you a home and a haven, to be sure. However, you, in the United States tradition of immigrants, are bringing us your skills, your talents and your cultures. We are grateful to you for broadening our scope and enriching our country which consists of newcomers just like you.' "

"Her offer to shake hands and greet the audience following her talk was met with overwhelming gratitude," Mrs. Neuman concluded her letter. 'You Americans cannot possibly know what this means to us,' she was told. 'To have your First Lady welcome us and to shake our hands after we were thrown out of our own homeland—no one will ever know how deeply we are moved!' Some of them stood in line twice. One young woman told her, 'I will not wash my hands tonight. I do not want to wash *that* handshake off.' "

Now, over twenty-five years later, Mrs. Janet Neuman still hears an occasional reference to That Evening.

I met Elena Priester on a ship going to Hawaii. Elena is twenty-eight years old, has long ash-brown hair, large dark eyes with thick black lashes, delicate features, and pearly teeth. She was seated next to me at the dinner table and we started to talk. Elena told me that she was an airline stewardess. When I told her that I had just about completed a book on Eleanor Roosevelt, her large eyes became even larger.

"Mrs. Roosevelt," she said, "helped me to get a mother."

"A mother?" I was stunned. In all the stories that had come my way, no one had said Mrs. Roosevelt had found her a mother.

"I was an Italian war orphan," Elena told me. "I grew up in an orphanage. My mother—that is, my adopted mother—saw me there when I was four years old. She tried to get me into this country for seven years before she finally succeeded. She could not have done it without the help of Mrs. Roosevelt."

"What an unusual person your mother must be," I said. "I wish I could meet her."

"Oh, that is very easy," said Elena. "My mother runs the dress shop on this ship. I am sure she will be glad to tell you the story."

That night I met Helen Priester. She was a calm, gray-haired woman in her late fifties. She too had dark eyes which looked, oddly, very much like those of her adopted daughter.

"It all began in January 1945," Helen Priester said in her pleasant soft-spoken way. "I was a professional singer and I was in Groseto, Italy, with the USO to entertain our troops. One day, one of our officers asked me whether I would come with him to visit an orphanage. He was taking candies and toys to the children. Of course I went along. By the time we got there it was late in the afternoon and the little girls were in their small beds in the dormitory, ready to fall asleep. The nuns were with them and when we came there was a great deal of giggling going on. The officer took off his helmet and put it on the head of one of the little girls; it fell down to her nose. When he took it off the child's head again she saw me. Instantly she threw her arms around me and exclaimed, 'Mamma mia!' And I held her and kissed her and from this moment on, I felt I was her mother. It was so strange," Mrs. Priester said while tears rolled down her cheeks, "that the little girl's name was Elena, Italian for Helen. For as long as we were in Groseto, I visited her every day. First I brought her a doll, but the Sisters said she could not have it since the other children had none. The doll would have to be for all of them and they would have to take turns playing with her. So I bought dolls for all the little girls.

"Then I brought shoes for Elena and the Sisters told me the same thing. So I bought shoes for all the children. I postponed my departure from Italy and gave more shows. The money I received for them went to the orphanage. Finally, I told the Sisters that I wanted to adopt Elena. The adoption went through in Italy without too much trouble. But when I tried to get a visa for the child at the American Consulate I was informed that it was impossible to obtain a visa for an adopted child: only a blood relation of an American citizen could be admitted to the United States." She was told that it was impossible.

" 'Nothing is impossible!' I told the Consul," said Helen Priester. She traveled to all the American consulates, from Rome to Florence, from Florence to Milan, but everywhere it was the same story. It was impossible. Finally, after she threatened to remain at one of the consulates until she had received some constructive advice, Mrs. Priester was told that the only way she could take her child with her to America was through an Act of Congress.

"Very well," declared Mrs. Priester. She took Elena out of the orphanage and put her in a private school. Then she returned to the United States to begin her work on an Act of Congress for Elena. After she had written about four thousand letters, she learned that the bill had to be written by a Congressman. At long last, she got Congressman Norris Poulson from California to write the bill and submit it to Washington. A bill of that order,

Helen Priester learned, has to go through the Judiciary Committee, the House of Representatives, and so forth. The danger was that the bill somewhere on its way would be shelved. She kept writing letters in order to prevent this.

"In 1946," Helen Priester continued her story, "I traveled again to Europe to visit my daughter. On the S. S. America were the delegates of the U.S. Mission to the United Nations traveling to the first General Assembly meeting in London. One of the American delegates was Mrs. Eleanor Roosevelt. After I had sung at one of the church services aboard ship," said Helen Priester, "Mrs. Roosevelt came to me to shake hands and to tell me how much she had enjoyed it. We talked a little more and Mrs. Roosevelt asked me what I was going to do in Europe. I told her the story of Elena. Mrs. Roosevelt instantly became interested. 'I will do whatever I can to help you,' she promised and soon afterward wrote letters of her own in order to prevent the bill from being shelved. We corresponded on that matter for several years.

"Due to Mrs. Roosevelt's constant urging, Senator William Knowland of California, after seven years, finally took the bill through the Senate. President Harry S Truman signed it."

Elena Priester was eleven years old when she stepped off the airplane in her new homeland, the United States of America. She spoke only Italian. In her arms she carried dolls and stuffed dogs and teddy bears which the other passengers had bought her. Elena's coat was covered with holy medals which the Sisters had pinned on her, certain that an airplane flight over the ocean would end the child's life.

Mrs. Priester wrote her thanks to Eleanor Roosevelt.

"I am so glad," replied Mrs. Roosevelt, "that your child finally has come home. With every good wish. . ."

Chapter Four

The New York

Cabdrivers

DR. SOPHIA M. ROBISON was one of the faculty of the New School for Social Research while I was working on this book. In her late seventies then, she was always rushing to or from a class when I met her in the elevator or in the corridors. Every time she saw me, she had another idea for source material on my book about Eleanor Roosevelt.

"Mrs. Roosevelt used cabs and must have had friends among the New York cabdrivers," she told me early one morning. "It would be fun to hear what *they* have to say about her."

It would be, I thought, with a shrug. There was, of course, no possibility whatsoever for me to find out. I rarely take a cab and, if I did, I could not really ask each driver whether he had ever driven Mrs. Roosevelt. But the idea of questioning the cabdrivers popped into my mind again and again. Why shouldn't there be a way to reach them? I leafed the pages of the telephone directory, foolishly looking for "Taxi cabs." There! "Taxi Drivers Union," it said. I dialed the number. A deep voice answered, "Yeah?"

"I would like some information," I said timidly. "Does your Union have a publication?"

"A what?"

Very conscious of my accent I tried again.

"You mean a newspaper," the voice at the other end of the wire said. "Yup. We have one. *The Voice.*"

"Would you know who the editor is?" I persisted.

"Yup. Frank."

"Where can I reach him?"

The voice at the other end gave me the number to call, then there was the click of the receiver as he hung up.

I tried the new number. Frank was out. I was advised to write to him. I did, explaining what I was doing.

I waited a few weeks. No answer. I phoned. Frank was out. I left a message for him. I waited several weeks. No word from Frank. I phoned again. I was told to hold the wire. Someone shouted, "Hey, Frank! Your lady-friend with the accent wants to talk to you!"

Frank came to the phone. "Yup." He got my letter, would try to publish my appeal in the next issue of *The Voice*. Click.

Late one evening a few weeks later, my telephone rang.

"I had her in my cab once," said an unfamiliar, throaty voice.

"You mean Mrs. Roosevelt?" I exclaimed.

"Sure. Who else?"

"Is my appeal for stories in your union paper?" I asked.

"Yup. Hit the street this morning."

"Tell me, what happened when you had Mrs. Roosevelt in your cab?"

"Nothing."

"Nothing?"

"Nope."

"You must remember something!"

"Well—just that she knew the fastest way to get to Idlewild Airport."

Before I could ask the driver's name he had hung up.

I did, however, get that issue of *The Voice*.

"Writer seeking info on Mrs. Roosevelt," it said. "Any cab-driver who has driven Mrs. Roosevelt in his cab is to get in touch with her." My name, address and phone number followed.

"I am Leon Katz," said my next caller. "Saw your ad in our paper. About four years ago I had Mrs. Roosevelt in my cab. Picked her up somewhere in the Sixties on Madison Avenue."

"Did you talk with her?" I asked.

"No, not really."

"Well, what happened?"

"Nothing. Just took her to a fruit shop where you buy those gift baskets and there were a few more stops. That was all."

"Don't you remember anything she said?"

"Naw. After all, it's four years ago."

"It was very nice of you to call me," I said to Leon Katz. "I appreciate it very much."

He did not hang up. "One thing sticks in my mind," he said, somewhat hesitantly. "I don't know whether this will mean anything to you. Anyway, Mrs. Roosevelt was such a tall woman and my cab is very small. Yet, she did not complain even once. When we made all those stops she went in and out like bullet. Boom, out she went, boom, back she came! I always think of her when some dame complains about my cab being so small. You should have seen Mrs. Roosevelt getting in and out, I tell them. *She* didn't even mention that my cab is so small!"

Abe is an official of the Taxi Drivers Union. "My wife saw your ad in the paper today," he told me over the phone. " 'Abe,' she said, the moment when I came home from work this morning, 'you call that woman right away and tell her about that time when you had Mrs. Roosevelt in your cab!' "

"Thank her for me," I said. "I am so glad you called. Did you talk with Mrs. Roosevelt when you drove her?"

"Sure enough."

"What did you talk about, do you remember?"

"Politics, natch! What else does a cabbie talk about? I told her that I was honored to have her in my cab, that I was very fond of her late husband. He was a great liberal!"

"What did she say to that?"

"Oh, I don't know the exact words. But she seemed pleased. Then we discussed some of the city affairs. Before she got out I asked her to sign my union card. She was very gracious about that. Eleanor Roosevelt was a very lovely lady. In every way. I never forgot her."

Although Abe Drogan did not remember exactly what he spoke about with Mrs. Roosevelt, she herself reported "An unusual encounter with a taxicab driver," in her column in the *New York Post* on March 25, 1960. It well might have been Abe. "A taxicab driver picked me up, recognized me, and at once began to tell me how he had always worked for my husband politically, and how much he had enjoyed my husband's political jokes over the years. Then in a more solemn moment he told me how he had always felt there was a particular tie between my husband and himself because he remembered the day he was working in the boiler room of a heavy Navy cruiser at the Brooklyn Navy Yard and suddenly he saw what seemed to be FDR standing beside him.

" 'He told me he was leaving me,' the cab driver said to me. 'And I should carry on and do the best I could. It was so real to me that I picked up my tools and packed them away and went topside and told the man that I had finished my work for the day. He said that I could not take off. But I replied that I had to. I had lost one of my best friends.'

"Stories such as these are strange," Eleanor Roosevelt concluded that column, "but they seem to indicate some supersensitive connection between people. They do indicate a sense of closeness, and the fact that the cabdriver has remembered it all these years shows how much it meant to him."

"I read your ad in the taxi driver *Voice*," " wrote someone whose signature I could not decipher. "I once drove Mrs. Roosevelt to Mark Cross on Fifth Avenue. I was so honored to have her in my cab that I did not want to take any money from her when she got out. But she got very excited and insisted, 'Oh, but I must pay!' She would not budge from her seat until I let her pay and took the money."

The next time I was on Fifth Avenue, I stopped at Mark Cross and asked for some salesperson who had been working there for a long time. I was referred to Miss S. to whom I explained that I was writing a book on Eleanor Roosevelt and that a cabdriver had told me she had been shopping there.

"Oh, Mrs. Roosevelt was a wonderful customer," Miss S. said with a warm smile. "She never brought anything back as so many of our other ladies, especially celebrities, do. She was always very pleasant and friendly. The last time I saw her was before her trip to Russia. She bought attaché cases for Mr. Khruschev and all the other dignitaries."

"Did you ever find out whether they liked them?" I asked.

"Oh yes," Miss S. said "When Mrs. Roosevelt returned from her trip she sent someone in to let us know how pleased the Russians had been with their gifts."

My last cabdriver-caller was Sol from Brooklyn.

"I had Mrs. Roosevelt in my cab on May eighth, 1945," he told me.

"You remember the exact day?" I asked, amazed.

"It was V-E Day," said Sol Schwartz. "We had won World War II in Europe. I was driving down Fifth Avenue and it was mobbed with people who were shouting, laughing, and singing. When I got to Twenty-third Street, a cop stopped me, told me that Mrs. Roosevelt was swamped by a delirious crowd, and asked me to wait while he brought her over. I felt so honored and privileged to have her in my cab, especially on that day, and told her so. She didn't say much in reply. In the mirror I saw that she didn't even smile. I took her to her apartment on Washington Square and when she paid me I asked her to sign the dollar bill. She did, but still without smiling.

" 'Mrs. Roosevelt,' I asked, "aren't you happy that the war is over?'

" 'Oh, of course,' she said. 'I am very happy for everyone. However, the war is not over for me. My sons are in the Pacific.'

"Then she said 'Good night,' very pleasantly and I could not see her any longer because it was so dark on the street."

Chapter Five

Fannie Hurst

"MRS. ROOSEVELT USED TO BE A GREAT FRIEND of Fannie Hurst, the writer," said a former school principal, a member of the Institute for Retired Professionals at the New School for Social Research in New York. "Miss Hurst lives in the Hotel des Artistes on West Sixty-seventh Street. I am certain she would have some stories for you . . ."

Into my mind flashed the image of Charles Boyer in the old movie *Back Street,* which had been adapted for the screen from Miss Hurst's book. I also remembered several other novels over which I had wept long ago. How fascinating it would be to meet this woman who had become a literary legend, I thought, and promptly wrote her a letter. I explained the idea of this book about Eleanor Roosevelt and asked her for an interview.

A few days later, at eight o'clock in the morning, my telephone rang.

"This is Fannie Hurst."

I almost choked on my piece of raisin toast.

"I received your letter," said a voice so young and light that I could hardly believe this was really Fannie Hurst who, I knew, was seventy-eight. "But I am afraid I won't be able to tell you anything about Eleanor Roosevelt that I have not written in my own autobiography," Miss Hurst added gently, regretfully.

I finally managed to swallow the dry crumbs of my toast. "Wouldn't you even see me, though?" My experience in interviewing people for this book had taught me that many individuals who claimed that they had absolutely nothing new to tell me often did come up with something meaningful without even being aware of it. "I won't take up much of your time, Miss Hurst," I assured her.

"Well . . ." the airy voice wavered, "I am a bit rushed right now before Christmas. Would it be all right after the holidays?"

"Of course."

We made an appointment, and I circled it in red on my calendar.

I myself went on a brief winter vacation, but before I left I managed to find in a secondhand bookshop in Greenwich Village a copy of Fannie Hurst's *Anatomy of Me.**

Before a crackling fireplace in a cottage in the snowy Pocono Mountains, I read about a chubby little St. Louis girl whose only yearning was to write about the oppressed of this earth, of injustices caused by prejudice and intolerance. This girl's talent and determination overcame the struggle with unresponsive editors and she became a literary legend. Her novels were widely read and her friends ranged from multimillionaires to truck drivers; she mingled with kings and queens and finally became a close friend of Eleanor Roosevelt.

It was during the Great Depression when, in spite of apple vendors and soup kitchens on street corners, there was a disturbing decrease of people available for domestic labor. "Long hours and unfit living conditions are responsible for this!" Mrs. Roosevelt declared in a newspaper. She urged domestic workers in the United States to organize a labor union. Fannie Hurst was deeply impressed. She knew that her mother in St. Louis would be outraged by the very idea. She would claim that "the truth is we spoil our maids! Willie has the best of food! Every other Friday and Sunday afternoon off and you should see how she rushes through the dishes on these days. Good wages: (They were four dollars a week) No living expenses! What else do they want?"

But Fannie Hurst knew that their Willie was on her feet twelve to fourteen hours a day, that her free time was so short

---

* Fannie Hurst. *Anatomy of Me.* New York: Doubleday, 1958.

that she spent most of it in her third floor room where the ceiling slanted and the day's heat beat through the roof. She also was aware that Willie's room, in comparison with what was given to other domestics, was elegant. There were many that were dark holes, opening from steaming kitchens, where the houseworker collapsed after cleaning, cooking three meals a day, and serving them. Fannie Hurst, thinking of her own mother, fully realized that the attempt to organize domestic workers would find few sympathetic ears. Because of this awareness, she wrote the first fan letter of her life to the woman who publicly supported this program.

As always, Eleanor Roosevelt answered at once. Unfortunately, nothing came of her suggested project, but out of the incident grew a long friendship between Fannie Hurst and the wife of the new President.

During the Hoover administration, Miss Hurst had been in the White House several times. Once she attended a luncheon for about twenty "key women." Earlier she had testified before a Senate committee, relating her experiences in a Pennsylvania coal mining town, and afterward there had been a luncheon at the White House with President Coolidge. Both occasions seemed impressive to her but were strictly formal.

But with the advent of the Roosevelt family, the climate in the White House changed. Informality had moved in. It was during her friendship with Eleanor Roosevelt that, for the first time, Fannie Hurst slept in the White House. She was invited for a weekend and arrived on Saturday morning. A car was waiting for her at the airport and en route to the White House they picked up Mrs. Roosevelt at a riding academy, following her daily early-morning horseback ride.

When Fannie Hurst discovered that her assigned quarter was the Lincoln Suite, she decided that she would not sleep at all that night, but would meditate on the spirit of Abraham Lincoln. At the moment of her arrival, however, she barely had time to glance around; she was instructed to report for breakfast at once.

Breakfast was served buffet style, in a screen-partitioned hallway outside of Mrs. Roosevelt's sitting room. The First Lady was deep in a stack of mail and was frequently interrupted by phone calls, secretaries, and ushers. A seating chart for a state dinner the following week had to be inspected, a miniature church made out of toothpicks arrived from an admirer in South Carolina, the housekeeper appeared for a conference. During all this, Eleanor Roosevelt kept talking with Fannie Hurst, asking about herself, her writing and her husband who, at that time, was in Europe. Then it was time to leave for a committee meeting, after which Mrs. Roosevelt took her literary guest to the Library of Congress and gave her a chance to gaze at a shelf of her own novels.

At lunch there were only the President, his mother, his daughter Anna, and Louis Howe. When Eleanor Roosevelt came hurrying into the dining room, Anna adjusted her mother's blouse. "There is sometimes a hopeless discrepancy between my mother and her clothes," she said with a smile to Fannie Hurst. The President seemed relaxed to Miss Hurst and she thought he ate with gusto. Between courses he smoked cigarettes in his long holder and kept the conversation well out of the tension areas of politics and affairs of state. However, Louis Howe related a recent conversation with a member of the State Department who had just returned from Russia. The details of the living conditions there were shocking and Howe apologized for introducing them at lunch. Franklin Roosevelt's mother put down her fork and knife, Fannie Hurst remembers in her memoirs. "I warned you," she said sternly to her son. "You should never have recognized the Soviet Union!"

In the midst of lunch, an usher entered and handed a note to Mrs. Roosevelt. She glanced at it and turned to Fannie Hurst. "You are wanted at the telephone."

"I?" Fannie Hurst exclaimed, amazed. To be sure, she had bragged a little to some friends about her visit to the White House, but who would have the temerity to phone her there? Certainly she was not going to leave the table during lunch with the President of the United States. "Will you ask the usher to take the message?" she appealed to Mrs. Roosevelt.

The young man left and returned a moment later.

"Queen Mary wishes to speak with you, Miss Hurst."

The First Family gasped. The President threw back his head and burst into laughter. Fannie Hurst sat petrified. "It is a joke, of course," she said. "I am not going."

"Oh, go ahead and find out what this is all about," the President urged.

Reluctantly, Fannie Hurst rose from her seat.

"Hello?" she said warily into the phone.

Her husband's voice came over the wire to her from the middle of the ocean. He was homeward bound from Europe and was calling from the Cunard liner *Queen Mary*.

After lunch was over, the day began in earnest for Eleanor Roosevelt. Fannie Hurst accompanied her first to the hospital where one of the Roosevelt sons was recuperating from an appendectomy, then on to the board of trustees' meeting at an orphanage, after that to an opening of a Picasso exhibit where she gave a speech, and then back to the White House just in time to receive a delegation of about forty educators from the Philippines, and finally a brief conference with a Negro Baptist minister from Atlanta. There were a few minutes to change clothes before venturing out again for dinner at the home of Henry Morgenthau, Jr. In the White House dining room meanwhile, the young Roosevelts, home for Easter holidays, had a large dinner party of their own, while the President dined in his suite. Mrs. Roosevelt and Fannie Hurst returned to the White House at eleven o'clock, just in time to see the first showing of a talking picture from a projector which the Metro-Goldwyn-Mayer corporation had newly installed for the President's use. It was long past midnight when Fannie Hurst found herself alone in her bedroom. Oblivious of her resolution of that morning to stay awake through the night, she sank onto the edge of Abraham Lincoln's bed, deciding that for once in her life she would retire without even removing her makeup. There was a knock on her door. "Come in," Fannie Hurst murmured weakly.

Clad in a black bathing suit, a towel over her arm, Eleanor Roosevelt entered briskly, holding a pad and pencil in her hand. "What do you want for breakfast tomorow, Fannie?" she asked.

After jotting down the answer carefully, Eleanor Roosevelt spread the Turkish towel on the floor. "Remember when I promised you this morning to show you my yoga exercises?" she asked. And the next instant she stood on her head, straight as a column, feet up in the air.

After I had read Fannie Hurst's autobiography, I was even more eager to meet her than before. The day which I had

circled in red on my calendar arrived. On my way to Miss
Hurst's apartment I bought a few yellow roses. The cavernous
lobby of the Hotel des Artistes was dim, with high ceilings and
stained-glass windows. It made me think of a Venetian palazzo.
A man at a desk phoned my arrival and an old-fashioned elevator
with a gilded gate took me to Miss Hurst's triplex penthouse.
The door was open. I entered and, for some reason, found myself on tiptoes. An enormous room opened before me. There was
a thirty-foot-high ceiling, paintings, sculptures, draperies in deep
reddish hues. My step was muffled by thick Persian rugs. Pale
light flickered through huge windows facing a wintry Central
Park.

A woman sauntered toward me. She was gracefully slim, her
hair was smooth and black, her face and complexion radiant and
unlined. Dark eyes, warm and luminous and young, took in my
appearance. This could not be Fannie Hurst! Her secretary
perhaps. This was not a woman of seventy-eight. My glance fell
on the jeweled calla lily she wore on her dress. It *was* Fannie
Hurst. In her arm she carried a small long-haired dog with a
pink bow on his brow. Her free hand was extended. "I am so
glad you could come." Her voice too was incredibly young and
vibrant. "I had a little accident and am housebound," she explained, pointing to her trim legs, one of which was bandaged
at the ankle. "For once I ventured out to do some shopping on
Fifth Avenue and I was in such a hurry that I failed to notice
a few steps. So silly of me. I hate to be laid up like this. There
is so much to do!"

I handed her the flowers.

"How charming and kind of you," she said and instantly began
to unwrap them. "I love surprises." She caressed the roses and
placed them in a little fan-shaped glass vase. "It's just right for
them, isn't it?" she asked happily. "Jack and I bought it one
year in Murano near Venice." She smelled the roses. "How lovely
they are. What I miss most with this leg," she said, and gestured
at her ankle with a graceful hand, "is my daily walk in Central
Park at five in the morning."

"At five?"

"But of course. Before I start to work. My dogs need the
exercise. So do I. When I was young," she confessed, "I used to

be fat. I was very unhappy about it and was constantly dieting. Once, after a very strict diet, I came to the White House and very proudly displayed my new figure to the President. He motioned me to turn around. 'The Hurst may have changed,' FDR said, 'but it's the same old fannie.' I was mortified!"

We both laughed.

"What a magnificent place you have," I said, as I looked around.

"It's really too large for just me," Miss Hurst said with some apology in her voice. "Come, I'll take you on a quick tour."

Fannie Hurst had one of the greatest private collections of religious articles of the late fourteenth and fifteenth centuries in the world. The paintings illustrated the various themes of the early Rennaissance period. "This is one of my most treasured possessions," Miss Hurst said as she pointed to a Medallion of Valor on the huge piano. It was presented to Fannie Hurst by Eleanor Roosevelt on behalf of the State of Israel Bonds. The medallion was surrounded by other objects of art: a faience horse under glass which, Miss Hurst explained, was from the fourteenth century; a Russian icon from Moscow; a Madonna which, I learned, was an eigthteenth-century wood carving. In front of the piano was an early Norman prayer chair with spool legs, and above the piano towered a seventeenth-century wood carving of Moses.

The dining room looked like a monks' eating hall. There was a long table of dark wood, a cup stood before each severe chair. Floor, ceiling, and wall came from the Davanzati Palace in Florence. The shelves in the library were filled with Fannie Hurst's novels.

"They are translated into fourtcen languages," Miss Hurst said with a pleased little laugh. "If I had listened to my mother, they never would have been written. She wanted me to marry a nice young man and have many children. . . . Let's sit down, shall we?"

We went back into the living room with its thirteenth-century tapestry which came from the Hall of Armor in an English Castle, as Miss Hurst explained. She led me to a red velvet window seat. Her dark eyes focused on my face. "Do you have a family?" she inquired.

Since she sounded as though she really wanted to know, I told her that I had a husband, a daughter, two grandchildren.

"How very nice," she said. "Then time is no problem for you as a writer, is it?"

I shook my head. "I so much enjoyed your autobiography, Miss Hurst." I produced the book for her autograph. "Do you mind?" I said.

"Of course not!" She opened it at once and wrote, "To someone with whom I share a great admiration for Eleanor Roosevelt." She then closed the book and handed it to me. "Mrs. Roosevelt was the only woman who made me feel inadequate," she said. "I often told her so. But she just laughed, looked at me with those magnificent blue eyes and said, 'But, Fannie, don't you see how easy it is for me to help other people? Where someone else would have to take forty steps to do something for someone else, I, as the President's wife, just have to take four.' This was true, of course," Fannie Hurst said as she gazed into the past. "But how many other First Ladies, for whom it would have been just as easy, dedicated their lives to helping others?" Fannie Hurst fell silent for a moment. "Women today," she said with a touch of anger in her voice, "simply do not have have Eleanor Roosevelt's courage and determination."

"Don't you think that American women have made a great deal of progress?" I asked.

Fannie Hurst shook her head. "It might seem that way, but it really is not so. Do you realize that American women, since they achieved the vote in 1920, have not only made no real progress in achieving any social gains but have lost ground? There are today fewer women Ph.D. candidates than there were in the 1930s, the Depression years. More than half of our population are women and there is today, out of one hundred Senators, only one woman, Margaret Chase Smith. In the House of Representatives there are eleven women, about two and a half percent. Forty-seven percent of women between eighteen and sixty-five now work outside the home, but most of them do routine or menial work. Where are our women in creative fields? In government? As judges and lawyers? Women should take more decisive voice in the reform of outdated abortion laws, in wider distribution of birth control devices, in the struggle for peace! I met a visiting delegation of West African women recently. They were shocked when they realized what discrimination against women exists in our country! Look at India, they even made a woman their Prime Minister. Could you imagine this happening here?"

"No," I said, "of course not. Would you blame this state of affairs on our society or on American woman herself?"

She pondered the question for a moment.

"Both, I suppose. Our society makes women feel so guilty when they have an interest outside of their house and children. We ought to stop the nonsense that there is virtue in having large families. With the population explosion, with overcrowed cities, freeways, educational institutions, hospitals and jails, the fewer children a family has, the better off society will be. We should stop making women who prefer not to have children at all feel like second-class citizens. We should stop deceiving women into believing that they will not have a good, or full, or complete life unless they marry."

"Why is it then," I asked, "that women in Russia, in Israel, in the Scandinavian countries, even when they do have families, do not seem to have the feelings of guilt when they work outside the home?"

"Society in those countries approves of women working outside of their homes," Fannie Hurst said. "More than that, the government requests it and makes it possible by creating nursery schools for small children who are being taken care of during the day. A woman cannot carry the double load of household and work alone. Society has to help and support her actively. The husband too has to pitch in. It is a pity that we are so backward in this respect in our country. Do you realize that in Russia, seventy percent of the doctors are women and here, where there is a severe shortage of physicians, it still is difficult for a woman to get into medical college? We only support women's work when there is a strong need. During a war, for instance, no one dreams of criticizing a woman for working outside of her home."

"I suppose when there is a fire," I said, "no one stops to ask the fireman whether he has a right to leave his family behind in order to put out the fire."

"Exactly." She nodded in agreement. "Although," she added, while the most charming, the most feminine smile I had ever seen, brightened her face, "they criticized Eleanor Roosevelt all the time while she traveled those thousands of miles to visit our soldiers during World War II. All the Hearst newspapers urged her to stay home where she belonged."

"It seems to me," I said, "that Mrs. Roosevelt did not pay much attention to their advice."

The lovely smile still was on her face.

"Eleanor Roosevelt did what we all should be doing—listen to no one but our inner voice. If this voice tells us that what we are doing is right, no power on earth should be able to change it."

It was about a year later that I read in the newspaper that Fannie Hurst had died. I went to the funeral.

A long line of mourners stood in the rain on Madison Avenue. They were elderly women mostly, several Negroes, a few girls in miniskirts. Inside the funeral home, the coffin of Fannie Hurst was covered with a blanket of calla lilies. They seemed to embody her spirit with their petals, so pale and graceful and mysteriously exotic. The people, some two hundred of Miss Hurst's friends, were very still. All one could hear were the gentle strains of Bach. The music faded away.

Dr. Abram Sachar, President of Brandeis University, stepped onto the podium behind a lectern.

"There is a story in the Talmud," he said. "When the angel of Death comes, he places the last letter of the Hebrew alphabet on the eyelids of the deceased. Whether young or old, rich or poor, it always is the same letter. However, the letter has two meanings. With a person who had led a selfish life, caring for himself only, the letter means 'He Is Dead.' But with a person who has cared for the human race, a person who has helped others, helped to make the world a little better, it has a different meaning. The letter which the Angel of Death has placed onto the eyes of Fannie Hurst means 'She Shall Live.' "

Chapter Six

The Reporters

IN MY QUEST FOR STORIES about Eleanor Roosevelt, I found out that reporters are busy people. Very busy people. I wrote first to the "big" names, the newspapermen who, as I knew, had had a lot to do with Mrs. Roosevelt. They replied with nice notes; they wished they had the time to give me a story, my book certainly sounded like a worthwhile undertaking. Alas, they had their own deadlines to meet. A very kind letter came from Art Buchwald. "I did not know Eleanor Roosevelt at all," he said candidly. "I met her once or twice but, unfortunately, I have nothing that could add to your book. If I did, I certainly would be happy to add to it, but I must be honest and say that I don't have any stories." Russell Baker also replied that "regrettably, I have never met Mrs. Roosevelt, but I wish you the best of luck with your project."

When I realized how very harassed a breed reporters are, I decided to give up doing a chapter about them. But then letters began to arrive from newspaperpeople across the country who remembered that Mrs. Roosevelt had given them their first break when they started out in this turbulent profession.

"I have interviewed many celebrities," wrote Alex Gildzen, who is a member of the English Department of Kent State University in Ohio. "Often I found them arrogant, rude, and impatient.

Each time I was confronted with one of the less gracious of the species termed 'famous,' I found myself remembering my very first interview in 1958. I was fourteen, a staff member of my high school newspaper *The Herald*. Mrs. Eleanor Roosevelt was in town for an evening speech sponsored by the Elyria, Ohio, Women's Club. That morning at 10:30, a mass press interview was scheduled at the club upon Mrs. Roosevelt's arrival and my editor sent me to cover the event.

"Television, radio, and newspaper representatives from the entire area news media were milling about the club, setting up microphones, taking meter readings and waiting for Mrs. Roosevelt. Punctual to the minute, Eleanor Roosevelt smiled her way through the crowd waiting outside the club.

"There was a great deal of interest in that interview because Mrs. Roosevelt had just returned from a trip to the Soviet Union. Almost instantly, questions were fired at her hard and fast. I was quite dazed by the speed and, although I had prepared several questions, they seemed too trivial to ask. Once or twice I tried to open my mouth but there was always another reporter ahead of me. The interview was almost over and I had not had a chance to pose a single question. I consoled myself with the thought that I had taken some hurried notes and would make a story out of them as well as I could.

"Abruptly, quite without warning, Mrs. Roosevelt looked directly at me and the friend who had accompanied me.

" 'How about these young people?' she asked. 'They didn't have a chance to ask anything.'

"Everyone looked our way. My own voice sounded small and high-pitched as I forced myself to pose a question. 'What kind of music,' I asked, 'do Russian teenagers like?' I thought I heard some snicker from the veteran reporters. Mrs. Roosevelt, however, gazed at me thoughtfully as she began to speak of Russian youths who, much as American young people, seemed to have preference for rock and roll.

"There were a few more questions and the interview was ended. Mrs. Roosevelt was at the door when a Cleveland newscaster came rushing in and pleaded with her to answer a few more questions for him. Even though every moment of that day had been planned for her, Eleanor Roosevelt sat down again and re-answered the major questions while squinting a little before the glaring television lights."

Marcia Levy of Philadelphia remembered when in 1956, she was a college senior and working for a weekly newspaper in Fall River, Massachusetts, as a reporter. Her editor burst into the newsroom one day to tell her that he just had heard that Eleanor Roosevelt was to make an unscheduled appearance at a Bonds for Israel dinner that evening at the town's hotel. He had also discovered that Mrs. Roosevelt was to stop off first for a rest at the home of a prominent citizen who was giving a cocktail party there before the dinner. The editor was determined to scoop the story. He handed Marcia Levy a small tape recorder, and ordered her to "crash" the party, find Mrs. Roosevelt, interview her on tape for the radio station (which the paper also owned), and finally write her story for the morning issue.

"I was nineteen," Marcia Levy wrote, "I had never operated a tape recorder. I had never interviewed anyone. Certainly, I had never before met Mrs. Roosevelt. My job was important to me. I went to the party and hid my tape recorder in a hall closet. Then I mingled with the guests. After about half an hour of worrying whether anyone would discover me as an intruder, I heard the police sirens announcing Mrs. Roosevelt's arrival from the airport. Before anyone had a chance to even get a glimpse of her, I found out from a maid that she had been whisked into one of the bedrooms for a quick nap.

"I withdrew from the cocktail party, surreptitiously recovered my tape recorder and began to search for Mrs. Roosevelt. Stealthily opening the second door I saw her.

"Eleanor Roosevelt was lying on a bed with her eyes closed. She was fully dressed except for her shoes which were neatly placed under the bed.

"I must have made some embarrassed noise because Mrs. Roosevelt opened her eyes, looked at me and said, 'Hello.' Almost in tears, I stammered out my apologies for intruding on her nap and explained my mission for the paper. I was certain she would throw me out at once.

"Of course, my dear," said Eleanor Roosevelt after hearing me out. 'I will be delighted to help you.'

"As she got up and put her shoes on, I saw that she looked

very tired and very old. For a while she stood and watched as I fumbled with the tape recorder, then she smiled, gently took it from my hand, and set it to work. Finally, she led me through the interview, talking for half an hour about her recent trip to Israel, her great hope for Adlai Stevenson at the coming Democratic Convention and about politics in general. When we ran out of tape, I thanked her right on the reel for the kindness she had shown me. When I started to pack up all the equipment, Mrs. Roosevelt asked me whether I was going to attend the Bond Drive dinner. I now confessed that I had crashed the party, that I had not been invited either personally or as a member of the press.

" 'You have been invited now,' Eleanor Roosevelt said. 'Ask for your table number at the door and I will arrange everything.'

"I raced back to the radio station to drop off the tape, then rushed to the newspaper office to write the story while it still was fresh in my mind. Then I hurried home to shower and change my clothes. She will have forgotten, I told myself as I ran to the hotel.

"But she had not. Mrs. Roosevelt had arranged for me to sit at the Press Table. After the dinner she made her speech. The crowd seemed mesmerized and listened to each one of her words as she spoke about her trip to Israel and pleaded for contributions that this wonderful work in a young country should be continued. When she had finished, the pledges poured in.

"I still have the tape of our talk together," Marcia Levy concluded her long letter. "Every once in a while I play it. It serves two purposes. First, it keeps me from getting too cocky about my interviewing qualifications, and second, it reminds me of the kindness shown to a very brazen and very scared teenager by Mrs. Roosevelt."

"The first time I saw Mrs. Roosevelt was in 1930, when I was a Boy Scout in Ithaca, New York," wrote Frederic Hillegas, news editor of WSYR-TV in Syracuse, New York.

"I saw Mrs. Roosevelt again many years later when she was the First Lady and I was a reporter for *The Cornell Daily Sun,* covering what the State Agriculture College called 'Farm and Home Week.' Mrs. Roosevelt often came to give speeches for these occasions. One of the topics I remember was 'The Role of the American Woman in the World of Today.' The audience consisted of real *old-soil type* farmers. They would bring sandwiches and apples in brown paper bags to the auditorium and listen to Mrs. Roosevelt's speech while they ate their lunches. But when the brown paper bags were empty, they drifted away.

"One time it was announced that Mrs. Roosevelt would speak about 'A Day in the White House,' and also that she would model the gowns she wore in Washington. The auditorium was overflowing on that occasion, the farmers gaped at the velvet and silk evening gowns of Eleanor Roosevelt, and they listened so intently to her talk about the White House, the daily life there, the exotic dinner menus required for various foreign dignitaries and the difficulties of protocol seating on those occasions, that they forgot completely to eat their own sandwiches and no one left early. The photographs of the First Lady modeling the White House gowns in the State Agriculture College went all over the country.

"Once, Mrs. Roosevelt almost broke up one of my romances," Frederic Hillegas continued his report. "During one of her visits to Cornell, a girl I knew was in charge of escorting her on her tour. I wrote about her time schedule in the Syracuse paper where I was employed, and my report read something like this: 'Mrs. Roosevelt arrived at 10:28. Left Press building 10:29. Had conference 10:30. 10:30–10:32 inspected food exhibit. 10:35 concluded her visit.' My girl friend did not think my description very funny. But Mrs. Roosevelt saw it too and, I was told, laughed as she read it.

"The last time I saw Mrs. Roosevelt was one of the most embarrassing moments of my life. When I was working for *The Syracuse Post Standard* as a student helper, I got an assignment to cover Mrs. Roosevelt on one of her visits to Syracuse. The editor ordered me to ask Mrs. Roosevelt during her press conference whether she was going to stop at Chittenango on her way back home. Chittenango was where a disability-retired state trooper lived; he had been severely injured when, on a cycle escort of the governor's traveling party, there had been an accident. Back of this was a leering rumor that Mrs. Roosevelt had some sort of romantic interest in, attraction for, or some such vague and undefined intimate contact with that man. At the press conference, after Mrs. Roosevelt had replied to questions pertaining to war and peace, woman's role in the United States, and similar matters, I finally asked the question I had been assigned to ask. Was she going to stop at Chittenango to visit that injured trooper?

"The room grew silent and there was a long pause before Mrs. Roosevelt spoke. She drew herself up to her considerable height and looked straight at me. 'This,' she said with great dignity, 'I consider my *personal* business.'

"I always thought that the reports of Mrs. Roosevelt's ubiquity were highly exaggerated," wrote Don Chatfield of High Point, North Carolina. "Especially when, in 1936, a cartoon appeared in *The New Yorker* which showed some miners looking up from their chores. One was exclaiming, "Look, here comes Eleanor!' But about that time, I myself went with a friend to cover the Boulder Dam dedication. As we were about to step into the bucket that was taking visitors to the base of the gigantic dam, who should come out of it but the First Lady herself, Mrs. Eleanor Roosevelt, in a rubber coat."

"I spent nearly two hours in May 1935, touring the interior of the Williow Grove Coal Mine in Bellaire, Ohio, riding side by side with the First Lady in one of those small mine cars, wearing a miner's cap as she did," wrote Helen Waterhouse in an article in *The Christian Science Monitor,*** on November 14, 1962. "While the rest of us all wore overalls, Mrs. Roosevelt decided it would be more fiitting for a President's wife to wear an old black dress with a faded sweater. When we emerged from the mine she was as dust covered and disheveled as we all were. And there was to be a tea given for her in the one big house of the town immediately afterward. When we entered the house, women were already gathered around the silver teapots. Running up the stairs, Mrs. Roosevelt called back to me, 'I am going to take a quick plunge in the tub, you can be second.' "

Jack O'Brian, the radio and newspaper reporter of WOR in New York, remembered the jokes which were habitually made

---

* From "A 'First Lady' Interview." Excerpted by permission from The Christian Science Monitor. Copyright 1962 The Christian Science Publishing Society. All rights reserved.

about Mrs. Roosevelt's constant traveling. Once, in 1944, he went to an Eddie Cantor charity affair at the Astor Hotel in New York. Henny Youngman, the M.C., welcomed the guests, then looked around searchingly. "Eleanor Roosevelt was supposed to be here, today," he said, then shrugged. "I suppose it was too near for her!" Jack O'Brian also recalled that, as a young newspaper reporter, he was often assigned to cover the appearances of Mrs. Roosevelt. "She made it her business to remember the names of the reporters who were assigned to her, even for a few days, and she always greeted us personally, singly, by name. I thought she was a fine lady," Mr. O'Brian, who writes a syndicated column for the Hearst papers, concluded his letter, "But I also felt that her niceness made her available to too many people who used her to her disadvantage."

On August 5, 1960, Radio Netherlands dedicated a commemorative program to the first dropping of the atomic bomb, fifteen years after Hiroshima.

The station asked their United States correspondent at the United Nations, Bernard Person, to try to get an interview with Mrs. Roosevelt on that topic.

Mr. Person walked over to the American Association for the United Nations where Mrs. Roosevelt had her office. "I talked to a charming and pretty young secretary," said Mr. Person, "and explained my mission. She promised that she would ask Mrs. Roosevelt about it. A few days later I got a call and was told that Mrs. Roosevelt would be glad to grant me an interview on that topic.

"I arrived equipped with a tape recorder. It was the first time that Mrs. Roosevelt spoke in an extemporaneous radio interview on this subject. The following is the authentic interview:

Q.: "Mrs. Roosevelt, I know that the first atom bomb on Japan was dropped under the administration of President Truman. But the—then secret—Manhattan project had of course been in development for some time. May I ask you this question: Were you aware of the development of the bomb during the administration of your late husband? And if so, how did you feel about its being used against Japan?"

A.: "I was never aware exactly of what was being developed. I knew from my husband that some work was going on which might affect the end of the war—that it was possible, in competition with Germany, that they would make a discovery which might end the war, and that we were therefore obliged to have research projects in the hope that we would at least make the discovery at the same time, or before. But what the discovery was, or the nature of it, I was never told. It was a very carefully guarded secret. Now when it was used for the first time, I think I had very mixed feelings. But I did know that the defense of Japan had been very carefuly prepared, and when Mr. Truman —after a great deal of debate and thought—said that it would cost not only millions of American lives, but it would probably cost millions of Japanese lives, and destroy many of the things in Japan which we had been begged by people in this country not to bomb, because they were artistic heritages for the whole world, not for any one people, I had the feeling that it was a terrible decision to take but that nevertheless the cost in the long run of human lives was probably less, and therefore the President could make no other decision.

"Now for a long while I questioned whether he should have dropped the second bomb on Nagasaki, and that bothered me for a long time, until I went to Japan, and saw the nature of the defenses and talked to one of our old, old consular people. He had lived most of his life there and had been in prison there during the whole war, and he told me that he felt it was an essential thing to do, because they had been taught that they were so invincible that he doubted if the Japanese people would have given up without the second bomb being dropped. That made me feel much better. I was always very worried about that second bomb."

It seems that Mrs. Roosevelt restrained herself to some extent on the topic of Hiroshima in this interview. This is what she said in her autobiography:* about her visit to Japan in 1953.

To arrive in Hiroshima is an emotional experience. Here is where the first atom bomb ever to be dropped on human beings was actually used. The people of the United States believe that

---

* *The Autobiography of Eleanor Roosevelt.* New York: Harper & Brothers, 1958.

our leaders thought long and carefully before they used this dread weapon. We know that they thought first of the welfare of our own people, that they believed the bomb might end the war quickly with less loss of life everywhere than if it had not been dropped.

In spite of this conviction, one cannot see a city and be shown the area that was destroyed by blast and fire and be told of the people who died or were injured without deep sadness. To see the home where orphans were being cared for was to wish with one's whole heart that men could learn from this that we know too well how to destroy and must learn instead how to prevent such destruction. It is useless to say that Germany started the war and even started the research that led to the atomic bomb. It is useless to remember, as I did, the feelings of my husband and of the people of the United States when he heard the shocking news of the Japanese attack on Pearl Harbor. Pearl Harbor was only the climax of years of mounting misunderstandings and antipathies throughout the world. And out of all this came Hiroshima. But it was not just here in this sad Japanese city that men women and children suffered. All the world suffered. So it seems to me that the only helpful thing we can do, as we contemplate man's adventure into the realm of outer space, is to pledge ourselves to work to eliminate the causes of war through action that is possible only by using the machinery of the United Nations. If we do, then the people may understand each other a little better; they may have a better chance to be heard. Contemplating the fate of Hiroshima, one can only say: God grant to men greater wisdom in the future.

Robert S. Pirk used to be the theater critic for the *Staats-Herold*, an American German-language newspaper. He is now retired and lives in Switzerland, but somehow he heard about my search for Eleanor Roosevelt stories. "It was quite a few years ago," he wrote, "that I went to the opening of a play called *Sunrise at Campobello*. It was written by Dore Schary and presented by The Theater Guild at the Cort Theater in New York City on January 30, 1958. Mr. Ralph Bellamy as FDR, certainly was deeply moving. But for me, as obviously for many other people in the audience who craned their necks, the highlight of this first night was not the Eleanor Roosevelt on the stage played by Mary Fickett, but the *real one* seated in a loge. The severe and almost masculine character of the figure on the stage, seemed to have nothing at all in common with that artless, modest woman in the loge who, after the last curtain, smiled a little as she applauded courteously."

"It was the summer of 1956 and the Democrats had gathered in Chicago to select a champion to challenge the seemingly invincible Dwight D. Eisenhower," wrote Roy Thompson, staff reporter at Winston-Salem, North Carolina. "Many names were being suggested. Mrs. Roosevelt was for Adlai Stevenson. 'Madly for Adlai,' as the convention slogan had it. There was a big reception for Mr. Stevenson on convention eve, and Mrs. Roosevelt was in the thick of it, shaking hands. There was nothing striking about her dress. It was blue, and it had flowers on it. Later that evening, there was a strategy meeting at the Blackstone Hotel and Eleanor Roosevelt was there. So was the flowered blue dress. She wore it the next morning for a television appearance. And again that afternoon for the opening session of the convention. And she wore it again, and again, and again, until it became clear that wherever Eleanor Roosevelt went that week, the blue flowered dress was to be there also. She was still wearing it—and a triumphant grin—as the delegates finally put their collective hand on Adlai Stevenson's shoulder.

"The reporters became curious about the blue dress with the flowers. Certain major-league ballplayers have been known to wear some attire for weeks rather than risk breaking a lucky streak. Perhaps Mrs. Roosevelt was also superstitious about the dress. One reporter directed a couple of discreet questions at one of Mrs. Roosevelt's aides about the dress. Mrs. Roosevelt heard of the questions and, apparently unwilling to entrust such high-level communication to an aide, summoned the reporter.

" 'I have been so busy,' she said. 'I brought other dresses, of course. Frankly, I had not realized I wore only this one. I promise to wear something else tomorrow.' She paused, smiled at the reporter and said, 'How interesting that a man should have noticed. Perhaps one of the women did also but was too polite to say anything. I promise, tomorrow I'll think of it and wear something else.' "

"I first met Mrs. Roosevelt when I was ten years old," wrote Harry Golden in the *New York Post* on November 14, 1962. "I recalled her as one of the 'Christian' volunteer workers at the University Settlement house on the lower East Side, during the great wave of Jewish immigration from 1905 to 1914. Fifty years later, in October 1962, she asked me to fill in for her at a speaking engagement at Alfred College. But the meeting I remember most vividly was when Mrs. Roosevelt and I met at Chattanooga airport, both of us on our way to speak at the Highlander Folk School in Monteagle, Tennessee. The Highlander Folk School was the first interracial school in the South, a place where Negro and white social workers taught together. Mrs. Roosevelt had just returned from Europe and one of the newsreel clips from her trip showed Queen Juliana of the Netherlands rushing down the steps of the palace with arms outstretched to greet Mrs. Roosevelt. Nine days later she was in the mountains of Tennessee eating her lunch from a paper plate while she sat on a harsh wooden bench."

Florence Pritchet Smith reported on the 1961 inauguration in Washington. John F. Kennedy was to become President of the United States. The day was cold. Even honored guests had to be in their seats in front of the Capitol by 10 A.M. Miss Pritchet Smith stopped at an Army-Navy store for boots, earmuffs, scarves, and blankets. Also at a liquor store to fill a flask with brandy as a bracer for the bitter cold. When she arrived in front of the Capitol and found her seat, she discovered a lady seated already in the one next to her. Eleanor Roosevelt. Miss Pritchet Smith offered her blanket to share and Mrs. Roosevelt gratefully accepted. "I wish they could hold the inauguration at a more seasonable time of the year," said Mrs. Roosevelt. "I remember one of Franklin's when it was raining. I had ordered a velvet hat in my favorite color, purple. Franklin insisted we ride in an open car so as not to disappoint all the people who had waited to see him. When we reached the White House I quickly took off my hat to greet five thousand people at a reception, only to discover the dye had run and my hair was purple. Back went the hat and it had to stay on the entire day."

While Miss Pritchet Smith shivered in the cold in spite of the blanket, ushers appeared and invited Mrs. Roosevelt inside.

"I would rather stay here," she said firmly. "I have never seen an inauguration from here."

Chapter Seven

Fala and Others

FALA ACCEPTED ME AFTER my husband's death, but I was just someone to put up with until the master should return," Eleanor Roosevelt said in her autobiography.

Fala, of course, was the best-known Scottish terrier in history. His full name was Murray the Outlaw of Fala Hill. He had been given to President Roosevelt in 1940 by his cousin Margaret Suckley. The political opponents of President Roosevelt often used the little black scottie as their target for slander. This led to one of FDR's greatest campaign addresses, one which became known as "that speech about Fala." President Roosevelt started by saying, "The Republican leaders have not been content to make personal attacks about me—or my wife—or my sons— they now include my little dog, Fala. Unlike the members of my family, Fala resents this. When he learned that the Republican fiction writers had concocted a story that I had left him behind on an Aleutian Island and had sent a destroyer back to find him— at a cost to the taxpayer of two or three or twenty million dollars —his Scotch soul was furious. He has not been the same dog since. I am accustomed to hearing malicious falsehoods about myself, but I think I have a right to object to libelous statements about my dog." This address made millions laugh at the Republicans and upset Dewey's self-assurance. Many came to identify the contest as between Dewey and Fala.

In the cottage at Hyde Park, Fala always lay near the dining room door where he could watch both entrances for his master. From there he would be ready to spring up and join the President when he suddenly decided to go somewhere. Fala continued to keep watch on this spot even after F.D.R. no longer was alive.

General Eisenhower once came to lay a wreath on President Roosevelt's grave. As his car approached the house, the wailing of the police escort siren sounded up. Fala pricked up his ears, straightened up his legs and it was obvious that he expected to see his master coming down the drive as he had so often.

"Many dogs eventually forget," Eleanor Roosevelt said. "Fala did not." He died soon after the death of the President.

When Mrs. Roosevelt moved to New York, it seemed that Fala could not get accustomed to city life. Many of her neighbors on Washington Square in Greenwich Village often saw her walking with her famous scottie on the leash.

Mrs. Gerald Carson, who lived at 387½ Bleeker Street at that time, reported that one morning when she opened the door of her house to "dash across the street for some groceries," she found Eleanor Roosevelt walking her dog, waiting patiently for Fala to inspect each tree.

Mrs. Carson and Mrs. Roosevelt exchanged greetings just like any two housewives, and then Mrs. Carson watched as Mrs. Roosevelt continued her early walk. At each step she was surrounded by men in shirtsleeves and women in housedresses who gathered to shake hands with her and to chat about community interests and politics.

New York University students, too, became accustomed to see the tall figure of Mrs. Roosevelt, walking her little black dog through Washington Square Park.

"I am indeed sorry to hear of the loss of your own little dog," Mrs. Roosevelt replied when a stranger reported to Eleanor Roosevelt the death of his scottie, "for I understand how much you must miss him. Dogs are wonderful friends and we tend to forget their short life span and depend too much on their companionship. It is a difficult thing to do, but I would advise you to get another little dog immediately. When Fala died I too got another dog very soon."

Tamas, the scottie which followed Fala, came to Mrs. Roosevelt in an unusual way. Bernard Solomon, fourteen, and his sister Susanne, twelve, read in their Toledo newspaper of Fala's death. They wrote to Mrs. Roosevelt, expressing their sympathy as fellow scottie fanciers, and offered her one of the pups from a litter expected by their pedigreed pet, Bonnie Lassie. About two weeks later Bonnie Lassie became the mother of six black puppies. At the same time the children received a reply from Mrs. Roosevelt, indicating that the former first lady would be happy to have the dog as soon as it was old enough to ship. "You are very generous," Mrs. Roosevelt said in her letter to the children, "and I am most grateful to you. I will, of course, gladly pay the expenses for the shipping of the puppy."

Tamas's sire was Billy Boy, a pedigreed animal owned by James O'Reilly, former Lucas County sheriff. When, in due course, Tamas too left this earth, she was succeeded by another black scottie of her line whose name was Duffy.

When Mrs. Vermes walked her black scottie on Sunday afternoon on Madison Avenue in New York, she noticed the most handsome Duffy, without being aware of his illustrious background or ownership.

Mrs. Vermes had phoned me and told me that she had a story of how she had met Mrs. Roosevelt through her dog. We made an appointment to meet at the Museum of Modern Art.

Mrs. Vermes was an attractive blonde Hungarian in a white suit and flowered blouse. "I was heartbroken when, some years ago, my little scottie died of cancer. I got a new dog at once but made up my mind that this one must stay healthy. If a little dog had to have puppies to survive, I thought, I simply would find her a husband!" Mrs. Vermes laughed gaily, in Zsa-Zsa Gabor fashion. "My dog and I were walking near East Sixty-fourth Street, when we saw this magnificent scottie coming toward us. The two began to sniff each other and to wag their tails excitedly. 'Is it a girl or a boy?' I asked the woman who was holding the other dog. She was very tall and wore a plain dark coat. I was so enraptured by the dog that I did not even take the time to glance at the woman's face. When she replied that her dog was a male, I immediately told her that mine was a girl. I explained what had happened to my first dog and asked if it would be all right with her if the two would get married.

"What a fool I was not to realize who she was," she continued with a faint blush to her cheeks, "but I just didn't. When she said that it would be quite agreeable to her to have the two dogs mate, I even hesitated and inquired whether her scottie had a good pedigree. She assured me that he did and added that I should contact her when the proper time came around. Then I asked her for her name and address.

"I almost fainted," Mrs. Vermes said, her Hungarian accent suddenly more pronounced than before. "Can you imagine, all she said was, 'I am Mrs. Franklin Roosevelt.' I thought I would die of embarrassment!"

"Did the two dogs ever get together?" I asked.

"Yes, of course," Mrs. Vermes said. "Mrs. Roosevelt gave me her phone number and I called her just as soon as, as, well you know . . . The secretary gave us an appointment and the meeting took place in the backyard of Mrs. Roosevelt's house. But she herself was out of town at the time, I believe on a journey to India. But for some reason my dog had changed her mind about Duffy and the marriage never took place. I later got her another very handsome husband with an excellent pedigree. But"—Mrs. Vermes sighed a little—"he had no Roosevelt connections!"

A few days after my meeting with Mrs. Vermes, a woman called me with another dog story. Oddly, it had taken place in India.

To welcome Mrs. Roosevelt to Bombay, an American women's organization had arranged a tea dance and cocktail party. They also planned to hold an auction to raise money for poor Indians. One of the women came up with what seemed to be a great idea. First prize in the raffle would be a little black scottie. They would ask Mrs. Roosevelt to sponsor the puppy and name him Fala. Much work went into the preparations. An American kennel was contacted and a suitable dog chosen; TWA agreed to fly the raffle prize to India. All that remained to be done was to get Mrs. Roosevelt's agreement to sponsor the dog. Surely the women assumed, this could be taken for granted, it would be a mere formality. Eleanor Roosevelt was famous for being agreeable when it concerned a cause to help the needy.

One of the women of the organization was elected to submit the plan to Mrs. Roosevelt at the cocktail party. As always, Eleanor Roosevelt listened attentively. But when the woman had finished explaining her gimmick, Mrs. Roosevelt emphatically shook her head.

"I certainly will not do such a thing," she said almost with indignation. "If you like, I'll give you some books written by my husband, the late President, and sign them for your raffle prize. But I will not sponsor a dog who is going to be auctioned off to someone I do not know. There would be no way for me to find out what kind of master he would get and I would keep wondering and worrying whether he is being treated all right." She paused. "I believe," she then added, a little more gently, "that dogs have feelings just as strong as, if not stronger than, people have."

Chapter Eight

People
from Other Lands

FRANZ JONAS IS CHANCELLOR of Austria. In 1952 when he was the Mayor of Vienna, the Association of American Mayors invited him to visit the United States. He went to Washington, Baltimore, Philadelphia, Milwaukee, and New York. In New York he got together with many old friends who, because of the political events of the thirties, had moved from their native Vienna to the United States where, as he wrote to me, "They had found a new home."

Among those friends was Dr. Ernst Papenek. At that time he was Director of the Wiltwyck School and he asked Mrs. Roosevelt whether he could bring Franz Jonas to meet her at Hyde Park. She invited the Austrian Chancellor at once to her home at Val-Kill. Dr. Papanek suggested to me that I write to Franz Jonas and ask him about his memories of that visit. I did write and the Chancellor replied at once in his native language.

"Very gracious lady," he wrote, "I thank you for your letter in which you told me that you are writing a book about Mrs. Roosevelt. It is true that, through the intervention of my friend,

Dr. Ernst Papanek, I had the honor of meeting Mrs. Eleanor Roosevelt. However, I spent only a few hours in her company. When I got to Hyde Park with Dr. Papanek, we first went to the grave of President Roosevelt to place a wreath there in the name of the City of Vienna. I recall that we had some difficulty in obtaining a red-white-red ribbon—the Austrian national colors —for the flowers. But a kind florist finally obtained it for us. After we visited the grave we went to see the former Roosevelt home and went through it on a tour. I was impressed by the simplicity and by the lack of pretentiousness displayed in the home of so illustrious an American family. I also liked the idea that it was now something like a National Shrine and supported by the government.

"After the sight-seeing tour, we were invited for lunch at Mrs. Roosevelt's home at Val-Kill and I was looking forward a great deal to meeting the venerable former First Lady. I immediately felt at home in Mrs. Roosevelt's country house. It was furnished in a style which we Viennese would call *gemütlich*. As I recall, also present at that lunch was the Lebanon representative to the United Nations. Mrs. Roosevelt was so animated and natural a hostess that I soon forgot to be conscious of my limited knowledge of the English language. She made me feel that a topic in which she was not interested simply did not exist. She spoke of various world matters with such assurance and such matter-of-factness that it was evident she had studied the problems thoroughly. Her main interest seemed to be the question of peace and international understanding. But equally important to her seemed to be the question of schools and education in the United States. After lunch we went for a walk in her garden, and she confessed to me that she had a great deal of trouble with the local police. Mrs. Roosevelt, it turned out, was a very impatient driver and repeatedly was reprimanded by the state troopers for speeding."

This confession of Eleanor Roosevelt's, Franz Jonas concluded his letter, taught him more about democracy than anything that he had read about the United States or seen in person during his visit. "I was deeply impressed," wrote Mr. Jonas, "that Mrs. Roosevelt, in spite of her position as First Lady, is treated by the police like any other American citizen, even to the extent of having to pay a fine."

"After thirty-three months in the concentration camp Theresienstadt, we were liberated by the Americans in 1945," wrote D. Albert A. Hess, of Amsterdam, Holland. "A few days later the Russians also came, but only with a sanitation crew while the regular army avoided Theresienstadt because of an epidemic of typhoid fever. Once we were free, I was put to work as a coal miner. From a few shreds of my shirt and of some material which I begged from the soldiers, I fabricated the first blue-and-white-and-red Dutch flag in Theresienstadt. As soon as it was finished I put it up in front of my coal shack. When I finally was free to return home, the flag was the most cherished of my possessions. In April 1948, the Dutch Queen received a distinguished American visitor at Palace Soestedyck, Mrs. Eleanor Roosevelt. I packed up my flag and sent it to Mrs. Roosevelt with a letter explaining its history. 'I am glad to accept the flag which you sent me,' wrote Mrs. Roosevelt. 'I will put it in the Franklin D. Roosevelt Library at Hyde Park where many people will be able to see it. I know my husband would be interested to have it.'

"This little epilogue to the entire epoch of Nazi history seems to carve out some semblance of sense from the chaotic senselessness of war, at least to me."

"When I came to England in 1940, as a refugee," wrote Mrs. Martha C. Mayer, "I knew how to play the piano and to cook. It was easier to find a job with the latter ability. Eventually I became a chef at the American Women's Club in London. One day I was told that Mrs. Roosevelt would be visiting us. Everyone was very excited, but I had no idea what to cook for this illustrious American guest. At that very time I expected some relatives from the United States myself. I left word for them at their hotel to phone me immediately upon their arrival, for I had to consult with them on a most important matter. They contacted me that night and I told them about my problem. 'You can cook whatever you like,' my American cousins told me. 'Just be certain to include some corn at every meal in any form whatsoever!'

"For the duration of Mrs. Roosevelt's visit to England, I served corn on the cob, creamed corn, corn fritters, and corn muffins. I never saw Mrs. Roosevelt in person. I just prepared the food and then gave it out to the waitresses who carried it from the pantry into the dining room. On the last day of Mrs. Roosevelt's visit, while I was working at the large table in the pantry, the manager informed me that Mrs. Roosevelt would be coming out of the dining room now and I was to withdraw from the pantry. Since I wanted very much to get at least a glimpse of America's First Lady, I just went to the most remote corner of the pantry where, I thought, I would blend with the furniture.

"Mrs. Roosevelt emerged from the dining room, took a quick glance around, and came straight at me in my corner. 'Thank you very much for the lovely meals you have given me,' she said, holding out her hand. 'I have enjoyed them very much. But I never knew,' she added, and her blue eyes seemed a little puzzled, 'that the English are so fond of corn. Don't they think it too fattening?'

"I was so flabbergasted that I did not know what to say," wrote Mrs. Mayer. "I am an old woman now and I no longer cook for a living. But I have never forgotten Mrs. Roosevelt and her kindness. You should have seen the manager's red face when the American First Lady came to me in the pantry to thank me for my work!"

"The day we arrived at the airport of Geneva in 1951," wrote Mr. Samuel R. Lavine from Trenton, New Jersey, "hundreds of Swiss people were waiting for Mrs. Roosevelt to land. I mentioned to my wife that I hoped we would meet her and a few days later, as we entered the League of Nations building, Mrs. Roosevelt and her secretary came over to us to greet us as Americans. Later that week we were invited to a dinner given by our daughter's Smith College group in honor of Mrs. Roosevelt. After dinner there was a question and answer period. Someone asked Mrs. Roosevelt what she thought about President Truman's relieving General MacArthur from his command of the army. Mrs. Roosevelt gently but firmly insisted that the military could not usurp the control of government."

Mr. Colitt is the Danish owner of Old Denmark, a small shop of foreign delicacies located on East Fifty-seventh Street in New York. There are a round wooden table and a few chairs in one corner were people can relax for a while for an unusual lunch of imported cheeses and all manner of salads.

I somehow had heard that Mrs. Roosevelt used to eat there quite often and stopped by one day to question Mr. Colitt.

"Sure," he said with his comfortable Danish accent, "Mrs. Roosevelt came here all the time. She sat right there"—he motoned to the round table—"and she never minded when other people sat with her. She was always pleasant and friendly with everybody. Except"— Mr. Colitt stopped and wrinkled his forehead—"she just couldn't stand it when people tried to butter her up or acted too deferential. Then she would freeze." He grinned. "We never made a big fuss over her and this was what she seemed to like. I never greeted her even by her name. 'How was Denmark?' I asked her once when I knew she just had returned from a trip there. 'I see you ate too much! You gained some weight, didn't you?' She chuckled then. Mrs. Roosevelt always ordered her hors d'oeuvres for her cocktail parties here. Her check was in the mail the next day! Oh, I just remembered, each month she sent a box of our special cookies to her personal physician." Mr. Colitt shook his head. "It doesn't seem possible that she is gone. I still see her sitting there at the table in the corner." We both looked at the six empty wooden chairs.

"I never really liked Eleanor Roosevelt," said a women whose name I have forgotten. "The first time I saw her was in Saratoga Springs while I was a student at Skidmore College. I was eighteen and, well, you know how a teen-ager feels about clothes and looks. Eleanor was really a homely woman. She wore a horrible brown dress, I think it was velvet with something like a big white bib around her neck and an atrocious hat. Besides, my family always was Republican. Anyway, Mrs. Roosevelt came to Skidmore to give an assembly speech. At that time her husband was Governor of New York. She came late and all she said was that she had been at an orphange already that morning and it was a hurried day for her and now she had to rush away again.

"I remember how I giggled and made fun of her to my friends. 'Wouldn't you like a hat like hers?' I asked the girls as I mimicked the high-pitched voice of Mrs. Roosevelt.

"'Next time I saw her was in about 1950, in India. She came

for a visit to that country and the American women's organization to which I belonged was part of the welcoming committee for the First Lady. She greeted us courteously but, it seemed to me, somewhat absent-mindedly. I could almost sense how she dismissed us in her thoughts as a bunch of golf- and bridge-playing committee-women. I watched her as she approached the Indian delegation. When she greeted them, Mrs. Roosevelt very carefully avoided reaching out for a handshake. Instead, she just touched her fingertips to her brow in Indian fashion. I felt my face turning uncomfortably warm because I had a tendency to forget, even after almost a year in that country, that Indian people cannot bear to be touched physically. Then I listened as Mrs. Roosevelt talked with the members of the Indian delegation, obviously deeply and thoroughly informed of the problems of that country."

On that occasion, the woman said that she remembered the first time she had seen Eleanor Roosevelt at Skidmore. "In the years that had passed, Mrs. Roosevelt's taste in clothes did not seem to have improved. She wore a nondescript jersey dress and white, sensible shoes. Her hair had obviously not been attended to by a French hairdresser and her face was perspiring. The members of the Indian delegation did not seem to notice. 'What a beautiful woman she is,' said a handsome young Indian official to me later. 'I have never seen such magnificent blue eyes in such a lovely feminine face. She is the personification of a beautiful soul. You Americans must be very proud of her!' "

"I remember Mrs. Roosevelt giving an interview in the BBC film of 'This Is Your Life,' which featured the life of Father Borelli, the 'Little Priest of Naples,' " wrote Mrs. M. D. Heckscher, from Utrecht, Holland. "If you want to find out more about him I urge you to read Morris West's book *Children of the Shadows*, on Father Borelli's work."

Mario Borelli was the son of a laborer in the slums of Naples. He was one of ten children who lived as did too many others, in crowded, unsanitary back-street tenements. When World War II began, he was a clerical student, no different from any other pale and emaciated youth one can see in the old-fashioned seminaries of the city of Naples. By the time the war ended, Mario

Borelli was a priest. A priest of the poor. The poor whom the wealthy tourists staying in the luxury hotels do not see. Oh, they do see the charming little urchins begging at the tables of the outdoor cafés, and they toss them a coin. They do not know that these small boys of six, or eight, or ten, ran away from homes where a family of twelve lived in one dingy room. Where girls bore children fathered by their own fathers or brothers, where a skinny little boy was supposed to work in any way he could, to add a little to the family income. The tourists do not know, and perhaps do not care, that these boys, if lucky, found a haven in the beds of prostitutes for whom they found customers on the streets. But the ones who were not so lucky, they were the ones who lived on the Street of the Two Lepers. On the cold winter nights they huddled together on gratings over bakeries where some warm air drifted up from the ovens.

Father Borelli had a deep concern for these small boys. The awareness of the *scugnizzi* on the Street of the Two Lepers would not let him sleep at night in his own clean cot. It was in the year 1950, when Father Mario Borelli was just twenty-eight years old, that he became so tortured about these children, hungry and alone, that he decided he had to take some action.

He went to his superior, Cardinal Ascali, Archbishop of Naples, to tell him of the *scugnizzi* and their way of life.

"We'll take these children off the street at once," said the Cardinal. "We'll put them into an orphanage."

"This is exactly what cannot be done," Borelli replied. "These boys are no longer children, yet they are not men. They live without love. They believe every woman is a whore, every man a thief. They believe every priest is a liar. A home to them—is a house of correction. They would only run away."

"What do you propose to do?" asked the Cardinal.

Mario Borelli asked for permission to take off his soutane for some time. He wanted to live with the *scugnizzi* as one of them.

He wanted to win their confidence.

The Cardinal was stunned. A priest, a man of the church, wanted to live in the squalor of the Street of the Two Lepers? With thieves and pimps? In the world of the prostitutes? How could a young man like Borelli remain unstained by it?

"Christ ate and drank with thieves and street women," Mario Borelli replied. "How can I be wrong if I do the same as Christ?"

The Cardinal was moved. He asked for time to think this unusual request over.

A few days later, a new *scugnizzo* joined the gang on the Street of the Two Lepers. His clothes were filthy rags, his face was grimy and unshaven, his hands stained with grease and tobacco. After some careful investigation, the *scugnizzi* accepted Mario Borelli as one of them. He kept watch and whistled a warning signal while the others stole, he ran with them like a hunted animal, he ate the bread that was bought with money stolen from the church poor boxes. He helped to steer foreign soldiers to brothels, he talked and joked with the prostitutes and he took his share of the money that was paid in commission by the whoremaster. For four months Father Borelli lived this life. He came to understand that the house he hoped to build for them would have to be of a very special kind. It would have to be a place to which they would return willingly. He watched them at night huddled over their fire, their thin bodies shivering with cold while their pinched faces were intent on a card game or the tally of their day's takings.

The first thing these children needed, Father Borelli realized, was food and shelter. Big bowls of spaghetti, a roof, a blanket. As he watched them, one of the little ones trembled violently. His teeth chattered and he tried to draw closer to the tin dish full of coals. Mario Borelli bent over him. "What's the matter, Nino?"

The child looked up, tried to swallow his tears. "I'm cold. I'm cold." He began to cough, blood ran from his mouth.

Time was running out, Mario Borelli realized. The child suffered with tuberculosis. A house must be found!

The place was an abandoned church. It was filled with dirt and rubbish. But it had a roof and stout walls. In the old days it had been dedicated to the Mother of God and this was its Latin name, Materdei. Somehow, by begging and pleading with the more substantial citizens of Naples and the American authorities, straw was provided to make mattresses, some blankets were found, a cook pot and a pan. Finally all was ready. On the cold tiles of Materdei was a row of old sacks filled with fresh straw. Each sack had a thin gray blanket. There was a wooden table and one chair. A pile of firewood, a sackful of macaroni and a can of tomato paste. A pile of rusty tin dishes and a few old forks and spoons.

It was late at night when Mario Borelli returned to the *scugnizzi*. He wore his black cassock and round priest's hat. The boys were huddled over their fires. Father Borelli drew closer to the boys. They stared at him with incredulous hostility. "You know me, don't you?" he pleaded. "I'm Mario. Your friend!" He explained what he had been doing. The faces of the *scugnizzi* turned savage with anger. They jumped up and jeered. They spat at Father Borelli's face.

"Nino here is sick," Mario Borelli said while he wiped the spittle from his face. "If he stays on the streets he will die. I have found a place for us. It's not much, but there are beds and blankets, a fire and a pot of spaghetti."

The boys remained hard, hostile. They shrank away from the black garb of Father Borelli.

"I know what you are thinking," he said. "That I want to take you into an orphanage where they close the gates and send you to school and read you lectures and let you out on Sunday afternoon in a long line which you call a 'Crocodile.' I give you my word that this is not so. This place I have found will keep the rain out. You can stay there for the night and leave in the morning. If you like, you can come back any time. There will be a pot on the fire and the soup will be boiling."

The *scugnizzi* kept staring at him silently. They had stopped jeering.

"I'm going there now," Mario Borelli said. "I won't force you to come with me. You can stay here or follow me, just as you want. But I am carrying Nino back with me. I'm going to try and find a doctor and medicine for him." He hoisted the sick child to his shoulders, abruptly turned around and began to walk down the dark alley.

He hardly dared to breathe so intent was he on listening to the sounds of the night. It was not until he turned the corner to the Via San Gennaro that he heard the footsteps behind him.

One at first, then two and three. Halting and hesitating, little by little getting faster, until finally, all the *scugnizzi* came running to catch up with Father Mario Borelli.

At present, a new casa for the *scugnizzi*, the Materdei Center is under construction at the Lago S. Gennaro A Materdei outside of Naples. It is large, well built, and sunny. Father Borelli trains his boys as apprentices to tradesmen in the city, as electricians, cabinetmakers, welders, and automotive engineers. The boys like the work. The life of the street has made them conscious of the dignity of work and the good fortune of being able to get it. The money for the new Casa delle Scugnizzi had been raised from private charities, from Australians, and from Americans, many of whom, one can safely assume, had heard of "the little priest of Naples" from Mrs. Eleanor Roosevelt, hearing her speak of him on television or picking up the book *Children of the Shadows* because *she* had endorsed it.

Last Christmas I received the *Casa delle Scugnizzi News*. The New Year's message on the first page was written by Val Norris, eleven years old. This was that message:

THE URCHINS OF NAPLES

> The sky was dark, and the night was cold,
> And huddled together, like sheep in the fold.
> Close to each other, snuggling down,
> Were the homeless urchins of Naples town.
>
> No bed had they, but the cobbled streets,
> No shoes to wear on their aching feet.
> They fought and squabbled, and how they lied!
> They stole their food—or of hunger they died.
>
> There was one priest who really did care,
> For the children who slept in the street so bare.
> He wanted a place where they could be fed,
> Where each tired child could rest its head.

---

* *Children of the Shadows*, Morris L. West. William Morrow & Co., New York, 1957.

A beggar he pretended to be,
And in amongst the boys went he.
He slept with them through the wintry nights,
He joined in their quarrels, he joined their fights.

At last he brought them from the street,
To a place where they could drink and eat.
And when he thought they feared him least,
He told them that he was a priest.

Though many children still roam the street,
At Father Borelli's they rest their feet.
And many a lucky urchin shares,
The home of a priest who really cares.

Chapter Nine

The Handicapped

"I SAW A MAN WHO WAS BORN WITHOUT LEGS," my friend Dorothy told me. "I heard that Mrs. Roosevelt had a great deal of influence on his life," she added, and went on to explain that the night before she had been invited for dinner at the home of Dr. Robert Yanover, Director of Surgery at Parsons Hospital. His home is in Kings Point, Long Island, and on his grounds is another large house where the man whom Dorothy had seen lives with his wife and four daughters. "His name is Henry Viscardi," she told me and handed me a slip of paper. "I got his telephone number for you. He has a school and factory for crippled people called the Human Resources Center."

I thanked her for her trouble, and took the piece of paper, but somehow was too busy to phone the next day.

I jotted the number down on my long list headed "phone calls to be made," and each day I managed to avoid dialing that particular number. But it kept staring at me. A man who had been born without legs! And he even had a wife and four children! I finally phoned. When I asked to speak with Mr. Viscardi, I got his secretary on the phone. I explained what I was doing and asked if I could have an interview with Mr. Viscardi. "I am so sorry," she said, "but Mr. Viscardi is away on a lecture tour in Europe. If you call back in a month or so—"

I said that I would be very interested to learn more about the center and she promised to send me some literature. A few days later, I found a thick envelope in my mailbox. It said: ABILITIES, INC. Human Resources and Training Institute—Human Resources School, Albertson, New York.

The first folder that came into my hands showed a paraplegic boy in a wheelchair. He was studying electricity in a physics class. The caption underneath said, WHERE THE DISABLED FIND THEIR ABILITY. There were more pictures. A small arthrogryposis victim with a huge head and withered arms and legs stepping into a swimming pool; a muscular dystrophy patient wheeling his small wagon through the library as he searched for books; another child creeping to the school on his belly; an amputee working in the wire factory with hands that were metal hooks.

It took me quite a while to make myself phone again for an appointment. In fact, it was a whole year later when I called the Human Resources Center to find out whether Mr. Viscardi could see me. The same secretary to whom I had spoken before remembered me, and said that Mr. Viscardi was in town. He was very, very busy, but she would try to arrange an appointment. A few days later she called back and asked whether I could come to the Center the following morning.

It was snowing that next morning and I wondered whether the driving would be hazardous. For a moment I contemplated canceling the appointment. "Mr. Viscardi is very busy but he will be happy to talk with you about Mrs. Roosevelt," I recalled the secretary saying, and quickly got dressed.

"What are you going to do today?" my daughter asked when she phoned that morning. "I'm just on my way out," I told her. "Frankly, I am frightened. I have an appointment out on Long Island at a school for crippled children, and I just hate to look at anything like that."

The snow on the road made me still more uneasy and tense as I drove out on the Long Island Expressway. I turned off at Searing Town Road, a pleasant, quiet street. At the corner of the second block I saw a complex of modern, low buildings. I parked my car and walked to the entrance. A school bus pulled up, the driver assisted a boy with a red woolen cap that matched his cheeks into a wheelchair and off he zoomed to the glass-and-metal door which sprang open as if a wand had been waved before it. I followed the child inside. Although it was a gray and dismal day, the corridors seemed filled with sunlight. From somewhere came cheerful muted music. Large windows gave a view of a greenhouse which substituted for a central courtyard. Children and adults were wheeling themselves busily through the hallways. Doors to the classrooms stood open. Students in wheelchairs formed a semicircle around the instructors; the young students listened in rapt attention. I came to an indoor swimming pool such as I had never seen before. Not only was it larger than any ordinary pool, and bluer, but it had slides leading into the water and all kinds of special attachments to make it possible for the handicapped children to go swimming.

Finally I got to the offices. They were no different from any other busy offices with typewriters and file cabinets and such, except that the people who worked there were in wheelchairs.

Miss Dorothy Fisher, Henry Viscardi's secretary, greeted me with a smile. "Mr. Viscardi will be with you shortly," she said. "Will you wait in here for a little while?" She led me into a small paneled conference room with a long table in the center. "Here is something for you to read in the meantime," she added and handed me some newspaper clippings which told of a recent visit to the Center by Mrs. Hubert Humphrey. "Our granddaughter Vicky is probably the most famous little mongoloid child in the country," Muriel Humphrey, wife of the Vice-President of the United States was quoted. "This is because Grandma and Grandpa talk so much about her," she explained. "We do this because so many people still don't understand how handicapped and retarded children can learn to fit into their communities." The pictures accompanying the article showed the silver-haired Mrs. Humphrey learning to bowl with her nose in a bowling alley designed especially for people without the use of their limbs, and eating ice cream at a birthday party with the children in wheelchairs.

Yet, as I leafed through the clippings, my uneasiness of earlier that morning returned. How do you behave with a man who has no legs? Would he be seated behind his desk. He wouldn't try to get up when I came in, would he? But what if he did? Could I say, please, do not bother? No, probably not. He might be insulted . . .

A man of medium height strode into the conference room. He had a strong body, short dark hair, an open and very alert face. He held out his hand. "I am Hank Viscardi. So good of you to come. Please come into my office."

I followed him into a large square room. The clouds from that morning had disappeared and sunlight flooded through the large windows. The first thing I noticed were the photographs on the walls. Mrs. Roosevelt with Henry Viscardi. Mrs. Roosevelt with a Negro woman touching her face. "This is Esther," Henry Viscardi said. "She was born blind. Still, she earned a Master's degree in sociology. Then she became deaf. There was nothing left for her but public relief. Finally she wrote to Mrs. Roosevelt and told her that she did not want to live off the taxpayers. She wanted to be one. Eleanor Roosevelt sent her to us."

Henry Viscardi pulled out a chair for me and then sat down behind his desk. His dark lively eyes focused on my face. "Now what can we do to make you happy?"

"I would like to know all about your friendship with Mrs. Roosevelt," I said instantly.

A smile came to Henry Viscardi's face. "It's a long story," he said very gently, "and it would take a long time to tell it. Unfortunately, time is the only thing I haven't got. But I'll tell you what we shall do," he added. He rose swiftly and took two books from a shelf. "This one is my autobiography,* and that one is the story of Human Resources.† If you read both, you will know everything about me and Mrs. Roosevelt's influence on my life." He wrote something in each volume, handed them to me. I thanked him. "You have a wonderful place here," I said. Then, as we stood, I saw on Henry Viscardi's desk the photograph of his four daughters. "You must be a very happy man," I said.

"I am," he said simply.

---

* Henry Viscardi, Jr. *A Man's Stature.* New York: John Day Company, 1952.
    † Henry Viscardi, Jr. *Give Us the Tools.* New York: Paul E. Erikson, Inc., 1959.

When I was seated in my car again, I opened the books, curious to see what Henry Viscardi had written in them for me. "To my friend," it said in a strong and firm handwriting.

As soon as I arrived home my telephone began to ring. "Was it very horrible?" my daughter asked worriedly. "You must be depressed after *that* visit."

That night I began to read Henry Viscardi's story, *A Man's Stature*.

Henry Viscardi, Jr., was born on May 10, 1912. The second child and only son of an immigrant Italian barber and his wife, he was born with underdeveloped legs. In medical terminology this was described as "arrested development of the lower limbs resulting in incomplete growth of the bones and spasticity of the immature, ill-formed muscles." The baby's short thighs ended in two small stumps twisted across each other on the abdomen. In the right limb there was a kneecap, imperfect but sufficient to allow for action. Below that was a small mass of tissue containing two inadequate pieces of bone, a rudimentary tibia and fibula. From this hung what should have been a foot, with three small nodes of flesh for toes. The left limb was worse; it lacked both the kneecap and the "foot." Both legs were tightly enfolded by the muscle pull so that they could not be straightened without severe pain and without reverting immediately to the original position on release.

The birth of this handicapped child was a great shock for his parents, since both were normal and they had one perfectly normal baby girl. The mother was a very devout Catholic and immediately after the child's birth she dedicated him to St. Anthony. As soon as possible after her confinement, she bought miniature wax legs at a store and took the long trip to St. Anthony's Church to place them on the saint's altar. As she prayed to him that her son would one day have legs and be able to walk, she promised that she would bring him flowers every year in June on his feast day. It was a promise that she faithfully kept all through her life.

Before little Henry Viscardi was two years old, he was admitted to the Hospital for Deformities and Joint Diseases in New York. He stayed there until he was five.

Through a succession of operations the short tight muscles of the "legs" were lengthened and held in position with casts and splints. Except for the pain of these operations and the traction, heavy weights and steel splints, the hospital was a happy place for little Henry Viscardi. The nurses smelled like flowers, there were toys to play with and books and teddy bears and, best of all, all the ice cream he wanted to eat. By the time he was four, his limbs were reasonably straight and he began to walk around in a pair of casts. Finally, these casts were replaced by leather ortho-pedic boots. With these boots on Henry could walk and run.

It was then that his mother took him home.

Life at home with his mother and father and two sisters was quite different from life at the hospital. But everyone was kind to Henry, and in time he got used to it. He soon entered first grade at a public school. The other children at first stared and made fun of him, but Henry Viscardi came to realize that all children have to go through a similar share of hazing on their first day. The family moved to Elmhurst on Long Island, and Henry got a little wagon in which he could push himself around as fast as other boys rode on their bicycles. One day a new young doctor in the neighborhood who had just opened his office, stopped him on the street. "That's quite some wagon you've got," he said. "I'm Dr. Robert Yanover. Nice to meet you, Hank." Thus started a lifelong friendship.

Henry Viscardi finished high school and then went to Fordham University. Money was scarce in the Viscardi family, however, and Henry got a job in the treasurer's office of the university and also worked as a busboy in the freshmen dining room. Money continued to be a problem. Henry's father died, one sister worked, another got married, two were still in school. Henry wanted them to stay there. He found a job in a law firm as a clerk. The only problem was getting to work. Subways are crowded in New York City at the rush hours—especially for someone like Henry, who saw other people as pushing, shoving giants. They rarely saw *him.* The ones who did, however, either stared at him as if he were something out of a circus, or peeked from behind a newspaper and then quickly looked away. Worse than either, however, were the ones who looked at him with pity. The subway was a problem for a man who was less than four feet tall, but Henry Viscardi managed to live through it. Then he bought a car, and a friendly mechanic grafted long extensions on to the clutch, brake, and accelerator, and added new pedals to them. For the first time in his life, Henry Viscardi could get around as fast as anyone else.

But then his "legs" began to hurt. They became swollen and tender until it was almost impossible to walk around on them.

"Your legs are burned out," said Dr. Robert Yanover. "I don't believe you can walk around for more than six months the way you are."

"What happens afterward?" Henry asked.

"A wheelchair."

"My family is depending on me," said Henry. "I just can't become an invalid!"

"There is a slight possibility that we can fit you with artificial limbs," said Dr. Yanover. "Let's give it a try."

"Nothing can be done in this case," was the verdict of the first designer of prosthetic appliances.

Dr. Yanover took Henry to another one.

George Dorsch was Prussian. His shop was under the Third Avenue el. Displayed in the window were a false nose, shiny steel splints, a detached hand wearing a golden wedding band. Mr. Dorsch examined Henry Viscardi with German thoroughness. He measured and probed, he worked over a drawing pad. Finally he nodded his head. "Yes, it can be done."

It took many weeks until the aluminum legs were completed. Finally the day came. At twenty-five, Hank saw himself in a mirror—at long last a man. He was five feet eight inches tall.

He had to learn how to walk, though. At first it was as if he stood on stilts, stilts it would be impossible to manipulate. There was the dead weight that had to be hoisted from a chair, muscles to be trained, balance to be learned. After a step forward, there would follow a fall to the ground. Little by little, his uncoordinated feet took some steps, first with crutches, finally without.

Henry Viscardi burned his old clothes. His sister taught him how to dance. He began going out with girls. He bought a boat and went sailing on the Sound.

One day while he was with his best girl, Elaine, the Sunday afternoon symphony on the radio was interrupted by a news special: "The Japanese Air Force and Navy have just attacked Pearl Harbor."

Henry Viscardi offered his services to his country. "But what can you do?" The authorities asked.

"There is something I can do better than anyone else," replied Henry Viscardi. "I can teach men who lose their legs how to walk again."

The Marine Corps said No. The Air Cadet Training School said No. The Coast Guard and the Navy said No. They did not want a cripple. Even the Red Cross interviewer shook his head. "We can't give you a job doing physical therapy with amputees. That requires skill and special training. But we might possibly use you in our Field Service."

Henry Viscardi, the man who was born without legs, now received the rank and pay of an Army captain. He was put on duty at Walter Reed Hospital in Washington to work with the amputees. One day he was called in to see Dr. Howard Rusk, who headed the Air Force's Convalescent Training Division.

"They tell me you are teaching the men to walk," said Dr. Rusk. "Now I'd like your report on Walter Reed."

"It is not a favorable one," Henry Viscardi replied and went on to tell the doctor that the hospital was poorly equipped to meet the great volume of amputees. The prosthetic shop was tiny and totally inadequate. The limb maker wanted to build a cart for a man who needed legs. The legs the patients did get after an unconscionably long period of waiting were usually so poorly constructed that they often broke the first time they were used.

Dr. Rusk listened to all the complaints and made some notes.

Henry returned to his job teaching a Major Robinson how to walk. The major, who had been a fighter pilot, one day cut short his lesson because he was invited for dinner at the White House.

A few days later, Henry Viscardi received a phone call.

"Mrs. Roosevelt would like to invite you to tea day after tomorrow at three-thirty," he was told by Malvina Thompson, secretary to the First Lady.

Maybe I'll get a decent meal, Henry Viscardi thought to himself, tired of mess-hall food.

"But I completely forgot about eating," he said, "as soon as I set eyes on Mrs. Roosevelt in her sitting room."

"I hear you are doing some wonderful work," Eleanor Roosevelt said, with an outstretched hand and the gentlest of smiles.

"Tell me, are you having difficulty putting your program over?"

"Before I knew what I was doing, I had told her the complete story of my life. My childhood, my artificial legs, the hospital, everything." Henry Viscardi wrote in his book.

Mrs. Roosevelt listened thoughtfully for a whole hour to him. He finally finished by telling her that the present system just was not geared for this war emergency. It had to be changed—inside the army hospital and, even more important, outside—when the amputees return to private lives. "They don't want pity," Henry told Mrs. Roosevelt, "and they don't want handouts. They want to be treated like men. They want a chance to make a new life for themselves, to work in order to regain their self-respect. I would like to talk to the people in industry."

"I think perhaps I can help you," Eleanor Roosevelt said.

Three weeks later, Henry Viscardi was called to tell his story to the chief of the Air Force. Pressure for improved conditions for pilots started at once. Parents from all over the country were writing to their congressmen and complaining about the amputee program. Congress began to move. Walter Reed expanded the shop for prosthetic appliances to three times its former size. They hired a large staff of physical therapists. A new amputation center was put into operation in Michigan. The National Research Council set up a committee to work on the improvement of artificial limbs. This was the beginning of a program that today provides disabled soldiers with the finest prosthetic appliances the world has ever known. Henry Viscardi's work in Washington was completed. He said good-bye to Dr. Howard Rusk and went home to New York to be married.

But his girl had a frightened look in her eyes when Henry, for the first time in civilian clothes, saw her again.

"When will you marry me?" he asked.

The frightened look became desperate. "I can't," she said. "I wanted to marry you but I can't make myself do it. I could not marry a man who has no legs."

"The world is full of women," his friends kept telling Henry Viscardi. He did not reply. What was true for them was not so for him.

Mrs. Roosevelt invited him for a visit to Hyde Park.

She walked with Henry in her quiet garden, she talked with

him about the improvement that had come about through him for the amputees. One day she touched his personal problem. "I've heard about that girl you were engaged to, Hank," she said gently. "Surely, it is hard for you now. A disappointment. But when you marry I think it is very important that both people have maturity and understanding of each other's problems. And when you do find the right girl you will realize what I mean."

Henry did when he met Lucille. They were married on November 16, 1946. It was after World War II and there were no empty apartments or houses for newly married couples. Hank and Lucille built their own on the grounds of their friend Dr. Robert Yanover's. A year later, their first daughter was born.

After a variety of jobs in industry, Burlington Mills offered Henry Viscardi the position of Director of Personnel Administration. It was a well-paid executive position with many financial benefits such as profit sharing, bonuses, and others. Best of all, though, the job was challenging. Henry's office was thickly carpeted and well air conditioned. Through his organization he hired thirty thousand employees. He almost forgot that the legs he walked on were artificial. He no longer thought of himself as a part of the world of the handicapped or crippled.

But then one day Dr. Howard Rusk phoned and invited him for lunch to meet Orin Lehman to discuss a very special matter. Henry went to Dr. Rusk's office at *The New York Times*. After his release from the Air Force, Dr. Rusk had joined the staff of New York University to head the first department of physical medicine to be established in any medical school. At Bellevue Hospital he set up the rehabilitation wards and in 1948 Dr. Rusk was named director of the Institute of Physical Medicine and Rehabilitation at the New York University-Bellevue Medical Center.

Henry Viscardi had no idea what this meeting was to be about when he and Dr. Rusk went into the dining room. They were met there by Orin Lehman, grandnephew of Mrs. Roosevelt's good friend Senator Herbert H. Lehman. Orin Lehman was a tall, large-framed man of about thirty. He had blond hair, blue eyes, and he walked with crutches. As an Air Force captain in World War II he had lost a leg. The other one had been badly shattered.

"Orin has formed a committee of young businessmen," Dr.

Rusk explained to Henry. "It is called J.O.B.—Just One Break. It is an organization to find jobs for handicapped people in industries like IBM, General Motors, and others. We need jobs for people like Ernie who is one of our former patients. Ernie lost his hands in an industrial accident three years ago. We have fitted him with a set of hooks. He has learned how to dress himself and feed himself. He can travel alone and is able to take care of all his daily needs."

"We can get pity for him," Orin Lehman said, "and handouts. This is not what he wants. He has a wife and three small children. He wants to support them like a man. This is why we have started J.O.B.—to give people like Ernie just one break. We are looking for a trained executive director who can run it as a business. We would like to know if you would be interested in the position, Henry."

The job meant less money and Henry Viscardi now had three children to support. It meant that he would have to return to the world of the crippled. He could not say Yes right away—he could not say No either. The thought nagged at him; his wife Lucile urged him to accept the new challenge. He still could not make himself do it. He and his wife went for a visit to Hyde Park.

"I like the sound of it, Hank," Eleanor Roosevelt said after she had listened carefully to all the details of Just One Break. "Of course I know Orin. I think he was about ten when I visited the Scarborough School, where he was a student. He presented me with some flowers. I thanked him for being so kind and recall expressing my hope that he would always be as kind to everyone else." She paused. "This position is something I feel you are particularly well suited for, with your personal background and your experience. But I think it is you who must make the final decision."

Mrs. Roosevelt's words made Henry Viscardi realize that he had known all along what that decision would be. He could not turn his back on the world of the handicapped.

This was the beginning. The organization, which did not even have a typewriter at the start, grew. Eleanor Roosevelt helped as she was particularly interested in the undertaking because of her personal experience when her husband fell ill with polio. Bernard Baruch helped as a tribute to the memory of his father, a Civil

War surgeon. Many, many others became involved. But Henry Viscardi was still not completely satisfied. Too many people who came to Just One Break seeking help had to be turned down because of the severity of their disabilities.

With four men he set about to find an opportunity for them to work. They set up a grimy shop in an unfurnished garage with only five good arms and one good leg among them. They called the company "Abilities, Inc.," for they were certain that their abilities outweighed their disabilities.

The company grew into today's modern, streamlined Human Resources Center on Searing Town Road, where four hundred and fifty "unemployable" workers are running a factory, where handicapped and retarded children are being taught from pre-kindergarten through high school.

"Despite their disabilities these people constitute a vast reservoir of skills, talents, and energies," said Bernard M. Baruch on the jacket of the book *Give Us the Tools.* Society does itself a disservice, even in an economic sense, by its reluctance to employ these willing and able hands. They are men and women who want neither pity, nor parades or pensions. They only want a chance to work, to regain the dignity which idleness and a sense of uselessness destroys."

As I finished reading the two books, I saw in my mind Henry Viscardi standing before me on his two artificial legs. I heard his forceful voice saying: "I am a happy man."

The students at The Clark School in Northampton, Massachusetts, are different from other children: they are deaf. On February 7, 1941, the school had one of the most exciting visitors of its history. Eleanor Roosevelt came to visit Joan, the daughter of her good friends, Margaret and Morris L. Ernst. Mrs. Roosevelt brought Joan a little pottery donkey of flowers and told her that it represented the Democratic party.

"Joan was very much excited to get it," reported one of the other pupils in *The Clark School Bulletin* in the issue of May 1941. "We were so thrilled to see Mrs. Roosevelt in person that we could not find our tongues," she continued. "Mrs. Roosevelt is quite tall and has a very charming manner. As soon as we saw her, we liked her. She had such a friendly smile and pleasing appearance. The students lined up on both sides of the long corridor down toward the chapel and Mrs. Roosevelt passed down the line saying 'Good Morning,' or 'How are you?' to every one of us. Joan Ernst is very fortunate to have a friend like Mrs. Roosevelt."

Mrs. Roosevelt's interest in the deaf was sustained throughout the years, long before she herself became hard of hearing.

On February 3, 1948, she gave an address to the Midtown Supper Club, an organization formed by a group of alert deaf adults. It was her first experience speaking before an audience of deaf people. Mrs. Roosevelt's appearance drew a crowd of 150—members of the club, their parents, relatives, and friends. When Eleanor Roosevelt entered the huge ballroom at the George Washington Hotel in New York, the audience gave her a thunderous standing ovation.

Mrs. Roosevelt began to speak about her work as the chairman of the United Nations' Human Rights Commission. Not once did she act awkward as so many people do when in company of the deaf. However, she spoke a little too fast and many of the lip-readers could not keep pace with her speech. Almost as though she sensed this, she paused now and then and supplemented her talk with gestures and facial expressions. She herself was wearing a hearing aid at that time. The Midtown Supper Club considered Mrs. Roosevelt's visit the most memorable affair of its history.

In her column, 'My Day,' on February 6, 1948, Mrs. Roosevelt reported on that visit herself.

"I had a unique experience last night," she said. "I went to the Midtown Supper club for dinner and found myself with the most cheerful, talkative people who were nearly all completely deaf. There is an organization called the League for the Hard of Hearing, but this group is starting a foundation for the totally deaf. They have an added handicap because, if they never could hear, learning to talk is a most difficult accomplishment. They talk to each other a mile a minute without any signs or sounds. They just form the words with their lips. This has advantages because they can carry on lengthy conversations and, unless you are watching, you are none the wiser!

"The president of the organization, Robert L. Swain, Jr., is a young man of ability and charm. One sees his cartoons every now and then in the subway. He has a wife and a baby and earns a living for them. I found him difficult to understand but, when he got up to introduce me, the audience understood him perfectly. On my other side was the vice chairman, Martin L. A. Sternberg, whom I found easier to understand. He is studying at the school of journalism at Columbia University and expects to go into magazine work. I was told he is getting all A's and B's in his courses. If you are deaf, you must do things better than the average person in order to get ahead. Once you have overcome the difficulty of persuading someone you can do a job and are given a chance, you must do it very well indeed to keep it. One of the advantages of being deaf is that the loss of one faculty sharpens all your others and gives you the perceptions that many hearing people might not have. The only difficult thing is that so many people think there is something the matter with your mind because it takes you a little while to get accustomed to the way they talk; to be looked upon as a moron when you are extra bright and extra disciplined must take a lot of patience."

Chapter Ten

Children and Schools

"THE FIRST LADY, MRS. FRANKLIN D. ROOSEVELT, enjoyed a strawberry ice-cream soda at Schrafft's in Greenwich Village last Saturday," reported *The Villager* on March 11, 1943. "Eleanor Roosevelt was with three friends, two of whom were children."

It seems significant that the reporter made no distinction between the adult and the youngsters in referring to them as Mrs. Roosevelt's "friends." Children always gravitated to Eleanor Roosevelt for apparently she never talked down to them but treated them with the same respect and courtesy she extended to everyone else. Perhaps she even stressed this attitude with young people because, to her, they represented the future of America.

One of her main concerns was that children must learn how young people live in other lands. "The world is smaller than you think," she often used to say. "It is essential that children are taught the cultures of various countries in our schools."

It was this concern that made her respond at once when Gertrude Selkowe, the principal of Junior High School 135 in the Bronx, New York, and Dr. Loretan, Associate Superintendent of Schools at that time, appealed to Mrs. Roosevelt to help start a pilot program concerning Latin America, Africa, the Middle East, and the Far East. Gertrude Selkowe, because of her extensive travels and study in the Far East, was asked to head the program on Asia.

"As soon as it became known that Eleanor Roosevelt was to appear, everyone was eager to participate," said Mrs. Selkowe. "Five hundred teachers and principals from schools all over the city came to the launching of this program. The children of our school were hanging out the windows when Mrs. Roosevelt arrived," Mrs. Selkowe still remembered vividly. "I asked her whether she would speak briefly to them over the microphone and of course she did."

Later, on the dais, while preparations were being made it seemed as if Mrs. Roosevelt was taking a quick nap. But she was fully alert the instant it was time for her to speak. She talked about the United Nations, about the world and how small it had become through the development of modern transportation and news coverage on radio and television. Of the five hundred people present in the auditorium, no one moved or made a sound.

The program Mrs. Roosevelt launched was designed to educate seventh, eighth, and ninth grade students in Far Eastern Cultures. All the departments of Mrs. Selkowe's school participated in making this a worthwhile undertaking. In the sewing class, the children learned to drape saris; in the cooking classes they concocted Eastern dishes using curry; in shop class they built a three-hundred-pound dam; in the science classes they learned of the monsoons. At a special festival the children gave an Eastern party, inviting their parents, to whom they served Eastern dishes while attired in Far Eastern clothing that they had made themselves. The children glowed with pride over their achievements and the opportunity to teach their parents something new; the parents glowed in return.

"Some of my children still write to me," said Gertrude Selkowe, who now teaches Far Eastern Cultures to adults at the New School in New York and spends her vacations traveling in the Far East. "They are adults now and several are working at consulates in India. Many others are in the Peace Corps. I like to think that their interest was sparked by our program."

It was in 1958 that twelve-year-old Claremont Carter, a junior high school student in Miami, Florida, made a survey of the teaching profession, comparing living standards of teachers with persons of other professions here and in the rest of the world.

He sent a copy of that report to Mrs. Roosevelt, who devoted one of her columns to praising the author. Several letters were exchanged and finally Mrs. Roosevelt invited Claremont Carter and his mother to visit her in her New York City apartment.

"For a moment I felt a little frightened to meet such an important person," the young man reported later in an interview. "But Mrs. Roosevelt made me feel at home at once. I had so much to tell her that for one half hour I didn't get a chance to sip the tea she served. 'Claremont,' she said after a while, 'you had better strengthen yourself a little and eat something.' But there was so much to tell her about my plans that I interrupted my story only for a little tea. When I finished, she escorted me and my mother to the door and invited us to visit her at Hyde Park."

When he got to Val-Kill about a month later, Claremont had started an international pen pal project sponsored by the U.N. He told Mrs. Roosevelt about it, and again she wrote in her column about her "young friend's" international pen pal project.

"When I arrived at Val-Kill," Claremont Carter recalled, "Mrs. Roosevelt greeted me with open arms. She said, 'How nice to see you again, Claremont!' This time I did not feel at all nervous.

"She served us lemonade and tea and cookies and, although several maids were standing around on the veranda, Mrs. Roosevelt handed us the refreshments herself. The only trouble was," he concluded, "that when she took me around the grounds, I could not keep up with Mrs. Roosevelt's pace."

"Mrs. Roosevelt recorded for RCA Victor a wonderful record," wrote Mrs. Mollie Seletski, a retired schoolteacher who lives on East Eighty-seventh Street in New York. "It is called *Hello, World!* and is a musical trip around the world. Mrs. Roosevelt is the narrator. She takes a group of American children to various countries and teaches them to say 'Hello' in each individual language. The recording is a beautiful lesson in brotherhood, friendship, and understanding. As a teacher in the New York Public Schools, I used this record for teaching purposes and also as the basis for a play which my class and I wrote. The children wore the costumes of the different countries and they sang along with Mrs. Roosevelt's narration. They performed it in the auditorium of our school three times and it was a huge success. For many months everyone walked around the school whistling the melodies."

Intrigued by the story, I went on a search for the record. "I remember it well," most of the salespeople in the record shops said. "But we no longer have it. It came out in 1959 and is now out of print."

After miles of walking and many phone calls, I finally did discover the record in a small record shop in New York. It was now a collector's item.

"Hearing this musical travelogue, you will stop with Mrs. Roosevelt in such countries as France, Ireland, Austria, the Belgian Congo, Russia and Japan," was on the cover. "You will learn the word for 'Hello' in the language of each country and you will hear a piece of the original music which captures the flavor of the individual land. Commissioned by Thomas Scherman, Conductor of The Little Orchestra Society, *Hello, World!* had its world premier at the opening of the Young People's Concerts of The Little Orchestra Society on November 10, 1956. The following day it was performed by CBS-TV, with the help of UNICEF, on the program 'Let's Take a Trip.' It was enthusiastically received by both children and adults, and has since proved popular in schools and with symphony orchestras."

I wrote a letter to Thomas Scherman asking him whether he would be willing to tell me the story of how the record came about.

"I will be delighted to share with you the enormously exciting experience I had in making that record," replied Mr. Scherman, and I went to see him in his office high above Columbus Circle.

Thomas Scherman, founder and director of The Little Orchestra Society, has been hailed repeatedly for his important contributions to the musical life of New York. His extraordinary ingenuity in programming has given concert audiences of New York, as well as other cities in the United States and abroad, invaluable opportunities to hear masterpieces never before presented by an orchestra. Mr. Scherman has appeared as guest conductor with many major orchestras in different parts of the world:

the London Symphony, the BBC Orchestra, Orchestre de la
Suisse Romande, the Berlin Philharmonic, the Vienna Chamber
Orchestra. In 1959, under the auspices of the President's Special
International Program for Cultural Presentation, Mr. Scherman
conducted The Little Orchestra Society in an eight-week tour
of the Far East. In addition to The Little Orchestra, Mr. Scherman also founded the Young People's Concert series which have
come to be regarded by musicians and educators alike as unique
and supreme in this field; in 1957 it was awarded the George
Foster Peabody award, the only series of children's concerts ever
to be so honored.

I asked Mr. Scherman what made him commission *Hello,
World!*

"I wanted something that was educational as well as entertain-
ing," he said. "I also wanted a young people's concert with the
opportunity for audience participation. I feel that if we expose
children to music at an early age, we will educate a generation
which is just as responsive to music as the people in European
countries. My aim is that in the years to come, a cabdriver will
talk just as easily about an opera singer as he will about a famous
baseball player."

"It must have been most exciting to work with Mrs. Roosevelt
on the recording of *Hello, World!*"

"I did not meet Mrs. Roosevelt when we did the recording,"
said Mr. Scherman. "You know how very busy she was with her
own work and it was decided that we would record the concert
from a tape with Mrs. Roosevelt's narration. But several months
later I was having dinner in a restaurant in Boston with some
friends and who should walk in but Mrs. Roosevelt. She and her
party sat down at the table next to ours. I leaned over to my
friend and asked him to introduce me to Mrs. Roosevelt. Evidently
she overheard me and turned around instantly. 'There is no need
for an introduction,' she said in her gracious way. 'I am fully
aware of who you are, Mr. Scherman, and even though I was not
present during the recording of *Hello, World!*, I was completely
conscious of everything that was going on. You did a magnificent
job with the piece.' "

"Can you imagine?" Thomas Scherman said to me while his

gentle eyes filled with tears. "Can you imagine that she knew who I was? That I did not need to be introduced to her?"

"Oh, but you must meet William Mayer, the composer of *Hello, World!*" he said then. "Bill really had much more to do with Mrs. Roosevelt than I did." He promptly lifted the telephone and dialed a number in Riverdale. After explaining about me and the book on Mrs. Roosevelt, Thomas Scherman handed me the receiver.

"If it is urgent," said William Mayer, "I will come into New York at once. But I am working right now on a concert and if it could wait a week or two . . ."

I assured him that it could and we made an appointment.

Several weeks later I met William Mayer in his small studio on the West Side of New York. There was a piano, a chair or two. Nothing else. No telephone. No books. Just a piano.

"This studio is not large," he said as he cordially shook my hand. "But it is a wonderful place for me to work."

William Mayer has had works performed by a number of leading orchestras in the United States. In 1963, the Philadelphia Orchestra presented a preview of his opera. *One Christmas Long Ago,* and in 1964 it produced the entire opera. The Minneapolis Symphony presented scenes from *The Snow Queen,* based on the tale by Hans Christian Andersen, and programs at Carnegie Hall have included many of his works.

"We had so much fun doing *Hello, World!* with Mrs. Roosevelt," Mr. Mayer said. "When we planned the recording we did not know whom to ask to do the narration. Then, because she was so wonderful with children, I thought of Eleanor Roosevelt. My grandfather was a cousin of Senator Lehman's and, through this channel, we approached Mrs. Roosevelt and asked her if she would be interested in doing it.

"I received word to come to Mrs. Roosevelt's apartment with my music and she would make a decision after hearing it. It was my first face-to-face meeting with Mrs. Roosevelt and I was quite nervous about it. But she was friendly and pleasant and I took my place at the piano." William Mayer hummed the music as he went on to explain that, on this musical trip, the narrator would have to take the children from country to country. "As I played," he said, "I watched Mrs. Roosevelt from the corners of my eyes. When I got to Austria, I saw that she was taking a little nap. I thought to myself, She finds it boring, she won't do it! But then Mrs. Roosevelt raised her head again and listened carefully until the ending. She said she would let me know her decision.

"A few days later I got word that she would do it. We did the recording at the Olmsted Sound Studios on East Fifty-fourth Street. I was terribly anxious that everything should go smoothly." "When we had finished the work I took Mrs. Roosevelt to the elevator. I was so eager to please her that in my nervousness I pushed the button for the service elevator by mistake. I was appalled when it stopped and I realized what I had done and told Mrs. Roosevelt that we would wait for the other one.

"She said, 'Nonsense! Why should we waste the time?' and stepped right in. Two garbage men were standing there with their tall containers filled with refuse. It was just at the time of the Suez Crisis, and, when the garbage men saw Mrs. Roosevelt, one of them said casually, and as though he had seen her just the day before. 'Oh, hi, Eleanor! Do you think we're going to have a war over this Suez business?'

"I almost fainted," said William Mayer, "but Eleanor Roosevelt did not seem a bit surprised. She said, 'Well, the situation is a serious one, but—I don't really think it will develop into anything large.' She then plunged into a long-drawn-out political discussion with the two garbage men." "It was quite noisy in that elevator," he added. "The lids of the garbage cans were not on very tight and they made a hard, metallic noise, something like bang-bang-bang. And then there was Eleanor Roosevelt's high pitched voice as she talked and the deep, resonant voices of the garbage men as they asked their questions. Maybe someday I will make a concert out of it," he said. "When the elevator finally got to the ground floor, Mrs. Roosevelt remained standing there until she had completed her discussion with the garbage men. Only when they had nothing more to ask her did she shake hands with them and step out of the elevator. It all was really quite incredible."

I noticed that Mr. Mayer was glancing furtively toward his piano and quickly thanked him for his story. "Oh, but you must meet Miss Susan Otto, the lyricist who wrote the words to *Hello,*

World!" He jotted down the address. "Susan was also present while we did the recording and she too might remember something that you can use." He wished me luck for my book and we said good-bye.

Susan Otto lives with her husband Bob Israel and her two young children on Riverside Drive and Eighty-sixth Street in Manhattan. She has done a number of children's songs in collaboration with William Mayer, among them a musical play, *The Pink Siamese,* and a one-act Christmas opera, *How Far to Bethlehem?"*

"Mrs. Roosevelt was marvelous with the children," said Susan Otto as she folded her slim, bare legs beneath her on the couch in her living room. "There were two children involved in the recording—Flip Mark and Phyllis Rosenthal. They took to Mrs. Roosevelt from the moment she entered the studio. . . . Oh!" Susan Otto exclaimed, "I just remembered! We have a tape of the entire working session. It might be interesting for you to hear it. Let me see, where is it? It's so long ago that we made it. More than ten years. I haven't thought of that tape since then. I think it is in my husband's studio. Let me check with him." She left the room to phone her husband. "Yes," she said when she returned. "Bob has the tape in his office. If you make an appointment with his secretary, he will be happy to play it for you."

A few days later I went to see Bob Israel in his studio where he sells the music for various television shows. He took me to his soundproof basement studio; there were several boxes of tape prepared on the desk. None turned out to be the one of Eleanor Roosevelt's working session of *Hello, World!*

"I can't understand it," he said, shaking his head. "I could have sworn it was here. But then, it was all so long ago. I must have it in my apartment after all. First thing when I get home tonight I'll look for it. Call me after ten o'clock."

I said that I was sorry to put him to so much trouble but he waved away my apology. "What you are doing sounds exciting," he said. "I really don't mind looking for the tape."

When I phoned him at ten o'clock that evening, Mr. Israel said that he was still looking. But he promised to phone me as soon as he found it, in a day or two.

At midnight my phone rang. "We've found it!" exclaimed Susan. "It's just marvelous. Do you want to hear it right now? I'll play it to you over the telephone."

And then the voice of Eleanor Roosevelt came over the telephone; it filled my small workroom. I heard a tape which no one except Susan and Bob Israel, not even Eleanor Roosevelt herself, had ever heard.

As Mrs. Roosevelt entered the recording studio she greeted the children. She talked about her own grandchildren and great-grandchildren, particularly about a little grandson who lived in the Adirondacks and loved to ski and to ride.

"How old is your grandson?" Flip Mark inquired.

"Oh," Mrs. Roosevelt said, "I think a little younger than you. About seven I would say . . ." And then she laughed at herself for not knowing his correct age.

"I love animals," Flip said. "But I am afraid they do not love me. I live on Long Island and one day I was on a big white horse and then a motorcycle came down the road and the horse raised itself on his hind legs. I was so scared that I thought it was the end of me," he declared.

Mrs. Roosevelt broke into warm laughter. "Oh, I can understand that," she said. "I have a little granddaughter who is only five years old and she rides her father's big horse. I must admit that I don't feel as confident as she does when I watch her." Again there was the laughter, a little rueful this time, though. It made me remember the story of Mrs. Roosevelt's granddaughter Sallie, who had died at sixteen after a fall from a horse.

Then the working session began in earnest.

"Do you want me to sit here?" Mrs. Roosevelt asked pleasantly. There was the sound of the shuffling of a chair. And then Eleanor Roosevelt began to rehearse the opening lines of the record: "Wherever in the world you go, to Maine, or Spain, or Mexico, it's most important that you know how people say hello. So let's take a trip, a musical trip in rhythms from all around the world—"

Eleanor Roosevelt had no difficulty saying *Bon jour* when they got to France, or *Buenos días* or *Guten Tag*. The problem started when she arrived with the children in the Belgian Congo where the word for "hello" was "M'Bote." "Could you make your voice a little deeper, Mrs. Roosevelt?" William Mayer asked.

"All right," Mrs. Roosevelt said pleasantly. "Let's try it over again."

"Now! That's perfect!" Mr. Mayer exclaimed after the eighth or ninth repetition. "Just perfect!" And Mrs. Roosevelt cheerfully ended her journey with the children in Japan by calling out, "O-hi-yo!"

There was the click of the recording machine and Susan Otto came back to the telephone. "Isn't it amazing how patient Mrs. Roosevelt was?" she asked.

I thanked Susan for her trouble and we said good night. My room suddenly seemed very still and lonely.

On Sunday, September 27, 1959, the following notice appeared in *The New York Times:*

"Mrs. Franklin D. Roosevelt has sent as a special gift to Premier and Mme. Khrushchev and to their grandchildren, an advance copy of her new long-playing record, *Hello, World!* It has a message close to the hearts of all peace loving people everywhere, old and young alike."

Chapter Eleven

Brandeis University

"I REMEMBER, when I was a student at Brandeis University in the late 1940s—it was, as I recall, just before the outbreak of the Korean War—Mrs. Roosevelt delivered a commencement address on campus," wrote Dr. Stanley F. Chyet, Associate Director of the American Jewish Archives in Cincinnati, Ohio. "I remember that she spoke on 'The Courage to Live in Uncertainty.' The very phrase made an enormous impression on me at the time; it still does. May I suggest that, since Mrs. Roosevelt was for years a member of the Board of Trustees at Brandeis University and also taught a course there, you might contact Dr. Abram L. Sachar, President of the University, to ask what he might be able to make available to you."

I wrote to Dr. Sachar.

"I regret that we have no copy of Mrs. Roosevelt's address in 1952 at our first Commencement," Dr. Sachar replied. "She threw away her prepared address in order to reply to the pessimism of a twenty-one-year-old valedictorian! But I am sending you an anniversary address that I gave on Mrs. Roosevelt which includes some special anecdotes that you may wish to use."

Eleanor Roosevelt was a long-time member of the Brandeis Board of Trustees" [Dr. Sachar wrote in what he called "An

Affectionate Portrait"]. It was no perfunctory assignment, the honored name loaned for prestige purposes. Mrs. Roosevelt took her trusteeship very seriously. She never missed a meeting if it was possible for her to get to it. At one session the Chairman had just called for the minutes when the door opened and Mrs. Roosevelt appeared. She quickly counted the trustees who were present. Then she said, "I hope you have a quorum without me. I have just flown in from Minneapolis. We've been over the airport for more than two hours because of the weather. If you have a quorum and do not need me, please excuse me. I am to fly to Morocco within a few hours." Some of our busiest members received an unforgettable lesson in discipline.

Another time, just a few years before her death, we had asked Mrs. Roosevelt, as we so often did, to be our guest of honor at a large University affair. As the clock crept half an hour beyond schedule without her appearance, we became somewhat worried. She had never permitted us to send for her. Suddenly she limped in, her leg in a cast. Shyly, she apologized and said, "I was struck by an automobile. Oh, it was my own fault. I walked behind a taxicab in the middle of the street to cross over and the driver backed into me!"

I said, "Good Heavens, what are you doing here?" She quickly waved away my concern. "Well, it wasn't that serious. Fortunately, it happened right in front of my apartment building. My physician also has an apartment there and he quickly took care of me. I'll be all right. But I must ask that you permit me to speak sitting down." This was the only concession she was willing to make to her human frailty. After that she was laid up for three or four weeks when it was found that she had broken several bones. She had promised to come. A large audience had gathered. She was not going to disappoint them.

Additional information on this particular incident was contributed by Maureen Corr, Mrs. Roosevelt's private secretary. She said that Eleanor Roosevelt was determined to go to Brandeis University that day because she felt that people would feel sorry for her and therefore the University would be able to raise more money. "She was right!"

Reading Dr. Sachar's "Affectionate Portrait." I also learned that it was not enough for her to be on the Board of Trustees of

Brandeis University. Her real interest was in the students and she wanted to get close to them. Dr. Sachar suggested that she teach a course. At the age of seventy-five, Eleanor Roosevelt became a member of the faculty of Brandeis University. After her teaching appointment had been made. Dr. Sachar remarked, "Well, now you are in a new role, Professor Roosevelt."

"She flinched momentarily," said Dr. Sachar. " 'Oh, don't you call me Professor; I never went to college. I'd be embarrassed if you put me down in that role,' she protested. 'What role, then?' I asked. 'Can't I be put down as a Lecturer?' she suggested. And that remained her title, listed in the faculty roster after Professors, Associate Professors, Assistant Professors, and finally the Lecturers. Because the listing was alphabetical, Eleanor Roosevelt's name was near the bottom."

And so Mrs. Roosevelt became a Lecturer at Brandeis University, teaching a course in conjunction with Dr. Lawrence H. Fuch, Professor of American Civilization and Politics. I contacted Dr. Fuchs for more information on this matter and he immediately sent me a long report.

"Dr. Sachar consulted me on the possibility of giving a joint course with Mrs. Roosevelt. I had met her already and we got along extremely well. Since Mrs. Roosevelt had been Chairman of the Commission on Human Rights and also was a member of the United States Delegation to the United Nations General Assembly, I suggested that she join me in a course on international organization and law.

"We limited the enrollment for that course," Dr. Fuchs continued. "I interviewed the students and those who seemed qualified by virtue of seniority, motivation, background and career plans were admitted; it was held at midmorning.

"Mrs. Roosevelt would usually fly to Boston the night before and often stayed at the Faculty Center. She had dinner with us a few times, but often she had appointments for dinner at Boston or Cambridge. As a rule, I joined her in the early morning to plan the seminar for the day and occasionally we would have breakfast together in her room. The syllabus had been prepared by me and gone over by her. Mrs. Roosevelt was quite content to let me lead the seminar. She was typically modest about her training in international organization of law although she knew a great deal.

Her teaching tended to be anecdotal rather than systematic. She liked me to pick the topic and to take the lead in the discussion, but, naturally, the students were interested in *her*. They wanted to hear her talk as much as possible. She would sprinkle the anecdotes with wonderful portraits of people who were famous and with sparkling insights into problems in international affairs. She liked me to put her stories into a broader conceptual framework. We kept tossing the ball back and forth between us.

"Mrs. Roosevelt had a great desire to hear from young people," Dr. Fuchs continued. "She had an unusual trust in them and endless patience in listening to their opinions and judgments. Because of this attitude she was able to bring out the best in them. I don't think I can remember a single student ever telling me that he or she was disappointed in Mrs. Roosevelt. I remember one discussion in which she suggested an idea for international voluntary service abroad sponsored by the United States. She thought that that would be an excellent substitute for military service. Of course, several years later that idea became known as the Peace Corps.

"In the private conversations which we used to have before and after classes, and particularly over breakfast, I was impressed by Mrs. Roosevelt's political shrewdness," said Dr. Fuchs. "It was part of her shrewdness to pretend that she had none. I remember her telling me of her visit to Mr. Khrushchev and how she brought Franklin D. Roosevelt's Bible to show him. Mr. Khrushchev tried to impress her with various arguments in international affairs and she told him that she really had no power in the United States. And that, of course, was part of her political power; she disclaimed it.

"I also remember her telling me of the time she refused to shake the hand of Adam Clayton Powell and how he practiced one-upmanship on her by telling his Harlem audience that although Mrs. Roosevelt didn't seem to care much for him, he was just crazy about her.

"Apart from teaching what she knew as a person and as a student of contemporary international affairs, Mrs. Roosevelt wanted to participate in the seminar in order to get a sense of what young people were thinking, and I think that she accomplished her purpose. Mrs. Roosevelt invited me, my wife, and three daughters several times to Hyde Park. We enjoyed ourselves immensely there. She would tell my children stories about her own childhood, how she used to take ice-cold baths in order to toughen her spirit, and many others. We used to have such fun with Mrs. Roosevelt."

Eleanor Roosevelt speaks of her teaching experience at Brandeis University in her autobiography. "I was a little staggered by this assignment," she says. "There were only thirteen students in the class, all of whom hoped to go into foreign service either for business or for the government; five were students from foreign countries. I felt sure that many of these young people were better versed in questions of international organization than I was. But at least I could discuss with them the tangled problems of foreign politics."

Mrs. Roosevelt's special interest in Brandeis University was aroused because it was something new and fresh, something that had started out as an experiment. She wrote about it in her column "My Day," on June 18, 1952:

> It was an honor and a pleasure to address the 101 graduates of Brandeis University in Waltham, Mass., yesterday—the school's first commencement.
>
> The President explained in his address that the group had always been seniors because they had never had a class ahead of them. Many college freshmen can behave foolishly, perhaps secure in the thought that they have older classmates with two or three years of experience ahead of them to tone down any foolishness. But a new University and new students must be at a senior level from the start, even in a freshman class. These students were taking a gamble too. They could not be sure that the university would be successful, nor that it would reach standards that would be acceptable in the academic world. It was pioneering along certain lines, in searching for both new faculties and new students.
>
> No questions were being asked as to race, creed or color; registrants were being accepted on merit only. Some of them in their courses would lay emphasis on Hebrew and become rabbis; some of them would go on from this university to theological studies in Protestant religion somewhere else. Much opportunity

was to be available in the fields of the arts in this new university, and young people were attracted to it who had an interest in music and writing and drama and painting.

The university has won its way and gained its place in academic circles. Of the students who tried for acceptance in the best graduate schools throughout the country this year, not one was refused. Even the medical students were all accepted.

A highlight of yesterday's festivities was one student who was graduated summa cum laude and who made the address for the students. [That student came as a refugee from Germany and he has never received a mark below "A" in his whole period at the university.]

In his speech he said that probably none of the young people there would set the world on fire. That was becoming modesty, I suppose, and yet, just because of what he has been through, perhaps he is the one who should set the world on fire . . .

This, I instantly realized, must have been the "pessimistic valedictorian" of whom Dr. Sachar had spoken in his letter. I contacted Dr. Sachar again and asked for the name of that particular student.

"Gustav Ranis was the student," Dr. Sachar said, "and he is now Professor of Economics at Yale University.

I wrote a letter to Dr. Ranis.

"I would be happy to discuss my experience with Mrs. Roosevelt with you whenever it would be convenient to you to come to New Haven," he replied at once.

Shortly afterward, I took a pleasant train ride to Connecticut.

Gustav Ranis, Professor of Economics and Director of the Economic Growth Center at Yale, did not appear pessimistic at all. He was a pleasant-looking man in his late thirties and he greeted me extremely cordially. We had lunch together in a lovely restaurant high above the campus.

"Why did you view the world so bleakly at the time you graduated from Brandeis?" I asked Dr. Ranis.

"It was 1952," Gustav Ranis said, "and the world was in a sorry state. World War II was barely over, the United States was involved in a deadly struggle with the communists in Korea. Peace talks that had begun in July 1951 were deadlocked by July 1952. Certainly, it all was nothing to be enthusiastic about."

"Do you still recall what you said in your valedictory address?" I asked.

"Well, something to the point that 'The Atomic Age, undoubtedly, has brought with it a certain fear of the end, of the approaching cataclysm,'" he said. "It is easy to understand. Even Orwell's imagination cannot compete with some of the possibilities for destruction that lie within our reach now. Yet, actually, though we don't admit it, we don't really think so. The end of the world, a third and final World War—these are phrases which are on the tip of our tongues, but rest really only at the back of our consciousness. Except for the devastating reaction on the Continent, Colliers could publish its 'The War We Do Not Want,' in all its gory details without too many eyebrows being raised. Almost imperceptibly, as if by osmosis, we have become accustomed to a situation in flux, to recurring crises and hungry headlines. We have a generation which has become used to the sword of Damocles."

"It does not sound very cheerful," I admitted. "I heard that, following your speech, Mrs. Roosevelt tore up her prepared commencement address and replied to you instead. Do you still remember what she said, Dr. Ranis?"

"Of course I do," he said instantly. "Mrs. Roosevelt said that we must have the courage to live in uncertainty—"

"This is the speech Dr. Chyet wrote to me!" I exclaimed and told Dr. Ranis briefly how my interest in Eleanor Roosevelt's role at Brandeis University had started.

Professor Ranis smiled. "Well," he said, "if I recall correctly, Mrs. Roosevelt refuted my lack of optimism in the future. She said something to the effect that even though I obviously did not think so, *she* was convinced that I would go far in my chosen career and so would all the other Brandeis graduates of that day. 'The world always has been deeply troubled throughout the ages by adversity,' she said. 'It is up to the individual to overcome it.'"

"Did Mrs. Roosevelt's reply to your valedictory speech change your frame of mind?" I asked Gustav Ranis.

"It was not as dramatic as all that," he answered. "And it did not change my outlook all at once. However, it did make me feel that if a woman like Mrs. Roosevelt who had seen and suffered so much felt that the world was not in so bad a shape as all that, perhaps it really wasn't. Afterwards, Mrs. Roosevelt often invited me to Val-Kill, her cottage in Hyde Park, and we had many long talks. Over the years her confidence that we would ultimately manage to 'muddle through' had its impact."

"How have things worked out for you?" I asked.

Gustav Ranis grinned. "Personally, not too bad," he said. "I enjoy my work here at Yale; from 1965 to 1967 I held a presidential appointment at the State Department connected with our foreign aid program. I have a wife, three lovely children. I am about to become a member of the Brandeis Board of Trustees. Of course now, in 1968, we are again involved in a war, Vietnam. I suppose it never ends. But individuals are not so important as I once thought. This is what we must pass on to the next generation and the next . . ."

We left the skytop restaurant and I said good-bye to Professor Gustav Ranis.

Since the time Mrs. Roosevelt taught at Brandeis University and gave the commencement address to its 101 graduates, the student body has grown to two thousand five hundred. Its students come from twenty-nine states and four foreign countries. The original thirteen-member faculty has grown to three hundred seventy-five.

The students at Brandeis University in 1968 are different from the first graduates in 1952. They are not pessimistic, they are angry. They *do* want to set the world on fire. I think that Eleanor Roosevelt would agree with them more readily than with the former generation. For in her column, "My Day," on June 19, 1952, she quoted the words of another Brandeis University Professor, Max Lerner, who also had spoken of the "pessimistic" students graduating in 1952.

"I think what has happened to the college students of today," he said then, "is that they have seen so many dreams collapsing and so many wounds inflicted on the sensitive, that they have drawn a protective sheath around themselves. Who can blame them for a kind of animal wisdom that this shows? But they will learn in time that while people who try to light fires often get burned, they also with their blaze dispel some of the darkness. Of course, in this world, if you love much you probably will be hurt much. But in the end you will be glad that you really knew love. If you believe in the great and the good, you often will be disappointed and disillusioned, but in the end you will know that it was better to have beliefs and convictions and fight for them. You will find yourself, over and over again, up against situations that you don't seem to be able to understand, and where the answers to problems continue to elude you, no matter how much effort and thought you bring to their solutions. But with each effort you will grow, and in the end you will realize that while not all problems have solutions, the effort to solve them may be the thing that gives you the quality of mind and heart to attract the people who may solve the unsolvable and help you to greater understanding."

Today, in 1968, there is much talk and resentment against the young people who refuse to conform. I feel certain that Eleanor Roosevelt would have opened her arms to them.

Chapter Twelve

The Jewish People

"I WANT TO ASK YOU A QUESTION," Eleanor Roosevelt once said to her good friend Judge Justine Wise Polier, daughter of Rabbi Stephen Wise. "Whenever I seek help for people, whether unemployed miners in Virginia, sharecroppers, or Negroes in the South, the Jews are always among the first to offer aid. Yet, when they themselves are mistreated, they usually are most hesitant in asking my help and, on the rare occasions when they do, they seem very embarrassed about it. I am troubled by this and am always wondering why this is so. Can you explain it to me, Justine?"

Judge Polier told Mrs. Roosevelt that while the hurts of the Jews in America were not physical, their lives were still shadowed. While free superficially here, the Jews are not truly free because they live in a hostile world.

It was her concern for the inner freedom of all people that made Eleanor Roosevelt say in one of her speeches that "the promotion of better understanding among Protestants, Catholics and Jews in America is truly one of the most necessary tasks confronting us, not only for the sake of lasting, social peace and goodwill, but in order that the idealism of religion may make its most effective contribution to the welfare of the Nation. None of our children should grow up without respect for every other American citizen, but when you have schoolbooks that don't tell you what each different group has contributed to the making of the country, it is very hard for children really to understand what they have in riches of heritage."

Her sympathy for the persecuted, her sense of justice, and her respect for the struggle of the Jews to reestablish their own identity in their own homeland, led her to respond wholeheartedly to the creation of the State of Israel. Israel was to her, she used to say, "like a breath of America."

Mrs. Roosevelt spoke, raised funds, and gave whatever support she could to the embattled people of Israel. "It is not because they are Jewish people only," she said at a dinner given in her honor at the Hotel Sheraton by the Westchester Committee for the State of Israel bonds. "It is because they are a people building a nation which will be valuable to the world. Americans should support Israel because that country will some day spread Democracy throughout the Near East."

On November 6, 1949, it was announced that the proceeds from a lecture tour to be conducted by Mrs. Roosevelt would be contributed to the United Jewish Appeal in honor of the late Mrs. Henry Morgenthau, Jr.

"I have accepted the chairmanship of the United Jewish Appeal for Greater New York for the month of June," Eleanor Roosevelt declared in one of her columns. "I would like to explain to my readers why I have taken so much interest in this work. This organization has helped refugees to get to Israel to escape persecution in different parts of the world and has assisted those who were already settled in Israel to develop their country in order that they might carry this burden of refugees until they were assimilated and became part of the nation."

At the time she went to the first meeting of the United Nations in London, said Mrs. Roosevelt, she had very little knowledge of the land that was to become Israel. It was shortly after the end of World War II. There was a long discussion on whether the people in the Displaced Persons Camps in Germany should have the right to choose whether they could or would return to their countries of origin. The Soviet Union insisted that anyone who did not want to do that was either a "Quisling" or a traitor, and the Committee argued the question for weeks. To Eleanor Roosevelt it seemed to be a question of fundamental human rights. She approached the United States Ambassador and asked him if she could go to Germany and see the camps they had been talking about for herself. He arranged for her to spend three days in Germany.

"We landed first at Frankfurt," Eleanor Roosevelt wrote in her autobiography, "where there were a number of refugee camps, including one for Jews in Zilcheim. I was greeted by leaders of the Jewish refugee group. They had built a small hill with steps leading to the top where they had erected a stone monument inscribed: 'To the Memory of all Jews who died in Germany.' In all the Jewish camps there were signs of the terrible events through which these people had passed and of the hardships they continued to suffer. In the mud of Zilcheim I remember an old woman whose family had been driven from home by war and madness and brutality. I had no idea who she was and we could not speak each other's language. But she knelt in the muddy road and threw her arms around my knees.

" 'Israel,' she murmured over and over, 'Israel! Israel!'

"As I looked at her weather-beaten face and heard her old voice," said Mrs. Roosevelt, "I knew for the first time what that small land meant to so many, many people.

"And I saw something else," she continued. "I saw a young mother and her baby and I thought she was going to die. I also was quite sure that the baby could not possibly live. I think it was one of the saddest days which I have ever spent, and I have never forgotten it."

In 1952, Eleanor Roosevelt went for her first trip to the land the old woman in the mud had spoken of, Israel. She went to Haifa and was shown around by the Mayor. As they were finishing their rounds, he told her that there was a woman who had come to him insisting that she must see Mrs. Roosevelt. When they went back to the hotel, a young woman with a very attractive husband, a little boy of five and a lovely-looking girl of about seven, with long pigtails were waiting for her. Mrs. Roosevelt looked at them but she was certain she had never seen any one of them before.

"Mrs. Roosevelt," said the young woman, "don't you remember me?"

"I am afraid not," replied Mrs. Roosevelt.

"Do you remember the Camp in Uelzen?" the young woman asked. "You thought that I could not possibly survive and that my baby too would die. You spoke to the superintendent about us. This little girl is that baby. I came here and I am married again now, and this is my little boy born in Israel."

"There is an atmosphere in Israel that one does not find in many other countries," Mrs. Roosevelt wrote in her column during her second visit on April 17, 1959. "Its young people are partly responsible for it. They are excited by the dream of building a country, they are willing to work with their full youthful energy to achieve unbelievable results. They have imagination, they know how to handle people, and they have plenty of experience in adjusting themselves to the handling of people of different background, different religions and different customs. The United Jewish Appeal has been the principal instrument through which money has been collected for work in this country and for work in Israel. I believe that a country in which deserts have been reclaimed and where, despite a tremendous influx of immigrants, the standards of health have been raised and education is provided for the majority of the people, cannot help but be a growing democratic force in the area in which it is established. If this is so, then whatever is done in Israel will serve in the long run to help stabilize an area of the world that needs peace for its future development. A strong and democratic Israel can mean a strong and democratic Middle East, and for that reason I am willing and anxious to help the UJA."

Eleanor Roosevelt was eager to expose other people from many diverse backgrounds to the experience of Israel.

"Mrs. Roosevelt had promised to address a group of eighteen Episcopal clergy at our 'Monday Club' at the Parish House," wrote Reverend Gordon L. Kidd, Rector Emeritus of St. James Church at Hyde Park. "It was sometime in January or February, and the day before her scheduled appearance she was to speak at a function near Pittsburgh. The private car that met her at the airport became stalled in a heavy snowdrift and a police car was called. Soon it was also snowbound. By the time the road was cleared it was too late for Mrs. Roosevelt's appearance in Pittsburgh. It was suggested to her that she go to a hotel and rest. But Mrs. Roosevelt declared she had to take the night train back to New York because she had committed herself to give an early morning talk at St. James' in Hyde Park. She sat up all night in a coach, arrived at my church about half an hour late but just as fresh as though she had had a good night's sleep in her bed.

"Her talk was to be about the role of the clergy in community affairs. She began by telling us of her experiences during her travels in the various parts of the world. She spoke of the West Virginia miners in the days of the Depression, the trips to Russia and the Communist world, of the injustices and poverty of the Negroes in the South and about a journey to the Arab World where a sheik who already had eighteen wives submitted to *her* a proposition of marriage.

"While the group of clergy broke into delighted laughter, Mrs. Roosevelt light-heartedly urged them to be more active in their involvement in the problems of which she had spoken. The Church could do so much to alleviate them, she said, and create more unity among all people. The clergy should put all their efforts toward this goal, even if it should mean loss of status for some of them. And finally, Mrs. Roosevelt spoke at great length of her yearly visits to Israel, a country she greatly admired for the courage of its people."

But to Eleanor Roosevelt it was not enough that only she had seen Israel; it was not enough for her to just talk about it.

In the summer of 1957, at her own expense, Mrs. Roosevelt sent her good friends Reverend Gordon L. Kidd and his wife Claire on a journey to Italy, Greece, Turkey, Egypt, Lebanon, Syria, and finally Israel.

"The Olive Branch Tour to the Middle East" was sponsored by The American Christian Palestine Committee, an educational organization, designed to give Christians an understanding of the forces at work in the Middle East and a comprehensive, authentic picture of what is taking place in Israel and the Middle East. The American Christian Palestine Committee was organized in 1941. At that time the steady annihilation of European Jewry made starkly clear the need for a Jewish National Home and emphasized to every man deeming himself a Christian the inescapable fact that there must be a Christian concern for the Jewish tragedy. Meanwhile, working along parallel lines, there had been founded in 1942 the Christian Council on Palestine, under the chairmanship of Dr. Henry A. Atkinson, general secretary of the Church Peace Union and the World Alliance for International Friendship Through Religion.

In one of its first published statements of purpose, the Christian Council on Palestine declared: "The destiny of the Jews is a matter of immediate concern to the Christian conscience; the amelioration of their lot, a duty that rests upon all who profess Christian spirit and principles. But the Christian conscience cannot be content with expressions of kindly intentions and of goodwill. It must translate itself into programs of action." Inevitably, these two growing streams of Christian endeavor—the American Palestine committee and the Christian Council on Palestine—met and merged in 1946. The result was the re-created and present American Christian Palestine Committee under whose auspices the Reverend Mr. Kidd and his wife undertook their journey to Israel.

Reverend Gordon L. Kidd talked about his experiences in many sermons. Claire, his wife, wrote an article series about the trip for the *Hyde Park Record*, a weekly newspaper.

"I should say that the people of Israel," Claire Kidd says in the conclusion of her article, "are the most idealistic people I have ever encountered and they are putting their ideals into practice at great sacrifice to their own convenience and comfort. They have willingly limited themselves and their children economically and culturally in order to provide a home for all the Jews of the world who need a haven of refuge and they are willing to continue to do so as long as necessary. They are very proud of the fact that they now have a place which they can fight for and die for, if necessary."

In 1952, Mrs. Roosevelt agreed to become the World Patron of Youth Aliyah. "Aliyah" is a Hebrew word which in ancient times meant "going up to the temple." The opposite of Aliyah is "yeridah" which means going down from the temple or leaving it; it is applied when someone leaves Israel forever. In modern times the Hebrew word aliyah has come to mean immigration to

Israel. Youth Aliyah is an organization for the rescue and rehabilitation in Israel of homeless children throughout the World. It originated in Nazi Germany to save Jewish children in danger of extermination, and became the greatest child-rescue movement in history. Today in Israel one citizen in every twenty was once a Youth Aliyah child.

Mrs. Roosevelt immediately expressed her desire to see the work of Youth Aliyah, and, when she visited Israel a few months later, she was invited to the Rural Vocational Training Center in Kfar Vitkin. She was deeply interested in the developments that had taken place and she seized every possible opportunity to meet those responsible for the education of the children to see for herself how the children were educated and cared for. She had long conversations with the children, and she described as "astounding" the way in which young people were being integrated into the life of the nation. She also was heartened to see these youngsters were taught to appreciate the values of older generations. Mrs. Roosevelt stated at the end of her tour that, to her mind, the most important and greatest need of Israel was the integration of its youth into a united people, and not, as she had previously thought, its economic independence. Youth Aliyah decided to name this particular training center after Eleanor Roosevelt because of her special interest in it.

"When I was in Paris in 1952 for the Youth Aliyah, I arranged to meet Eleanor Roosevelt at her office at the U.S. delegation at the United Nations," wrote Moshe Kol, publisher of the *Jerusalem Post*. "I planned in my meeting to ask her to accept the World Patronage of Youth Aliyah. Mrs. Roosevelt received me most cordially. From the very first she seemed captivated by my story. But she did not give me an immediate reply. She told me that she would first of all like to visit the Arab refugee camps and then visit Israel. After that, she would let me have her decision.

"Mrs. Roosevelt arrived from Jordan via the Mandelbaum Gate in Jerusalem and proceeded immediately to Kibbutz Malaleh Hahamisha in the Judean Hills. Here she met with a group of youngsters from the Eddie Cantor home. Mrs. Roosevelt was most responsive to our educational and rehabilitational work with children and youth. She visited many places and absorbed everything. She saw our development and life-saving projects and her heart became linked to our activities.

"Since her first visit in 1952, Eleanor Rooscvelt came again to Israel several times. Each time she renewed her contacts with those same places she saw on her first visit in order to compare the development. She would also talk to people to learn whether they were content and to hear of their problems. When she received letters from Youth Aliyah wards, she would, as usual, ask me to check the particulars and she would always send an encouraging reply.

"Eleanor Roosevelt was not Youth Aliyah's patron in name only. She viewed her patronage as an important role in her public life and never once gave a negative answer to any of our requests. She traveled widely for Youth Aliyah in Great Britain, France, Canada, and Mexico. She participated actively in the Hadassah Conventions as well as those of other Women's Zionist organizations in the United States of America and accepted many speaking engagements for Youth Aliyah. She visited the Youth Aliyah camp at Cambus near Montpellier in the South of France where she asked to meet with children from Morocco. On her visits to Israel, she would sit with us for hours on end, listening intently and asking searching questions on matters large and small. In her introduction to my book on Youth Aliyah which was published in English by the International Federation of Children's Communities under the auspices of UNESCO, she wrote of Youth Aliyah, what it meant to her and how she contemplated its activities.

" 'I have always felt,' she wrote, 'that Youth Aliyah is one of the creative undertakings in history, significant far beyond the borders of Israel. It has offered a warm welcome to thousands upon thousands of children in need of love and acceptance.'

"When the Beersheba Youth Center that bears her name was inaugurated, she was radiant with happiness. When the Eleanor Roosevelt workshops in the Neurim Village were inaugurated, I presented her with the work of one of the wards: a rug woven in the workshop that bears her name. She was very pleased and whispered to me: 'You know, Moshe, I love to get presents.'

"Eleanor Roosevelt traveled to many countries to enlist help for Youth Aliyah. Her visit to Mexico City became an extraordinary event that conquered public opinion, press and official circles alike. Recognition of Youth Aliyah rose enormously on hearing what she had to say about this humanitarian and educational project. She came to France on a Youth Aliyah mission, and visited first of all the Youth Aliyah transition camp at Cambus near Montpellier in the South of France. She met children who had come from Morocco and other countries of North Africa, and who were being treated for ringworm, trachoma, and vitamin deficencies.

"When a reporter asked Mrs. Roosevelt in England in 1957 why she was so particularly interested in Youth Aliyah, she replied, 'I am interested in every child who needs help and I am ready to help him. The Youth Aliyah,' she said, 'crosses all frontiers and evokes the imagination.'

"Mrs. Roosevelt wrote to several institutions regarding the award of the Nobel Prize for Peace to Youth Aliyah. This took place after Professor Albert Einstein suggested to Oslo to award us the prize. Statesmen, politicians, and representatives of many countries were apprised by Mrs. Roosevelt of our venture.

"Eleanor Roosevelt's last visit to Israel took place in the year she passed away. She paid another visit to the youth center in Beersheba that bears her name. She praised the great development of the State of Israel and the humanitarian and educational mission of Youth Aliyah. In spite of her frailty, her voice was strong and clear. I had the feeling that she wanted to visit us a last time and take leave of our country, our people.

"Some weeks before her death, I was in the United States. Maureen Corr, her secretary, phoned me daily in the name of Mrs. Roosevelt to tell me that she soon hoped to be strong enough to receive me. She never could. Shortly after my return to Israel, I learned of the death of Eleanor Roosevelt.

"Her family cabled me asking me to attend the funeral at Hyde Park. The Sabbath prevented my attendance, but we published mourning notices in the *Jerusalem Post* and announced the establishment of a fund which would award annually, on the date of Mrs. Roosevelt's birth, scholarships to Youth Aliyah wards and graduates."

"Above everything else," said Eleanor Roosevelt after her first visit to the new country, "I think Israel's good fortune lies in its top leader, Premier David Ben-Gurion."

" 'Your David Ben Gurion always reminded me of my husband,' Eleanor Roosevelt once said to Dr. Haim Ginott.

Dr. Ginott told me the story over the telephone in a short interview which he squeezed in between lecture tours, writings of articles and books, teaching and working in his private practice as a psychologist. Dr. Ginott is Adjunct Associate Professor in New York University's Graduate Department of Psychology. His book *Between Parent and Child* was No. 1 on the best seller list for over a year. His new work *Between Parent and Teenager* was published in May 1969. His idea of bringing up children concentrates on creating human beings with concern, commitment, and courage rather than educated monsters. His ideal human being was Eleanor Roosevelt.

"I met Mrs. Roosevelt in 1959 when she came to Jacksonville, Florida, to give a speech for the United Jewish Appeal," Dr. Ginott said. As soon as she heard my Israeli accent, she said that about David Ben-Gurion. 'Ben Gurion reminded you of FDR?' I exclaimed amazed," Dr. Ginott recalled in his droll way of speaking. "How?"

" 'Well,' Eleanor Roosevelt said and laughed as she remembered, 'whenever my husband and I would drive through a countryside, he suddenly would put his hand to his forehead and say, 'Oh, oh, look at all this empty land there! Oh, oh, how I wish I could buy it! Imagine all the things that I could do with it!

" 'And when I visited Israel for the first time,' Mrs. Roosevelt continued, 'David Ben-Gurion drove me through the Negev and suddenly, in exactly the same way that Franklin used to do, he put his hand to his forehead and said, 'Oh, oh, look at all the empty land there, Mrs. Roosevelt! We'll make beautiful gardens out of it!' "

That story gave me the idea that David Ben-Gurion might have other personal memories about Eleanor Roosevelt, and so I wrote him a letter, telling him of what I was doing and asking for assistance. Just around that time, my appeal for stories had appeared in the *Jerusalem Post*. I got several responses, among them a small letter. "I am now finishing the history of twenty years of Israel," it said in painstaking handwriting on a thin piece of lined paper. "It will still take another four to six weeks. But I am an old admirer of Eleanor Roosevelt also." It was signed, "Sincerely yours, D. Ben-Gurion."

Shortly after I had received that letter, an article on David Ben-Gurion by C. L. Sulzberger appeared in *The New York Times*.

"David Ben-Gurion, Israel's first Premier, is now a gnomish old man living a simple life on this Kibbutz in Sde Boker, in the baked Negev. His wife died last year and, solitary by choice, far from his children, he works, contemplates and reminisces. Volumes and folders are piled around his study on chairs, tables, jammed into shelves. One leather-bound set contains all the secret records on the Suez expedition. Ben-Gurion today, in 1968, is diminutive, sturdy, incredibly active at 81, bouncing about like a squash ball. He dresses in austere khaki. The massive dome of his head is bald, flanked by wings of fine white hair. His face is pink, his eyes blue, most of his teeth are missing, but his firm jaw thrusts out more pugnaciously than ever."

On the death of Eleanor Roosevelt, David Ben-Gurion had written in *The Israel Digest* of November 23, 1962, "Her unique contribution to democratic and human values in the United States as helpmate of an outstanding President and in her own right, her deep and constant concern with humanity and with the problems of mankind and especially of the underprivileged in search of peace and welfare, have engraved her name indelibly in our consciousness as a great woman and great citizen of the world."

A letter came from Israel from Dr. E. Halpern, Deputy Director of the Asaf Harofe Hospital in Zerefin, Israel.

"Mrs. Roosevelt visited our hospital on March 27, 1959," wrote Dr. Halpern. "She was a guest of honor when our Institute of Hydrotherapy was dedicated to her. She visited outpatients at their bedsides, at the hydrotherapeutic pool, and while at other treatments. I vividly recall how the tears were rolling down her face. The plaque in her honor is worded as follows: "Gift to the future, the Mrs. Eleanor Roosevelt Room, dedicated by Canadian Hadassah with warmest admiration and highest esteem.' "

Not all the stories that came from Israel were solemn. Shortly after my appeal for stories had appeared in the *Jerusalem Post*, a young woman phoned me and introduced herself as Erica Stiefel. "I am a neighbor of yours," she said, "and I just this minute have returned from a trip to Israel. My husband Fred read in the paper there that you are writing a book about Mrs. Roosevelt. It was so strange," she continued, "to see your appeal so far away from home, especially as the address given was practically next door to me in New York. It was even stranger because on that very day of a sight-seeing tour, our guide had spoken about Mrs. Roosevelt. Our bus was riding through the desert and the guide pointed out the places where the Bedouins live. He said that many of them no longer exist huddled beneath rugs but have huts made of stone. When we came to Eliat Road at Beersheba, we saw a settlement of small buildings. 'A very wealthy Arab Sheik lives here,' the guide announced proudly. We noticed, with great astonishment, that some of the buildings had television antennas and inquired about them. 'Sheik Suleiman has thirty-nine wives,' the guide told us. He can be with only one each night and he wants to keep the others entertained. So he got them some television sets. But then the guide said something else," Erica Stiefel continued. "Sheik Suleiman, he told us, is a very intelligent and learned man. 'He was a close friend of your Mrs. Roosevelt. She once visited him here and, in fact, Mrs. Roosevelt's picture is hanging on the wall of the harem. There even is a rumor to the effect that Sheik Suleiman asked her to become one of his wives.'"

Obviously, this story is authentic since Eleanor Roosevelt herself used it to amuse the group of clergy at Hyde Park.

"When I was in Israel in November 1962," said Gertrude Selkowe, a former principal of a New York City school, "I took over a class of high school students for one day. We spoke about their country. 'Why do you think I came to look at it?' I asked the students. Most of them thought it was because I am Jewish. I replied that this was only a part of it. 'There is another woman who is deeply interested in Israel who is not Jewish,' I told the class. 'Don't you know who it is?' No one seemed to know to whom I was referring. I was amazed," said Gertrude Selkowe, "and I told the students so. 'How is it possible,' I said, 'that you really do not seem to know? This woman who is so very interested in your country is of course no other than Eleanor Roosevelt!'

" 'You mean she *was* interested in our country,' one boy spoke up abruptly.

"I looked at him puzzled," said Gertrude Selkowe.

" 'I heard it over the radio before I came to school,' the boy said. 'Eleanor Roosevelt died this morning.'

"And this was how I heard of the death of Eleanor Roosevelt," said Gertrude Selkowe, her voice choked.

But Eleanor Roosevelt was not only interested in the Jews of Israel. In her preface to the book *The Jew in American Life,** Eleanor Roosevelt wrote:

We in America at present stand before the world as their great hope for future peace and understanding among nations. Here in our land men of many races and many religions have lived side by side. They have learned something far better than tolerance. Tolerance implies a certain condescension. There should be no element of condescension between one American citizen and another American citizen. We have learned to treat people as individuals and to give them their due, regardless of race, religion, or background. You may say that this is not always an actuality and that of course is true, but in the great documents in which the aspirations of the people of the United States are recorded you will find that discrimination on racial or religious grounds is always openly eschewed. In Columbus' crew it is said that the first man to step ashore to the New World was a man of Jewish origin. And down through the history of our country Jewish people have held their place. They have fought in our wars; they have given us geniuses in the fields of art and literature, they have been great teachers, they have contributed to our scientific development, to our entertainment and our sports, they have contributed to our economic success. The Jews are part of the life of our nation. What the United States is today does not belong to any one of the racial and religious groups anymore than it does to the Jewish group. They make up a comparatively small percentage of our population, but their contribution is in some cases out of proportion to their numbers. For instance, in World War II, the Jewish people made up three

---

* James Waterman Wise, *The Jew in American Life.* New York: Julian Messner, 1946.

percent of our population, but four percent of our Jewish citizens served in our armed forces. Jews were represented in every facet of American life.

These were leaders in important fields: In labor, David Dubinsky and Jacob Potofsky. In industry, Meyer Guggenheim. In business, David Selznick and David Sarnoff. In science, the most famous of the immigrants, Albert Einstein. In law, Louis Brandeis, Benjamin Cardozo, and Felix Frankfurter. In journalism, Joseph Pulitzer, Walter Winchell, and Adolph Ochs. In music, Irving Berlin, Jascha Heifetz, Benny Goodman, Serge Koussevitzky, George Gershwin, Oscar Hammerstein, and Richard Rodgers. In literature, Gertrude Stein, Scholem Asch, Lillian Hellman. And in religion, Mrs. Roosevelt's own good friend Stephen Wise.

Like all races and faiths which make up the United States, Jews are both a group within and a part of the nation. To know their history—their early settlers, their outstanding citizens, their special contributions to religion and industry and science and the arts and to Democracy itself—is to know America better. Jews were once a people with a land, a language, a religion of their own. That was in Bible times. Today, Jews are citizens of many countries and speak the language of those countries. In England they are British, in France they are Frenchmen, in the United States they are Americans. Jews have lived in America since its discovery by Columbus. They have taken part in every phase of our national life. There were Jewish settlers in colonial days, Jewish patriots in the Revolution, Jews who fought for the Union and the Confederacy, and in both World Wars, Jews who helped build the cities of the east and open up the Western frontiers.

American Jews brought their historic memories and their heritage, Judaism, here. They and most of their descendants follow that religion and cherish a sense of fellowship with Jews everywhere.

In other things, in opinions, in politics, in occupations, in economic status, they are divided like other Americans and—in time of war and crisis—united like other Americans.

That Mrs. Roosevelt respected the Jewish people in the same way as she respected all other people is borne out by the following story: Rabbi Feldman heard that when Franklin D. Roosevelt was Governor of New York from 1928 to 1932, he was in the habit of inviting to luncheon conferences at the executive mansion in Albany various committee chairmen and important members of the State Legislature. Among these were two frequent Jewish guests, State Senator Philip M. Kleinfeld and Assemblyman Samuel Mandelbaum. After several such luncheons it came to the attention of the Governor and Mrs. Roosevelt that these men partook only of the fruit entree and the concluding dessert and coffee. Somehow the Roosevelts learned the reason for this abstention was that the Senator and the Assemblyman were strictly orthodox Jews and observed the dietary laws of orthodox Israel. Thereafter Eleanor Roosevelt served to these Jewish guests only dairy and vegetable foods in a new set of dishes especially reserved for them. Rabbi Feldman was told that this arrangement is available even now to Orthodox Jews invited to luncheon at the White House. The entire matter was done without ostentation by a characteristic spirit of broad-mindedness and respect for the religious scruples of those of another faith. Rabbi Feldman wanted to verify the story with a view to using it in a public address and so he wrote to Mrs. Roosevelt, gave her the story as it came to him, and asked whether it was true.

"Dear Rabbi Feldman," Eleanor Roosevelt wrote in her reply. "The story you sent me is true as it pertains to Albany. Since we have been in Washington I know of no occasion on which it was necessary to serve special meals, but I certainly would do it if I knew it would be desired."

Chapter Thirteen

The Entertainment World

"MRS. ELEANOR ROOSEVELT, like the sunshine, touched all lives," wrote George R. Spota, who had seen my Author's Query in *The New York Times Book Review*. "I think I may be able to help you with your project. Do call at my office. Warmest regards and good luck . . ."

The letterhead was that of a television production company on Madison Avenue. A few days later I was in that neighborhood and, on the spur of the moment, decided to look in on Mr. George Spota, who had sounded so poetic.

An elevator whisked me to a bright penthouse suite of offices. A girl with streaming blonde hair and pretty legs bared by a mini skirt greeted me. She said that Mr. Spota was out but would be back momentarily.

After a few minutes, a slim, well-dressed man with a graying crew cut entered. "George," the girl said, "this lady is waiting for you."

I introduced myself.

Probing dark eyes looked at me. "You are writing the book on Mrs. Roosevelt, aren't you? When I saw your Author's Query in the Times, I thought someone who is writing about Eleanor

Roosevelt is a person I should like to meet. Please come into my office."

Dominating George Spota's room was a bust of Abraham Lincoln.

He offered me a seat and then sat down behind his desk.

"You are a fortunate woman," he said as he lighted a cigarette, "that you are blessed with the perception of what Eleanor Roosevelt meant to the people of this world." He paused. "I always felt that she affirmed all that is noble and decent in the human race."

"What was your own contact with Mrs. Roosevelt?" I asked.

George Spota's eyes turned pensive. "It goes back a very long time. Actually, I am a product of the New Deal. In 1933, I was very young and very idealistic. I still was in high school. I'll never forget March 4, 1933, the Inauguration Day of President Franklin D. Roosevelt. As I was listening to his addresss I felt as if the clouds which were hanging over our country at that time were lifting. It seemed that a new era was beginning. I felt that this man's desire was to make life happier for people.

"A short time later I fell in love with Eleanor Roosevelt. It was when I saw a photograph of her in the newspaper. The new First Lady was paying a visit to the miners in the Appalachian area. She was simply dressed and wore a miner's cap. Later, I had several occasions to meet her in person. But usually it was at large functions. As the years went on, my love and admiration for her grew.

"In about 1956, I finally had the opportunity for closer contact with her. ABC Television had a weekly program entitled 'Women Want to Know.' We invited many famous personalities to talk on divorce, birth control, and similar topics. One program was to focus on women in politics. What more qualified person to talk on this was there than Eleanor Roosevelt? we thought, and approached her.

"She agreed to come. Faye Emerson was the hostess for the show. Everyone in the studio wanted to meet Mrs. Roosevelt before the show. Even the stagehands, who are a crusty lot and not usually interested in celebrities, pleaded for a chance to shake her hand. I tried to protect Mrs. Roosevelt and give her a little privacy and some rest, but I did ask her whether she would see the men for a moment. She said, 'Of course.' I offered her some coffee or iced tea and she said, 'Well, a little iced tea would be nice.' I also asked her whether she would be willing to see just one more person besides the stagehands. A fifteen-year-old high-school girl who had traveled thirty miles for the opportunity to meet her—my daughter. Mrs. Roosevelt smiled and said she would be delighted. When I brought George-Ann in, Eleanor Roosevelt asked her about herself, what school she was going to, and what interested her. The memory of this meeting is still a highlight in my daughter's life," said George Spota.

"You know," he said then, "Eleanor was very much beloved in the entertainment world. It would be fascinating to find out what some of the stars have to tell about their memories of her."

"A chapter on 'Eleanor Roosevelt and the Entertainment World!' I exclaimed. "What an exciting idea."

Abraham Lincoln, behind George Spota, seemed to smile a little.

"But," I said then, "all the show people seem so terribly busy and sophisticated. They would not take the time to write or talk to me."

"Eleanor Roosevelt was loved like no other human being of our times, and by more diverse people," George Spota said fervently. "Show people especially appreciated the way Mrs. Roosevelt immersed herself in the needs of humanity. It might be well worth your while to give it a try."

"I'll think about it," I said as we shook hands good-bye.

"Don't forget," George Spota called after me, "anything that I can do to help I will be most happy to do. Don't ever hesitate to call on me."

The next day I made a few telephone calls. The first one was to Harry Brandt of the movie houses. "How do I get the home addresses of the movie stars?" I asked.

"Get in touch with *The Independent Film Journal*," he said. "Tell them I sent you. You shouldn't have any trouble getting what you need."

Miss Charlotte Gross, who works at the *Independent Film Journal* as a secretary, was immensely interested in my project.

"Just write down for me the names you want and I will send you the addresses," she promised. I sent her a list and received the information I asked for by return mail. Sometimes she would add some extra names which she herself thought might be of interest.

And so I began sending letters out to the stars.

The first response came from Frank Sinatra. I had written to him because I found an old issue of *McCall's* in which someone asked Mrs. Roosevelt whether, like the Kennedy family association with Frank Sinatra's "Rat Pack," she and FDR had also had any such close friends in the performing arts.

Mrs. Roosevelt replied that from her earliest years she had been brought into contact with people in the entertainment world, and that she and her husband always knew a certain number of artists. Many of them performed for them and on occasion stayed in the White House. She added that she had known Frank Sinatra for a long time and had always found him to be a kind and considerate person.

Just the same, when I sent my leter off to Mr. Sinatra, I felt that I certainly could not expect a response. According to the columnists, Frank Sinatra was never long enough at any one place to receive a letter, much less to answer it, especially when the writer was someone completely unknown to him.

About a week later I found in my mailbox a letter postmarked "Burbank, California." The return address on the cream-colored envelope said "Frank Sinatra," in his own handwriting.

"Here is one memory of Mrs. Roosevelt that quickly comes to my mind," he wrote. "It was during World War II and there was a drive for Bundles for Britain at the Astor Hotel in New York. During the luncheon, the press asked that a photograph be taken of Mrs. Roosevelt and several of us who were seated next to her. They placed Mrs. Roosevelt in front of us—a group of about thirty—and Mrs. Roosevelt, being a fairly tall woman, suddenly seemed to become conscious of the fact that she might be blocking so many people behind her. Before anyone realized what had happened, she fell to one knee to get out of the way to make sure that everybody was in the photograph. It showed the kind of consideration and kindness she always had. Mrs. Roosevelt, at all times, was aware of everybody else."

"You can reword the above, as you wish," Frank Sinatra added as a postscript.

"I am fascinated by your proposed book on Mrs. Roosevelt," Allen Funt of "Candid Camera" replied by return mail. "On one occasion I directed a radio show given by Eleanor Roosevelt. Assembled in the guest booth was a group of some twenty blind children who had come to listen to the program and to present Mrs. Roosevelt with a piece of sculpture they had made. Upon concluding the program, Mrs. Roosevelt, feeling that words could not adequately communicate her sentiments for the gift, entered the guest booth. In her own inimitable way, she walked among the children, touching each. As she touched each child, he or she broke into tears. The booth was filled with a tenderness and unique *esprit de corps* that only she, in this spontaneous expression of thanks, could have generated."

"I knew that Mrs. Roosevelt had been criticized for traveling so much," wrote Bob Hope. "I too used to make a lot of jokes about her. Once, after a trip, I said that 'nothing passed us on this flight. We went so fast that just Eleanor zoomed by going both ways.' I also used to say that when Eleanor said good-bye in the morning to her husband, Franklin would look up and say, 'Where to now, dear?'

"But seriously," Bob Hope continued, "Mrs. Roosevelt had done a tremendous job during World War II. You only had to follow her into the hospital, say in Guadalcanal, to realize how much good she was doing morale. Because when they said, 'Mrs. Roosevelt is coming tomorrow,' the soldiers' faces would light up. After her visit the servicemen would boast, 'Guess who was up here yesterday? Mrs. Roosevelt! I got her autograph!' It made them feel important and not forgotten back home.

'In making wartime flights overseas to combat zones, Mrs. Roosevelt said she hoped, as the wife of the Commander in Chief, to represent to the servicemen their womenfolk at home. Upon her return from such trips she called or wrote to hundreds of relatives of the men to whom she had talked. When the voice on the telephone said it was the White House calling, a young government secretary was certain it was a gag. But the voice which came over the wire then was unmistakable. 'I met your boyfriend in Australia and he asked me to call you and say hello,' reported Mrs. Roosevelt who had just returned from the South Pacific war front. 'The boys are doing a wonderful job, but they are lonesome for their girl friends.'

"I had great affection and respect for Mrs. Roosevelt," Bob Hope concluded. "I have a photograph of her with myself. It is framed and hanging on the wall of my sitting room in my home in North Hollywood."

Earl Wilson wrote in his *New York Post* column that composer Richard Rodgers often used to be a guest in the White House. I sent a letter to Mr. Rodgers, asking whether he might have a memory to share with me. The creator of *Oklahoma, The King and I, South Pacific* replied by return mail.

"When my wife and I went to Mrs. Roosevelt's cottage in Hyde Park, I watched her dive into the pool at the far end and swim toward us. She got out of the pool and said to me, 'I have just learned to dive. My grandchildren made me feel ashamed.'

"Best of luck with your book and thanks for inviting me."

I had no clue at all when I wrote to playwright Arthur Miller. I simply felt that there had to be a link between a woman like Eleanor Roosevelt and a man like Arthur Miller. I treasure his handwritten reply.

"I had great respect for Mrs. Roosevelt. But I am afraid it was from a distance. I believe I met her only once, and then there was no opportunity to speak. I cannot say that I agreed with all her ideas, but her total dedication to a more humane world was nearly unique and moved me deeply."

I found out about Edward G. Robinson's deep feelings for Eleanor Roosevelt through a Congressional document.

At the first session of the Eighty-eighth Congress in Washington, it was resolved that the eulogies delivered in the House of Representatives as a tribute to the life and ideals of Mrs. Roosevelt be printed as a house document. When I heard of the book I wrote to Senator Robert F. Kennedy, asking him whether it would be possible for me to obtain a copy. Two weeks later I received a small package in the mail, from the United States Senate. When I unwrapped it I found a black volume on which was printed in golden letters, "Anna Eleanor Roosevelt, 1884–1962." Enclosed with the book was a brief note.

"Thank you for your letter of October 27, 1967. I am enclosing a copy of the house document on Anna Eleanor Roosevelt. All the material in the book is a matter of public record and no permission is necessary to reprint any of it. I wish you every success on your book, Robert F. Kennedy."

The document contains many deeply moving tributes to Mrs. Roosevelt. One touched me especially. Instead of delivering a eulogy, Senator McGovern of South Dakota spoke of the Eleanor Roosevelt Humanities Award Dinner which he had attended in Washington. That dinner honored the man who received the first Eleanor Roosevelt Humanities Award for his contribution to humane causes, the distinguished American actor Edward G. Robinson.

> We are not here to memorialize Eleanor Roosevelt [Mr. Robinson said in his acceptance speech], but rather to celebrate her, to rejoice that she lived. In that life she ignited a flame that will keep burning in the hearts of mankind around the globe. To be linked in this fashion with the name and life work of one of the greatest and most beloved personalities of our time is far more than I deserve. She practiced the philosophy of Thomas Paine who said that "those who expect to receive the blessings of freedom must undergo the fatigues of supporting it." And she regarded this as a sacred duty. In America we know the value of freedom. Our danger is that we sometimes take freedom for granted. Freedom was not part of my heritage when I was a child in Bucharest. It did not belong to me and to my fellow Jews in Rumania. Many years have passed since I came to the United States, but I have never ceased to remember my debt to this land of opportunity. I shall forever be grateful to Eleanor Roosevelt for helping me to relive that first exhilarating introduction to freedom.

I wrote a letter to Mr. Robinson, telling him how very much I had liked his speech. I also told him of my book and asked him whether he would contribute a memory about Eleanor Roosevelt of his own.

"Mrs. Roosevelt was the most wonderful woman I have ever known next to my mother, and perhaps equally as great," he replied. "I am not good at reminiscing and telling anecdotes but my memory of her is indelible and a photograph of her hangs in my study—not that I need a reminder. With best wishes for the success of your undertaking . . ."

"When I first became a comic I used to do an impression of Eleanor Roosevelt mainly because she was very much in the news," wrote Phyllis Diller. "But also because her voice and manner of speech were so individual and easily recognizable. During the time her husband was in office as President she traveled so much that her very mobility became something to kid. Her column 'My Day' was many times filled with gracious parrying of inane criticism of her and her children. Because of that I used to say, 'Eleanor Roosevelt is un-buggable!' It did work as a comic line, but it also epitomized my idea of the composure of a great woman. I remember that Mrs. Roosevelt once was asked how she chose a hat. Her answer was that she always inquired, 'Can I sleep in it?'

"It has always been my theory that to elevate one's self one can do so by identifying with great people. I identified with Mrs. Eleanor Roosevelt."

Agnes Morehead has performed over one thousand roles in her successful career. One of her favorite roles was that of Eleanor Roosevelt. "During the 'Golden Age' of radio the 'March of Time' was the major radio program on the air," she wrote. "I was selected from scores of actresses to impersonate Mrs. Roosevelt. In fact, I was the only actress ever to receive permission from the First Lady to impersonate her. She was always in the news and 'The March of Time' show was always anxious to do sketches about her. I was sent to the White House to be interviewed by her and found her just marvelous. I recorded a radio-tape of each impersonation to be sent to her for her approval and it always came back with a complimentary note. I did the impersonation many, many times, and during one program I approached the mike and the radio director in charge told me to look up in the 'fish bowl' [the glassed-in sponsors' booth]. There sat Mrs. Roosevelt and all of her family, except the President who was in Europe. I began the performance and, afterwards, looked up. Mrs. Roosevelt smiled and nodded her approval. After the show she came to my dressing room and told me how pleased she was that she had selected me to do the impersonation."

"I believe Eleanor Roosevelt and I were very good friends," wrote Jack Benny. "She always seemed grateful when I appeared at any benefit performance and particularly for 'The March of Dimes.' Whenever there was a testimonial dinner given for me in New York City, Mrs. Roosevelt usually was one of the members of the dais. Yet, we never had a real long conversation. I wish I did have some deeply moving stories that I could give you that would be good for your book. Maybe you can make up a little something . . ."

Reading that letter, I could almost see Jack Benny's deadpan face on television when he tells a story which he obviously does not really mean. But his tone was so kind that I instantly answered, telling him that this particular letter alone would be a nice story about Eleanor Roosevelt and Jack Benny.

"You have my permission to do whatever you like with the story," he replied at once.

Just then, by chance, I found an old cartoon in a newspaper. Mrs. Roosevelt is approaching Jack Benny for a contribution to a worthwhile cause. "Of course, I'll be delighted, Mrs. Roosevelt," he assures her as he digs in his pocket. "The only thing is—" he adds as he fishes out a quarter, "can you give me any change?"

Soon after this correspondence with Jack Benny, in December 1968, I was planning a trip to Los Angeles. Following up his letter in which he said that "perhaps I could make up a little story about him and Eleanor Roosevelt," I wrote him again and asked whether we couldn't make up something together while I was in California.

"When you arrive in Los Angeles, please phone Mr. Benny at this number," his secretary replied.

I arrived in Los Angeles on a Sunday and watched the "Jack Benny Show" on the television in my hotel room. The following morning I phoned Mr. Benny. "Hello?" the long-familiar and famous voice of Jack Benny came over the wire. "I will be in my office on Santa Monica Boulevard at five o'clock," he said pleasantly. "But I must warn you," he added, "although I met Mrs. Roosevelt many times and was very fond of her as she, I believe, was of me, I have no particular story that I can remember. But I will be glad to talk with you."

Jack Benny's office is in an unpretentious building on Santa Monica Boulevard in Beverly Hills. "The little Santa Monica Boulevard," he had told me. Since it is not easy in Los Angeles to find a taxi, I gave myself ample time to get there and arrived fifteen minutes before five o'clock. Mr. Benny's office is more comfortable than elaborate. I chatted for a little while with a pleasant gentleman in a red vest who is Mr. Benny's secretary and looked at the pictures and awards on the walls.

Suddenly, I heard someone outside humming a melody, the sound came closer, there were some footsteps, the door opened. Jack Benny! His face was California tanned, his blue shirt matched his eyes, he wore a maroon-and-black checked jacket. He looked, well—he *really* looked not much older than thirty-nine. In his hand he carried a violin case.

"So here you are," he said to me. "Come into my office. Sit over there, that chair is comfortable." Then he pointed to a photograph on the wall. "There is your friend!" It was Eleanor Roosevelt smiling at Jack Benny.

"I think this was taken at a benefit dinner given for me a long time ago," he said. "I forgot what the occasion was. But I do remember that we had four First Ladies present. Eleanor Roosevelt, First Lady of the Land, Helen Hayes, First Lady of the Stage, Gracie Allen, First Lady of Comedy, and the First Lady of my Life—my wife!"

I showed Jack Benny my chapter on *Eleanor Roosevelt and the Entertainment World*, and what I had written about him.

"Well," he said, "you wrote the truth. I don't have any particular story that I can recall about Mrs. Roosevelt. However, if the cartoon said I gave Mrs. Roosevelt a quarter and asked her for change when she appealed to me for a donation for a worthwhile cause, that is overdoing things, even for me. Couldn't you say that I gave her ten dollars?"

"Ten dollars?" I exclaimed. "Impossible! People would never believe it."

"All right then," he said. "Make it five. But this is as cheap as I could get ever, if Mrs. Roosevelt asked me for a donation!"

"In fact," I said, 'I took a sight-seeing tour through Beverly Hills yesterday. When the driver pointed out the house you used to live in, he said that 'you people probably won't believe it, but Jack is the biggest tipper in Hollywood."

"That gag of my stinginess is costing me a fortune," Jack Benny said dryly. "I do like to tip well. But in order to overcome that story of my stinginess I have to tip especially well. One day in New York I took a cab for a very short distance. I always feel badly when I have to do that and usually tell the driver before I get into his cab that it will be a short trip. That time the fare amounted to about sixty cents and I gave the driver two dollars to make up for it. 'Mr. Benny,' he said while he put away the money, 'I wish you wouldn't have done that!'

" 'Why not?' I asked him amazed. 'Well,' the driver said, "While I was driving you, I was planning in my mind how I would tell my wife tonight that I had Jack Benny in my cab. *And you know,* I was all set to tell her, *that son of a bitch gave me a dime for a tip!* Now you have spoiled that story for me, Mr. Benny.'

"I told him that I was very sorry about that and if he liked he could give me back the extra dollar and thirty cents.

"You know," he said, "money doesn't really mean a thing to me. If it did, I would have a fortune now. The truth is that I don't. I don't have all that money that people believe I have. I wish I did."

"What difference could that make to you?" I asked.

"Oh, a great deal," said Jack Benny very seriously. "Instead of giving ten thousand dollars for one particular charity I could give a hundred thousand." He rose and picked up his well-worn violin case. "My Stradivarius," he said and smiled. "I never take any money for the concerts I give. They all are for charity only."

"Danny Kaye will not see anyone," I was told by several people during my visit to Hollywood. "He is like quicksilver. You cannot pin him down to an appointment. Either he is traveling, working, or flying his airplane."

I could not give up that quickly. For many years I had watched his weekly television show, and I never tired of watching him perform with children. I was absolutely certain that a man like Danny Kaye would have felt a strong affinity for a woman like Eleanor Roosevelt.

I phoned the office of Mr. Kaye's business manager and explained to the secretary about this book.

"It sounds very interesting," she said. "But—what can I tell you? It is just impossible for me to make an appointment for you with Mr. Kaye. Impossible!"

"Doing this book I learned that nothing really is impossible," I said.

"Well—" the young lady wavered—"the only thing I could suggest is for you to talk with Dan Jenkins. Mr. Jenkins is one of Mr. Kaye's associates. If Mr. Kaye has a memory about Mrs. Roosevelt, he might be willing to tell it to Mr. Jenkins who then could tell it to you. Would that be all right?"

"Of course," I assured her. "It would be just fine."

Dan Jenkins came onto the wire. I explained what I wanted. There was a long pause. "I don't quite know what to say," said Mr. Jenkins. "You see, Danny Kaye—"

"I know," I said. "Mr. Kaye is difficult to pin down. But couldn't you try? If you just told him of my book and asked him whether he has a memory for me or—if he just were to say how he felt about Mrs. Roosevelt . . ."

"Very well," said Mr. Jenkins with some reservation, "I will try. But of course I cannot promise anything."

The following day a message awaited me at my hotel.

It read: "Mr. Kaye said that he would like to talk you. We haven't yet set the day or hour."

I phoned Mr. Jenkins. "What wonderful news!" I said.

"As soon as I mentioned Mrs. Roosevelt," Mr. Jenkins explained, "Mr. Kaye said that he would be glad to talk with you."

"When?" I asked.

"I don't know yet," said Dan Jenkins. "Danny spends a lot of time at the airport with his plane. How long will you be staying in Los Angeles?"

"Two more days," I said, then added hastily that I could postpone my departure if necessary.

Dan Jenkins promised that he would try to set the appointment for the following day.

The next message that awaited me at my hotel was laconic: "Mr. Kaye will see you tomorrow morning at nine o'clock at his house. Please meet me at my office at eight forty-five."

Slightly dazed, I went to bed early.

The streets of Beverly Hills were quite empty when I walked to Mr. Jenkins's office early the next morning. No other person was in sight. Even the elevator in Mr. Jenkins's office building seemed not yet predisposed to begin the workday; it only unlocked after nine o'clock in the morning. But Mr. Jenkins was ready and waiting for me. As we went out to his low sports car, I finally became a little uneasy.

However, while driving out toward Danny Kaye's house in Beverly Hills, I thought of my television image of him, his softness with children, his very special grace when he danced, his ever-present smile. The uneasiness disappeared and anticipation took its place.

The last trace of my nervousness vanished the instant we entered Mr. Kaye's white, somewhat old-fashioned and conservative-looking Georgian house. A tall, very thin figure clad in blue dungarees, white turtleneck shirt and blue wool-and-suede jacket came toward us. He had a blond beard and his blue eyes seemed a little tired. We shook hands.

"Would you like some breakfast?" asked Danny Kaye.

I saw a table set for three in a room that looked like a sun porch. "I would love some coffee," I said.

"That's *all* you want?" Danny Kaye sounded a little disappointed. "Don't you want an omelet?"

"An omelet would be wonderful," I said.

Then, not quite believing what I saw, I watched Danny Kaye heating a pan.

"It must be very hot before you put the butter in," he explained as he turned the pan expertly. "That way the butter won't burn and the omelet won't stick. Go and eat it right away," he said to me as he turned his handiwork out upon a plate which he handed to a pretty Japanese girl whose name was Yuki. "Eat it before it gets cold."

"How do you like my Chinese stove?" Mr. Kaye asked as he pointed to an enormous black stove in a corner. "I didn't realize it was too big to put anywhere in the house. So I had to put it into the back alley and build a sun porch around it. Come, I'll show it to you." He jumped up and took me to the door. Only then did I realize that the room in which we were sitting jutted out into what for the house next door was indeed the back alley.

When we had finished eating, Danny Kaye leaned back and looked at me. "Tell me about your book on Mrs. Roosevelt."

I explained how it had come about. He listened very intently. When I had finished he did not say anything; he seemed to wait for more. I told one of the stories that had come my way. It seemed that his eyes turned moist. He kept on listening with great interest as I told story after story.

"I loved and admired that woman more than I can say," he said, and stretched out his long legs.

"I guess I first saw her in person when we gave performances for 'The March of Dimes.' One day we were invited for lunch at the White House." His blue eyes became wistful as he remembered the occasion. "Imagine, *me*—a kid from Brooklyn—having lunch at the White House!" he said and smiled. "After lunch we were taken on a tour," he continued, the smile becoming wider. "We were shown the blue room, the red room, I don't recall how many other rooms. Finally we got to the swimming pool. A fine large swimming pool where the President took his daily swim. While the other people went on with their tour, I hung back and looked around. I opened a door. It was a dressing room. There on a hook was a blue terry-cloth robe. It had many large cigarette holes. The monogram said *FDR*. The President's robe! I quickly glanced outside to make certain that the other people had gone. Then I hastily took off my jacket and put on President Roosevelt's bathrobe." As Danny Kaye told the story, he touched the edges of his blue jacket to demonstrate how he had turned before the mirror in the dressing room of the White House. "Here I was," he said, the smile still lingering, "a boy with my background, having lunch in the White House, wearing President Roosevelt's robe! After a while I took it off again and put it back on the hanger. Then I joined the others in my group."

Danny Kaye fell silent. Neither Dan Jenkins nor I was able to say anything.

"For years and years Mrs. Roosevelt would call me 'Mr. Kaye.' But then one day when she saw me she embraced me and kissed me on the cheek and said, 'My dear Danny.' From then on we always embraced when we saw each other and she kept calling me 'My dear Danny.'

"One day—it was many years after that first lunch at the White House—I told Mrs. Roosevelt of that moment in the dressing room when I put on her husband's bathrobe.

" 'My dear Danny,' she said, 'would you like to have that robe?'

"I just looked at her. All that I could do was nod. Three weeks later a package arrived for me from Mrs. Roosevelt." He paused. "I had the robe treated so that it will never fall apart," he said then. "It is hanging upstairs in my closet wrapped in cellophane."

It took me several minutes before I could speak.

"Is it all right to use the story for my book?" I finally asked.

Danny Kaye gazed into space. "I am trying to think," he said slowly, "whether Mrs. Roosevelt would approve."

"Have you never told the story?" I asked.

"Once on television," he said. "But I asked Eleanor Roosevelt first if it was all right."

"What did she say?"

" 'Oh, of course!' " he said, imitating Eleanor Roosevelt's voice and manner; for a moment it seemed as if she were physically present with the three of us. We all laughed.

"I suppose it is all right," he said gently.

"Danny," said Dan Jenkins, "you told me that you have another appointment at ten. It is later than that now."

"Oh, yes . . ." Danny Kaye passed a hand over his face. As he got to his feet it seemed to me that he was somewhat reluctant to leave his memories of Eleanor Roosevelt.

I rose and thanked him. He nodded. Then his tall, thin figure disappeared inside the house.

Sidney Glazier is the man who had produced the documentary film *The Eleanor Roosevelt Story*. It was written by Archibald MacLeish.

"I would be most happy to be interviewed by you," Mr. Glazier replied to my request.

He had his office on West Fifty-sixth Street in New York, in a small old building which also housed the Eleanor Roosevelt Foundation.

Among the photographs on Mr. Glazier's desk was one of Han Suyin, the distinguished Chinese writer who also happened to be Sidney Glazier's mother-in-law.

"What made you do *The Eleanor Roosevelt Story?*" I asked.

"I loved her," Sidney Glazier said simply. "Mrs. Roosevelt stood for everything that was good in this world. When I attended her funeral I felt as if a light had gone out in the world. I knew that I had to do this film. Even if I didn't earn a penny with it. I devoted one year of my life to the picture and, in fact, it did not make much money. However, it did earn me the Academy Award for the Best Documentary Film in 1965." Mr. Glazier gently touched the bronze Oscar on his desk.

"The Eleanor Roosevelt Story is one of the finest the screen has yet offered," wrote Rose Pelswick in *The New York Journal* at the time the film was first shown. "Made with both skill and affection, it is deeply moving, a constantly absorbing film. History comes to life. It is a beautiful job."

"When I wrote my book on *Charm,*" said Miss Arlene Francis when I saw her in her television studio, "I recall asking Mrs. Roosevelt for *her* definition of it. 'I have no definition,' said Eleanor Roosevelt, 'unless it is to be kind.' "

"I remember when Mrs. Roosevelt was the Mystery Guest on 'What's My Line?' " said Mrs. Jean Bach, Arlene Francis's producer. "When the moment arrived when all masks were in place and John Daly announced, 'Here is our Mystery Guest!,' no Mystery Guest appeared. A search was made where the Mystery Guest usually was hidden, but Eleanor Roosevelt was not there. They finally found her all the way down the hallway. 'I was afraid I would cough or sneeze and disturb the show,' explained Mrs. Roosevelt as we quickly ushered her onto the stage."

Through the assistance of Harvey Granat, a friend of Cary

Grant's, I had one of the most unusual experiences with a personality in the entertainment world. I had written Cary Grant a letter in Hollywood, telling him of my book on Eleanor Roosevelt and asking him whether, by any chance, he too would have a memory for me.

Several weeks passed and there was no answer from Cary Grant. Then, one morning, my telephone rang. A deep and very cheerful male voice which sounded most familiar said, "This is Cary Grant."

It took me a moment to take that in.

"Oh my goodness!" I said then. 'I am afraid I am going to faint."

"Now don't you do that," said Cary Grant in his lighthearted way. "I am on my way back to the Coast and I wouldn't have time to wait until you come back again. I tried you all last week but could not reach you. You must have been out of town. I thought I'll give her one more try before I leave for the airport. I really just phoned to tell you that I never met Mrs. Roosevelt."

I had to think fast. You couldn't let Cary Grant get away so quickly.

"That's too bad," I said. "It's both your loss!"

"Yes," said Cary Grant, "I quite agree. I did meet her once at that, but only very briefly. We gave a performance in Washington and Mrs. Roosevelt came backstage afterward and shook hands with me. She was very kind, very gracious as always, but that was all. Absolutely no story for you."

"Mr. Grant," I said, "if you give me permission to tell in my book that *you* took the trouble to call *me*, just to tell me that you never met Mrs. Roosevelt and are sorry you didn't, this would be quite a story in itself."

"Of course," he said. "I'll be delighted. But now I really have to run . . ."

Chapter Fourteen

The Negroes

"THERE IS, I BELIEVE, A LEGEND in the Talmud which tells us that in any period of history the heavens themselves are held in place by the virtue, love, and shining integrity of twelve just men," Adlai Stevenson said in his tribute to Eleanor Roosevelt at the Democratic National Convention in March 1963. "They are completely unaware of this function. They go about their daily work, their humble chores—doctors, teachers, workers, farmers, (never, alas, lawyers—so I understand)," he added, and one can imagine his quick smile, "just ordinary devoted citizens—and meanwhile the rooftree of creation is supported by them alone. Can we doubt that Eleanor Roosevelt's standards and her integrity steadied our own? Long before the civil rights issue moved to the forefront of the nation's consciousness, she was there, earning public abuse for her quiet reminders of the inequalities practiced in our land. She would bid us to add to the civil liberties we guarantee, the extra dimension of opportunity without which even rights can seem so much emptiness."

How often I thought of these words when, in 1965, 1966, and 1967, the newspaper headlines screamed, "Riots in Harlem!" "Riots in Newark!" "Watts Is Burning!" Perhaps if we had listened to Eleanor Roosevelt, I thought, if we had done what she asked us to do, much of this tragedy could have been averted.

How did Negroes feel about Eleanor Roosevelt? I began to wonder. For years I had heard that she had many Negro friends. I knew of course about Mrs. Roosevelt's friendship with Marian Anderson, a friendship which began early in 1939 when the Daughters of the American Revolution made it known that they had refused the facilities of their headquarters, Constitution Hall in Washington, D.C., for a concert by the outstanding contralto. Constitution Hall was virtually the only auditorium in Washington suitable for concert purposes. The reason, the D.A.R. president stated, was the organization's desire to maintain conformity to "existing and still prevailing conditions and customs in the capital which the community itself must work out."

Protests against the D.A.R. policy were immediate, and they came from people of widely different social and political viewpoints. Chief Justice and Mrs. Charles Evans Hughes, Associate Justice and Mrs. Hugo Black, New York Mayor Fiorello La Guardia, Senator Charles McNary, Republican of Oregon, and Senator Bennett Champ Clark, Democrat of Missouri, were among those lending their names to petitions of objection. *The New York Times,* after paying tribute to Miss Anderson's artistry, declared:

"If Miss Anderson's inability to find a suitable hall in the national capital for her April concert is due to social or racial snobbery, all that can be said is that such an attitude is inconsistent with the best American traditions, including those which were born in the fires of the American Revolution. It is hard to believe that any patriotic American organization in this country would approve of discrimination against so gifted an artist and so fine a person as Miss Anderson. In fact, no organization could do so and still merit the adjective patriotic."

A group of New York clergymen signed a petition which called the D.A.R.'s policy "pagan." In Washington, Democratic Senator Robert Wagner of New York spoke at a protest meeting where resolutions condemning the D.A.R. position were drawn up. At Howard University, Senator Robert A. Taft, Republican of Ohio, promised a black audience that they would have the support of the great majority of white people, and of all the intelligent white leaders in their fight against certain narrow prejudices, such as those which excluded Marian Anderson from a proper auditorium in the city of Washington.*

Eleanor Roosevelt, however, as was her custom, did more than protest; she took action. In her column, "My Day," on February 27, 1939, she wrote:

> I have been debating in my mind for some time, a question which I have had to debate with myself once or twice before in my life. Usually I have decided differently from the way I am deciding now. The question is, if you belong to an organization and disapprove of an action which is typical of a policy, should you resign or is it better to work for a changed point of view within the organization? In the past, when I was able to work actively in any organization to which I belonged, I have usually stayed in until I had at least made a fight and been defeated.
>
> Even then, I have, as a rule, accepted my defeat and decided I was wrong or, perhaps, a little too far ahead of the thinking of the majority at that time. I have often found that the thing in which I was interested was done some years later. But, in this case, I belong to an organization in which I can do no active work. They have taken an action which has been widely talked of in the press. To remain as a member implies approval of that action, and therefore I am resigning.

Consequently, the Interior Department in Washington assisted Marion Anderson, and she was given use of the space adjoining the Lincoln Memorial for her concert. On Easter Sunday, April 9, 1939, Miss Anderson sang before the memorial to Abraham Lincoln to an audience of 75,000 people. The following July the great contralto was given the Joel E. Spingarn Medal, an award to the Negro who "shall have made the highest achievement during the preceding years in any honorable field of human endeavor." Chosen to present the medal was Mrs. Eleanor Roosevelt.

Another famous Negro friend of Eleanor Roosevelt was Harry Belafonte. She once wrote a column trying to find an apartment for him, and once even considered buying a house in Manhattan

---

* James R. Kearny, *The Evolution of a Reformer*. Boston: Houghton Mifflin Co., 1968.

where she could rent him a floor. She often invited him to Hyde Park; at the time when she was dying, she still was busy knitting a blanket for his expected baby.

"Pauli Murray is one of the finest of my Negro friends," wrote Mrs. Roosevelt in an article in *Ebony* magazine. "I met her when she still was a young firebrand and a warm friendship has developed between us."

Dr. Pauli Murray is a distinguished lawyer and poet. She has lectured, tutored in legal writing, practiced law in the most important law firms of the country, taught, written, and traveled widely, including a year of lecturing in Africa. The list of her accomplishments is endless. "I looked upon Mrs. Roosevelt almost as a mother," Pauli Murray told me at Brandeis University where, in the fall of 1968, she became a professor in the department of American Civilization, teaching a course titled "Law as an Instrument of Social Change."

"Mrs. Roosevelt often invited me to Hyde Park and several times asked me to bring members of my family," she said. "I'll never forget when, in August 1952, I took my Aunt Pauline along on a visit to Mrs. Roosevelt. Aunt Pauline was eighty-two years old at the time. After our visit to Eleanor Roosevelt, Aunt Pauline wrote a very long accounting of it in the form of a letter; it was sent to all the members of our family."

"Last week, Friday to be exact," Aunt Pauline started her letter, "Pauli was invited by Mrs. Eleanor Roosevelt to bring her aunt up to Hyde Park and take lunch with her at Val-Kill Cottage. Well, Pauli borrowed a dark blue car, a Ford sedan with every gadget you could think of in it. Hyde Park is about 80 miles in upstate New York. We went all the way up to Poughkeepsie on the Parkway. The roads were lovely and the scenery was beautiful. We kept near the Hudson River most of the way, the great Bear Mountain was far above and in front of us all the time. We left New York about 11 o'clock in the morning and traveled steadily all the way, through Poughkeepsie and on to Hyde Park about 3½ miles from there, and the famous Roosevelt home. We got lost and went about 5 miles too far because we missed the stone gateposts that lead to Mrs. Roosevelt's home,

Val-Kill Cottage. But we arrived about 1:15 o'clock. (It was all right because Mrs. Roosevelt had forgotten to order the fish and so lunch was delayed anyway.)"

Aunt Pauline's letter goes on for many delightful pages describing every single incident of this memorable visit.

When I visited Pauli Murray at Brandeis University, we talked for many hours. We came to realize that although we came from different backgrounds, we shared the same devastating experience of having been rejected by our native land, I, as a Jew in Austria during the Nazi regime, and Pauli—all of her life.

For the first time I was made really to feel what it means emotionally to be a Negro in America.

"Do you think that Mrs. Roosevelt inspired me to achieve what I did?" Pauli Murray asked just as we were saying good-bye.

I looked at the slender woman, the dark intense eyes.

"No," I said with absolute assurance, "you had the courage to go on and make something of yourself even before you ever met Mrs. Roosevelt. But—I feel that she accelerated what was there."

Pauli Murray seemed content with my reply.

But after having learned about three of Mrs. Roosevelt's famous Negro friends, I began to wonder about the others who were not famous. The people in Harlem, the people in the South, the Negroes all over the country who surely must have had experiences with Mrs. Roosevelt also. I decided to get in touch with the average Negro citizen to help me.

How? I had no Negro neighbors. Never before had it dawned on me quite so consciously that I was, in fact, living in a segregated community. Why had I never thought of this in the past? I had always fervently condemned the Southern style of segregation, more so the South African system of apartheid. I was appalled when I read of the South African laws in which a white man had no other contact with an African except when the latter came in his house as a domestic. Now, abruptly, I had to face the fact that the life I was leading in New York, the most integrated city of the United States, was not so very different from the way white people lived in Johannesburg. I tried to rationalize by telling myself that the American Negro did have opportunities, opportunities for schooling, for higher qualified jobs, no restrictions—

No restrictions? If this were so, how did it happen that I myself did not know any Negroes? I had no Negro friend or neighbor whom I could ask about their personal experiences or memories of Mrs. Roosevelt. To me, the doors to the black community seemed completely shut and I had no idea how I could open them.

Then I received a letter from Morris Milgram. M-REIT, the Mutual Real Estate Investment Trust, the letterhead said, was established to invest in housing open to all. "I noticed the item about the book you are writing on Mrs. Roosevelt in the *New School Bulletin*," wrote Morris Milgram, President of Planned Communities, Inc. "Eleanor Roosevelt served on the board of our company and I may be able to help you."

I promptly phoned Mr. Milgram to thank him for his letter and to make an appointment.

The offices of Planned Communities on East Forty-second Street were humming with people at work. Behind the desks and typewriters were an equal number of white and black faces. The room of the president was just a small cubicle. Morris Milgram was dictating a letter when I came in. "It'll take me a few minutes to finish and then we'll have lunch together," he said.

Morris Milgram was around fifty. He had a dark crew cut, horn-rimmed glasses, a stubborn chin. He hurriedly finished his letter and rose swiftly. "All right, let's go." Although it was cold outside, it did not seem to occur to him to put on a coat. Once we got to the street I realized that if you want to keep in step with Morris Milgram you have got to run. We went to a restaurant, ordered sandwiches and coffee. As I watched him eat, I had the feeling that he had not the slightest idea what he was swallowing.

"Tell me about Planned Communities," I said. "What made you start this?"

"Life is too short to do anything else but to build the kind of world one believes in," Morris Milgram said with a sudden smile. "My father-in-law was a builder. He asked me to become a partner in the business in 1947. I said okay, but only if I could build for *all* people, without racial discrimination. He said okay. That's how it began." He gulped his coffee. "My parents were poor Russian immigrants with six children. My sisters worked in the garment industry, the famous sweatshops. I grew up carried on the shoulders of union leaders. I suppose they gave me my convictions against all kinds of social injustice."

Morris Milgram took off his glasses to wipe them. Only then did I see the light of total dedication in his intense eyes.

"How does Planned Communities work?" I asked.

"We buy all-white apartment houses in good neighborhoods far from minority areas and open them to all, without fanfare," he explained. "The whites do not flee, for both white and non-white families come and rent apartments they can afford. Most of these buildings are now bought by M-REIT, the Mutual Real Estate Investment Trust which we organized in 1965."

"Your work must be enormously satisfying," I said.

"Developing and building integrated communities means a great deal to me. I find that everywhere in America there are what William Saroyan calls 'the beautiful people.' To me they are those who, given the facts, will do the right things and work for equal justice."

"I imagine it was a hard beginning for you," I suggested.

"It was," Mr. Milgram admitted. "The real estate dealers said no whites would voluntarily buy next door to Negroes, that my idea was an impossible dream. But I felt that nothing is impossible in the field of getting people to live together. If you can dream it, you can do it. For us, integrated housing is working. We now have Planned Communities in nine states. In Philadelphia, in Washington, in Princeton, New Jersey, in New York. We have communities of one-family homes and apartment houses."

"How did it happen that Mrs. Roosevelt became a member of your board?" I asked.

"Well, for years Eleanor Roosevelt served on Planned Communities National Advisory Committee," he said. "When we began to build in Deerfield, Illinois, a Chicago suburb, the community voted to take our two separate sites for parks to keep the village all white. Their Southern supporters called me a 'man who makes his living by making other people unhappy.' Mrs. Roosevelt did all she could to help us stop the condemnation of our fifty-one lots and two model houses in Deerfield. The White Citizens Council's national newspapers, of course, attacked her for this. I asked her, as long as she was blamed for running our company, whether she would like to become a board member. She did. Earlier, in July 1958, Mrs. Roosevelt wrote about us in her column, 'My Day,' and said she was waiting for us to build an apartment house in New York where she herself would like to live."

"I know that Mrs. Roosevelt had many Negro friends," I said. "I want to find them, hear how she affected them. Would you have any suggestion?"

While I searched for the words to explain what I had in mind, Morris Milgram pulled a piece of paper and a pen from his pocket. "Get in touch with . . ." and in a few minutes he had jotted down at least fifty names.

I looked at the list. "Before I met you," I said, "a chapter on Eleanor Roosevelt and her Negro friends seemed impossible for me to do. And now—"

The quick smile again appeared on the intense face with the stubborn chin. "To get things done you must ask a busy person," he said. Then he called for the check.

"Don't hesitate to call me if you need more assistance," Morris Milgram said as we said good-bye on the street. I watched him cross against the light as he raced back toward his office to the sound of screeching automobile brakes.

As soon as I got home I wrote to the first name on the list, Poppy Cannon, widow of Walter White, the former head of the NAACP. Miss Cannon writes a food column in the *Ladies Home Journal* and also a weekly column in the Harlem newspaper *Amsterdam News*.

On April 1, 1967, Poppy Cannon's entire column in the *Amsterdam News* was devoted to my projected book on Eleanor Roosevelt.

And then the letters began to arrive from Negro communities all over the country. There was also one phone call.

"My name is Calvin Johnson," said a husky, somewhat hesitant voice. "I met Mrs. Roosevelt in Brisbane, Australia, way back in 1942. I was an American soldier and I am a Negro. There was a lot of racial tension in the army there. Even the Red Cross had a white and a black division," he said, and I could hear the bitterness in his voice. "I was only nineteen and very impressionable. It was real bad there. They made me feel as though I were scum." He paused and I waited for him to continue.

"One day I was sitting in the canteen at the lunch counter eating an ice cream cone. Suddenly there was some commotion at the door. Everyone looked and stared and when I turned around I saw a tall lady walking in. 'What do you know," I said to myself, 'it's Mrs. Roosevelt!' She went behind the counter, shook hands with each of the men down the line, and asked them their names and where they were from. When she came to me, I still was eating my ice cream cone and I put it into my left hand to be able to shake hands with her. I told her I was from Pittsburgh and she smiled and said, 'What do you know, we have a Yankee here!' Everyone laughed and cheered. Then, Mrs. Roosevelt looked straight into my eyes and said, "May I have some of that ice cream?"

Mr. Johnson paused. I waited.

"It will be difficult for you to understand the turmoil that went on inside of me," he said then, his voice a little shaky. "I did not know what to do. I thought if I said No, I would hurt her feelings. On the other hand, if I were to say Yes, I would do her a grave injustice. For this, after all, was a white woman! She didn't really want to eat from *my* ice cream cone. So I guess I must have been sitting there just staring at her with my mouth hanging open, not knowing what to do. And then, very gently, Mrs. Roosevelt took the cone from my hand, took a big bite from it and handed it back to me. 'You see,' she said and smiled real wide, 'that didn't hurt at all, did it? You won't ever even miss it.' "

Calvin Johnson fell silent. "Would you mind," I said after a long pause, "if I asked you a personal question?"

"No." His voice was wary.

"What Mrs. Roosevelt did—did it change your feelings about white people?"

"Only about *her*," he instantly replied.

"But didn't it make you think there might be other white people very much like Eleanor Roosevelt?"

"Oh," Mr. Johnson said very casually, "perhaps there are. But if so, I have not met them."

There was something in his voice, something so final and so hopeless, that it would not let me argue the point. "It is a beautiful story," I said instead. "I sincerely thank you for your trouble in phoning, for sharing it with me."

"I always wanted to tell it to someone," Calvin Johnson said. "But I never had the opportunity. That day in Australia, Mrs. Roosevelt made me feel like a man again. I will never forget her."

After Poppy Cannon's column about my work appeared in the *Amsterdam News,* my post-office box began to fill rapidly. One letter came from a Mrs. Graham: "I like to remember when Mrs. Eleanor Roosevelt came to Atlanta, Georgia, and spoke in the city auditorium," she wrote. "I think I was about fourteen years old but we always read articles about her when possible. Thus, learning of her scheduled speech, we went to the auditorium. At that time public facilities in Georgia were fully segregated. We had to go to the balcony. As the auditorium was very large, it meant we would be a great distance from Mrs. Roosevelt and we worried that we would not hear her. Do you know what the Great Lady did? She walked graciously out to the center of the stage, looked straight up toward the balcony and said, 'I shall address myself to those who are in the balcony." All through her talk she kept looking up to us. We were thrilled beyond measure and could hear every word she spoke crystal clear."

"My uncle said they would not give colored people help," wrote Mrs. Effie L. Blue from Detroit, Michigan. "I was eighteen years old when Mrs. Roosevelt came to Michigan in 1937, for the ground-breaking ceremonies at the site of Detroit's first low-income housing project—Brewster-Douglas Homes. I was there two hours before she arrived. It was a very hot day. You see, my dad was very old and still was trying to work his farm down South, in Fitzgerald, Georgia, and I wanted to ask Mrs. Roosevelt to help us. My uncle was scared for me to come and said it was no use, but I came anyway. Mrs. Roosevelt was very friendly and said to write to her and explain everything in a letter. I did. Then I received a letter from the President himself! He said that anyone could get aid and I showed that letter to my uncle. He still would not believe it. But then we got shoes and clothes, and food and something they called commodities and finally he had to believe it!

"I will never forget that day when Mrs. Roosevelt came to Detroit and pulled the rope that was tied to a little old gray shell of a house. There were people all across and up and down the streets and packed in front of the Castle Theater. It was a real scorcher that day and I almost fainted. But it was the thrill of a lifetime to be able to talk with a great lady like Mrs. Roosevelt. Oh, I just remembered, she had on a brown hat stitched all around shaped like a turtle's back. I sketched it and had a lady that made hats on Beaubien Street, across from Wright's Funeral Home, copy it. I hope this memory of Mrs. Roosevelt will help you some . . ."

Another lady from Detroit, Mrs. Ateemese Lyons, remembered when Mrs. Roosevelt surprised the Detroit Spiritual Singers when she visited them at the Ebenezer Chuch where they were rehearsing under the auspices of the Michigan Music Project, WPA. In the middle of the song "Joshua Fought the Battle of Jericho" in walked a tall woman whom the singers instantly recognized. However, they finished their song and then remained standing, gazing at her, speechless.

"Mrs. Roosevelt explained that she had come to the church to hear another group, 'Wings Over Jordan,' sing," Mrs. Lyons wrote. "But during the time she was listening to them, she heard our voices float down the hall and simply followed the sound. She asked us if we would like to come to Washington and entertain her husband and some guests singing the old year out and the new one in on New Year's Eve. Of course we said yes—thinking that she never would remember us. But a month or so later, we received a telegram from Washington inviting us to the White House as Mrs. Roosevelt's guests and advising us as to the travel arrangements she had made for us."

Dr. Sophia M. Robison remembered the time when she worked

in Washington in 1941 with a Committee for Civilian Defense which was housed in the Du Pont Building.

"Mrs. Roosevelt participated in our group," Dr. Robison said. "Several Negroes from New York and elsewhere had gone to Washington and they had no place to go for lunch since the restaurants in the neighborhood refused to serve them. When we brought the situation to Mrs. Roosevelt's attention, she listened attentively, then she said, 'Very well, we'll all eat together in the lobby.' She arranged for a large urn of coffee and sandwiches every day at noon, and set up folding chairs in the lobby of the Du Pont Building to serve her and all the workers on the committee. Luncheon with Mrs. Roosevelt in the lobby became so popular that the restaurant in the building felt a sharp drop in their business and decided to lift their restrictions."

Mr. Will Maslow of the American Jewish Congress wrote to me about an incident in which Mrs. Roosevelt took action in a more tricky situation. In 1944, he was working as Director of Field Operations for President Roosevelt's Committee on Fair Employment Practices. In the Atlanta office, a white and a Negro secretary were employed. The other white clerical employees on the floor objected to the Negro girl using *their* ladies' room. Somehow, the story got to Washington and to Mrs. Roosevelt. Very soon, plumbers arrived in the Atlanta office building and they commenced to build a new ladies' room for Negroes. It was so superior to the existing one that the white girls soon asked for permission to use it also.

One day in the lobby of The New School I had an appointment with a woman who had seen my appeal for stories in the *Amsterdam News*. As I entered the building, I saw a young Negro woman seated on the bench near the information booth and I asked her whether she was the lady I was looking for. She replied that she wasn't and then said, "It must be difficult to wait for someone you do not know." I replied that I did this often and mentioned my projected book.

Her face lit up. "Oh, I have a story for you about Mrs. Roosevelt!" she exclaimed. "I am so thrilled to have the opportunity to tell someone about it.

"In about 1960," said Gwendolyn Lawrence, "I was living at the Kings View Bridge Housing project in Brooklyn. It was an integrated cooperative building. Peter Sturgen, white newspaperman, was also living there. When he heard about Mrs. Roosevelt's interest in integrated housing, Peter decided to invite her for dinner. He wrote her a letter asking if she would be interested to see for herself how such a project worked. We all teased him about it and, of course, were quite certain that there was not the slightest chance that Mrs. Roosevelt really would accept the invitation. But she did. You can't imagine our excitement. Peter invited a few other couples to his small three-and-a-half room apartment and we all helped his wife with the cooking.

"Peter picked Mrs. Roosevelt up at her apartment. She was so sweet and so simple that we were completely overwhelmed. She was totally at home in our group. She said that people are wronging themselves terribly, if they just communicate with their own kind. They must realize that there is a great deal to gain and to learn from other cultures. Familiarity with another history would give people the opportunity to broaden their views, open the windows to other writers, other thinkers. It would make people feel alive and at peace with themselves. They would come to realize that there was nothing to fear in each other."

Gwendolyn Lawrence smiled as she remembered.

"What was it about Mrs. Roosevelt," I asked slowly, as I remembered Calvin Johnson and his ice cream cone in Brisbane, Australia, "that made her one of the few white people whom Negroes really do not seem to resent?"

Gwendolyn Lawrence's forehead wrinkled for a few moments.

"Mrs. Roosevelt made us feel," she said at long last, "that she had respect for us like for any other human being."

"But how did she get this across?" I persisted.

Again Gwendolyn thought for a long time.

"Mrs. Roosevelt," she said then and gave me one of her lovely smiles, "did not talk about integration. She integrated!"

The lady with whom I had had the original appointment never showed up. But I had learned something more about Eleanor Roosevelt anyway.

Chapter Fifteen

The Depression

ON MARCH 4, 1933 Eleanor Roosevelt became First Lady of the Land. At that time, unemployment afflicted twenty-five percent of the population. College graduates were grateful for the opportunity to sell furniture for seventeen dollars a week. Harvard and Yale graduates worked for the Fire and Police departments of New York. A society matron reported that her butler had a master's degree in Engineering from M.I.T. Business School graduates were selling neckties at Macy's. Maids were paid twenty-five cents an hour and even at that wage they found it difficult to find work. Housewives tried to sustain their families by shopping for five cents' worth of rice and ten cents' worth of butter. Each day the newspapers reported more bankruptcies and suicides. Landlords could not collect their rents, people put off seeing their doctors and dentists, hospitals could not fill their private rooms.

"These unhappy times call for the building of plans that put their faith once more in the forgotten man at the bottom of the economic pyramid," Franklin D. Roosevelt declared during his presidential campaign. He solemnly pledged himself to "A New Deal for the American People."

The first task of the Roosevelt administration was to meet the urgent need for relief. People needed to eat; they had to find jobs.

While President Roosevelt set about creating his famous work projects for the masses who had been idle for so long, letters pleading for help came pouring in to Mrs. Roosevelt. Her deep concern was instantly aroused and, as always, she responded to every appeal that came to her. Now, thirty-five years later, many people still remember her attempts to help them.

"Many years ago, during the Depression, my daughter was very ill," wrote Mrs. A. I. Pollick from Bayside, New York. "We had spent all our savings for medical aid which had gotten us nowhere and we did not know to whom to turn. A relative finally wrote for advice to Mrs. Roosevelt. She replied at once and said she would have her personal physician look at my daughter; her doctor did pay us a visit soon afterward. Then she sent us a large box of roses with a picture of the White House on it. I think that Mrs. Roosevelt and her husband were the most wonderful and humane people in the world. We would have lost our home if it had not been for the H. O. Loan."

During the Depression living conditions were especially appalling in the Appalachian area of West Virginia. Dr. Frank Kingdon, the distinguished former newscaster and journalist, entered a coal-miner's hut in that section one day and was astounded to find Eleanor Roosevelt sitting on a shabby cot. She was holding a naked, emaciated child in her arms, while the mother was stirring a thin soup in a blackened pot on the stove. "The two women were discussing their household problems as though that Appalachian hut were no different from a Washington drawing room," Dr. Kingdon still remembers.

The evening after that visit to West Virginia,* William C. Bullitt, the American Ambassador to France had dinner at the White House. Mrs. Roosevelt told of the family she had met at the hut, the father who had shown her the weekly pay slip he received as a miner. A small amount had been deducted toward his bill at the company store, another small amount for his rent and oil for his lamp. These deductions left him with less than one dollar each week. There were six children in the family

---

* *The Autobiography of Eleanor Roosevelt.* New York: Harper & Brothers, 1961.

and they had ducked into corners when Mrs. Roosevelt came. On the table was a bowl filled with scraps ". . . the kind most people give to their dogs," Mrs. Roosevelt told the guests at the White House dinner table. At noon the children came running in, took a handful of scraps out of the bowl and ran out again. As Mrs. Roosevelt left, two of the children gathered enough courage to stand by the door. The little boy was holding a white rabbit in his arms. His sister, a little older than he, was thin and scrawny, and she had a malicious gleam in her eyes as she looked at her brother. "He thinks we are not going to eat his rabbit," she whispered to Mrs. Roosevelt. "But we sure are!"

"The little boy must have heard her," Mrs. Roosevelt said as she ended her story, "because he suddenly clutched his rabbit closer and fled down the hill."

The morning after the dinner, Mrs. Roosevelt received in the mail a check from Mr. Bullitt. The accompanying note said that he hoped the money might help to keep the rabbit alive.

The years of the Depression were especially hard and bewildering for America's young people who were just emerging into the adult world after high school. Many felt that they were a burden to their families, sensing that by their very presence they were taking food away from their younger brothers and sisters. There was no place for them in the labor market. Letters pleading for help came pouring in to Mrs. Roosevelt, and she took a very special interest in these unfortunate youngsters. She immediately devoted her time to various programs of the American Friends Service Committee and the government Civilian Conservation Corps which inaugurated voluntary work camps for young people. Today, thirty-five years later, some of these former campers still remember the woman who, during that unhappy period, made the world a friendlier place for them.

"My family had to go on welfare and my brother worked for the WPA." wrote Freeda Menschel of Arverne, Long Island. "I was promised a job by the government but, until one materialized, I was sent to Camp Jane Addams, a camp for jobless and homeless girls, which was sponsored by Mrs. Roosevelt and which she often visited. I had never met a President's wife and I was completely overwhelmed when Eleanor Roosevelt ate with us one Sunday, the chef's night off. Like everyone else, she took her plate, helped herself from the buffet on a big table and sat down to supper. At first, when she asked me about my problems, I was completely tongue-tied. But she spoke to me in a quiet, kind way; she was not at all condescending and she made me feel that at the moment what I said was vitally interesting and important to her. I forgot all about being shy and I never forgot how she put me at ease. What I felt was so very special about Mrs. Roosevelt was that she didn't just go around making speeches; she truly did help so many people by doing so many wonderful things."

Freeda Menschel is one of the many young people who were given a chance for a better life during the Depression through the efforts of Eleanor Roosevelt. The idea of the work camps outlived the days of the Depression. In 1939 it took the form of the Work Camps for Democracy. In 1940 and 1941 this citizenship training program expanded under the name of "Work Camps for America," and, in the years following World War II, the program evolved into its present form—"The Encampment for Citizenship"—an undertaking in which Eleanor Roosevelt was vitally interested.

I heard about it for the first time when I received a letter from Algernon D. Black, Leader of the Society for Ethical Culture in the City of New York. "Mrs. Roosevelt was involved with the Encampment for Citizenship from the earliest days," wrote Mr. Black, and suggested that I contact a former friend of Mrs. Roosevelt, Mrs. Alice K. Pollitzer, who, at the age of seventy-five, had chaired the first Board of Directors. "Mrs. Pollitzer is now ninety-seven years old," Mr. Black added.*

When I dialed her number the next morning, a pleasant voice answered and said, "Good morning, this is Alice K. Pollitzer speaking."

I introduced myself and explained what I wanted.

"I am awfully sorry but you caught me at a bad moment," Mrs. Pollitzer said pleasantly. "I am just leaving the house for a luncheon appointment. Please call me tomorrow."

When I phoned the following day, Mrs. Pollitzer again an-

---

* Mrs. Pollitzer celebrated her one hundredth birthday on May 31, 1970.

swered the phone herself. I inquired whether it was more convenient now to talk for her and she chuckled. "Please don't think
that I am rude, but I am just leaving the house again for an appointment." However, we did make a date for the following day.

Mrs. Pollitzer lives with her daughter in a large apartment on
Broadway and Eighty-sixth Street. When I rang the bell on the
dot of noon, a voice called out, "Coming!," and, without inquir-
ing as to the identity of her caller or glancing through the peek-
hole, Mrs. Pollitzer herself opened the door.

A slight, very erect, white-haired lady dressed in a neat black
dress shook my hand. She led me into a pleasant living room
which, with its Oriental rugs, paintings, books, and photographs,
had a somewhat European atmosphere. Mrs. Pollitzer asked me to
sit down and she herself took her place on a sofa behind a coffee
table. To be sure, she did not give the impression of a young
woman. However, nothing in her appearance or her attitude
indicated that she was almost a hundred years old.

"I did not know Mrs. Roosevelt very well," Mrs. Pollitzer said
as she looked at me through very thick glasses. "But whenever
I would come to visit her at Hyde Park with the young people
from the Encampment, she would see to it that there was a chair
for me to sit on."

I told Mrs. Pollitzer that I would be very much interested to
hear more about the Encampment for Citizenship.

"I, like Mrs. Roosevelt, was always interested in young people,"
Mrs. Pollitzer began.

In 1946, she, Dr. Algernon D. Black, and others in the fields
of education and social welfare became concerned that American
youth had little knowledge or appreciation of the experiences and
aspirations of people of different racial, religious, and economic
backgrounds. There was an alarming lack of clarity among young
people about the meaning of democracy, and there was little
understanding of how young men and women might help solve
pressing socioeconomic problems. Too, they showed little understanding of what Fascism and Communism really were all about.
Therefore, under the sponsorship of the American Ethical Union
and its affiliated societies, the Encampment for Citizenship was
launched at the Fieldston School in Riverdale, New York.

One hundred and twenty-eight young men and women from

eighteen to twenty-three years of age took part in the first Encampment. They came from all parts of the United States and
from several other countries. There were Caucasians and Negroes
and Indians; Japanese-Americans and Mexican-Americans; North-
erners and Southerners; Protestants, Catholics, and Jews, farmers,
office workers, factory workers, miners, veterans, students. The
Encampment program was based on the assumption that to learn
to be a citizen the individual must have an actual experience in
living in a democratic community.

Upon arrival, every camper is recognized from his picture and
greeted by name. This gives him a sense of belonging from the
very first moment, a sense of being an important person in his
own right. Then he is assigned to a dorm group, which is religiously, racially, vocationally, and geographically mixed. A
member of the very minority group he has been taught to hate
may be sharing his double-deck cot, sleeping above or below him.
But in all the years of the Encampment's existence, no one ever
asked to be shifted because of this. This is especially meaningful
since many of the campers came from towns which were almost
entirely Protestant or Catholic and had never before had contact
with a Negro or a Jew.

At some point during the Encampment, it should be possible
for campers to say, "Here one does not feel himself to be a Negro,
Indian, or anything but a person. People are valued as people."
This does not happen entirely by itself and it does not happen
right away.

"It is one thing to believe in equality intellectually," said a
white girl from the South, "yet another matter entirely to live
with other races as intimately as we do in the dormitories. One
morning the Negro girl who slept in the bunk next to mine
woke up with severe menstrual cramps. I was amazed to find out
they were exactly the same kind of cramps that I had every
month." For this girl it was a very great discovery to find out that
a Negro girl not only suffered the same pains but also took the
same medication for her discomfort.

"It is amazing how well we all got along," said a young American Indian about the Encampment.

"I have lost my stereotypes and learned to accept people as
individuals," said a Negro from Harlem.

"I have learned respect for other people's different ideas," was the discovery of a young Puerto Rican.

"The Encampment enriched my life in many ways," said a girl from Kentucky. "I hope I can convert others with such ideas when I get home." *

Many of the campers were quite uninformed about other people's beliefs. Some had distorted ideas and stereotyped images of members of other faiths. Even those who were liberal and open minded on other problems, such as labor or race or foreign affairs, were quite intolerant about religion. Others, who were tolerant toward religions different from their own, were intolerant of people from faraway places.

"What do we know in Holland about Negro problems and Indians?" said a young girl from Europe. "All I ever saw in a Dutch weekly were some pictures of guardsmen in Kentucky and Tennessee who had to protect Negro students who wanted to go to school. Everyone in my town was outraged. But it gave a completely superficial picture of the race problem in the United States. I discovered that during my six weeks at the Encampment."

The Encampment tries to demonstrate that democracy offers more to the individual but also requires more from him than any other form of society. Citizenship is not merely a matter of voting and obeying the laws. The entire process of self-government requires awareness of the community process.

As a test, Dr. Black once gave a speech that was actually a Fascist program.

"We have all been brought up to believe in democracy as a wonderful way of life," he began. "Now I am going to tell you the truth about it. Freedom can be a cloak for selfishness. A free people might be a people without restraint or discipline. Take the phrase 'the sacredness of the individual'—do we not become more worthy if we live for something bigger than ourselves? As for the idea of 'all men created equal,' is this not a completely false premise? As we all know, men are created completely unequal in abilities . . ." He went on to point out that democracy meant corruption in government and politics, a materialism and com-

---

* Algernon D. Black, *The Young Citizens*. New York: Frederick Ungar Publishing Co., 1962.

mercialism that corroded all that was sacred in life, and a waste-ful conflict among capital, labor, finance, and industry, each group out for itself. His conclusion stressed the need for recognition of the absolute sovereignty and authority of the nation. From now on, he stated, there should be stress not on freedom but on obedience and order and discipline, not on rights but on duties, not on rule by majority but rule by a competent elite.

At the end of the talk, two thirds of the young people broke into applause. After it died down, Dr. Black asked quietly, "Do you people really think that I believe what I have been saying?" There was a sudden embarrassed silence.

At last one of the campers spoke up. "Wasn't this a Fascist program?" he asked timidly.

"Correct," Dr. Black replied. "I wanted to test you. How can you be on guard against a person like me? I did not wrap myself in the American flag. I did not use a scapegoat. I did not use Fascist slogans."

"You only spoke of the weaknesses of democracy and you made no mention of its strength," another student added. His objection started a lively discussion in which all the campers participated.

"I feel that, channeled constructively, the power of youth can bring great strength to the democratic way of life," Mrs. Alice K. Pollitzer said in her pleasant living room. "Mrs. Roosevelt completely agreed with me on this. She was chairman of the Sponsors Committee of the Encampment for Citizenship for seventeen years. I think"—Mrs. Pollitzer chuckled a little—"she always forgot to think of herself as old. The last time I saw her was at Carnegie Hall. When I said 'hello' to her, she looked at me amazed and said, 'What are *you* doing out at *this* hour of the night, Mrs. Pollitzer?' Then she began to laugh and said quickly, 'I suppose we *both* should be in bed!' "

Chapter Sixteen

The Labor Unions

"THE LAST TIME I SAW MRS. ROOSEVELT was on a blustering day day in 1961," said Mrs. Wakefield, an English lady who worked at the Information Center of New York University on Washington Square. "She had come down here to dedicate a plaque. It was such a cold day and I shivered while I listened to her brief speech. All that Mrs. Roosevelt was wearing was a thin brown dress. I still remember thinking to myself, She never worries about herself, does she now?"

"What kind of a plaque was it?" I asked.

"It's right around here on Waverly Place," said Mrs. Wakefield. "Why don't you go and take a look at it?"

The day was cold, too, and rain was coming down heavily. But I did walk to Twenty-nine Waverly Place.

"THE TRIANGLE FIRE," said the heading on the bronze plaque. "On this site one hundred and forty-six workers lost their lives in the Triangle Shirtwaist Company Fire on March 25, 1911," was engraved beneath. "And of their martyrdom came new concepts of social responsibility and labor legislation that have helped make American working conditions the finest in the world." That text was signed, "International Ladies Garment Workers Union, March 25, 1961."

One hundred and forty-six workers! I stood in the chilling rain and gazed at the innocent and calm gray building. I imagined the screams, the flames. And Mrs. Roosevelt had come down on a cold day to dedicate the plaque. Why? I began to wonder and soon started to explore Eleanor Roosevelt's close contact with the labor unions.

Long before Eleanor Roosevelt was the First Lady, even before she was married to FDR, she came down to the lower East Side of New York to work in a settlement house on Rivington Street. And thus she came to know the sweatshop, the home industries of women and small children sewing buttons on pants, making paper flowers, earning a penny here and there; falling asleep at the table, falling off a bench, many children crowded in one room.

Eleanor Roosevelt then went to work with Florence Kelley of the Women's Trade Union League which was battling for equal pay for equal work, for protection for pregnant women who had to work under horrible conditions for a livelihood. "Eleanor Roosevelt could have run away from this life at its rawest," wrote George E. Sokolsky in his column in November 1962. "She chose not to. She devoted herself to rectifying the faults which appeared in our society."

I realized that labor leaders must have known Mrs. Roosevelt well. I wrote a letter asking for an interview concerning Eleanor Roosevelt to David Dubinsky, President of the International Ladies Garment Workers Union.

I got an appointment at once.

I had my appointment with David Dubinsky on July 11, 1968. At eleven o'clock in the morning I entered the building on 201 West Fifty-second Street, where he had his office. I gave my name to a girl at a desk, Miss Krisberg, and Mr. Dubinsky's secretary came out and said she would find him for me in a moment.

And there he came, stocky, silver-haired, and brisk, the man whose face was so familiar to me from newspaper pictures and the television screen.

He glanced at me sharply and held out his hand.

"Come along now," he said, "and don't forget your pocket-book."

We entered his office. David Dubinsky sat down behind his desk. "So you are writing a book about Mrs. Roosevelt?" he asked as he leaned back comfortably.

"Well . . . ask me some questions!"

"Do you remember when you first met Mrs. Roosevelt?" I ventured.

His eyes turned pensive, as if gazing into the past. "That was a long, long time ago," he said. "When Franklin D. Roosevelt was Governor in Albany. Oh," he said and chuckled, "I do remember a story then. One day I went back to New York from Albany by train and I could not get a private compartment. So I had to go coach. Guess whom I met there? Eleanor! She was seated very comfortably at a window seat, going through her papers. She always was careful with spending money for herself. I remember how she once phoned me just before Christmas and said that she had a lot of sweaters to buy as gifts for her children and grandchildren. Could I send her somewhere to buy them wholesale?" David Dubinsky shook with mirth and wiped his blue eyes.

I too laughed and asked whether I could use the story.

"Of course," he said, "it's true. I even remember the foreman I sent with her on that errand. He was a very stubborn fellow and he always wore a cap, never a hat. I told him that if he went with Mrs. Roosevelt he must wear a hat and gave him the money to buy it. But after he had gone to the wholesale house with Mrs. Roosevelt he came straight back to my office, threw the hat on my desk and said, Here! I don't want it! Then he put his cap on again and left.

"In all the years I knew the Roosevelts, I never asked them a personal favor. But Eleanor and I really were very fond of each other. I remember how she phoned me once to ask whether a strike at Milgrim's on Fifty-seventh Street was a legitimate one. I said that yes, it was. 'Oh, dear,' Eleanor Roosevelt replied, 'I had a fitting for a gown set for this afternoon. But of course I couldn't possibly go there now. Oh, well, I suppose I'll just have to order one elsewhere.' "

David Dubinsky drew a packet of colored photographs from his coat pocket and handed them to me. "My granddaughter at her wedding," he said. "How do you like her?"

I examined the photographs. David Dubinsky's granddaughter looked like a young movie star and I said so.

The grandfather beamed. "What do you think of all that nonsense they are writing now about Franklin D. Roosevelt's supposed romance?" he asked. "I know how FDR felt about his wife! There was an incident just about the time of Pearl Harbor. I wanted the CIO and the AFL to merge. The President was against this. Apart, the two unions were weaker, and he could play one against the other. I was mad at him, and I let him know that I was mad at him. The President did not like Dubinsky to be mad at him, so he gave me an appointment at the White House. I went to Washington. The war had just broken out and you can imagine how busy the President was. His secretary told me he could not possibly give me more than twenty minutes. But Roosevelt talked with me for an hour and a half. In all that time—obviously on his order—no phone calls came through. That is, none except one!" David Dubinsky grinned. "Eleanor, of course! This told me a lot about the relationship between President Roosevelt and his wife."

He then asked me about my book and I told him more details. He got some papers and magazines together and gave them to me. "They will be good background material for you," he said. Then he handed me a large, beautiful magazine. It was the *ILGWU News History* of the International Ladies Garment Workers Union from 1900 to 1950. "This is the very last issue we have," he said. "Can you read it in a week?" I looked at the size of the magazine. "All right," he said, watching my face. "I'll give you two weeks. But if you don't bring it back then, I'll—oh, I'll throw a picket line around your house!" He chuckled. His secretary stuck her head in. "Mr. Dubinsky," she said, "we do have one more issue."

He gave her a reproachful glance. "Did you *have* to squeal on me?"

I thanked him for his time and we said good-bye. "Don't forget now," he said with an impish grin, "in 1933, two good men became President. Dubinsky and Roosevelt!"

The next Labor Leader I met was Jacob S. Potofsky, General

President of the Amalgamated Clothing Workers of America which represents the workers in the men's clothing industry.

It was on a hot day in July that I entered the building of the Amalgamated Clothing Workers at 15 Union Square.

Mr. Potofsky's secretary looked up from her desk. "Go right in," she said. "Mr. Potofsky is expecting you."

I went into a large room. Behind his big desk sat Jacob S. Potofsky, holding out a hand. President Potofsky has gray hair, a short gray beard, a powerful face, and remarkably blue eyes. "Sit down," he said. In front of him on his desk was a folder containing gathered material on his contact with Mrs. Roosevelt. "Here," he said, as he handed it to me. "We have prepared this for you. Mrs. Roosevelt often came to see me right here in this office. She sat in the very chair you are sitting in right now. Whatever she wanted us to do for her we always were most happy to do. Whether it concerned the Wiltwyck School, the Citizens Committee for Children, the UN, or any other of her favorite charities, the Amalgamated always was ready and eager to help her."

He asked me how far I was with my book and I explained that the first draft was almost completed. The bright blue eyes looked at me astonished.

"So why have you waited so long before you came to us?" he inquired. "Why were we at the bottom of your list? Are we not big enough for you?"

I gasped. "Mr. Potofsky," I said, "I did not dare to bother the *big people* before I had a contract with a publisher."

A twinkle came into Mr. Potofsky's blue eyes.

"Big people are little people," he declared. "You must not forget that."

He turned me over to his Associate Director of Education, Miss Connie Kopolov. We had a brief talk about her work in rural counties where many workers still labor in nonunionized shops and where she conducts summer school sessions. "The students attending the Amalgamated training institutes in upstate New York for the past dozen or so summers, always looked forward so much to the one big feature of the week's schedule," Miss Kopolov told me. "It was a visit with Mrs. Roosevelt at nearby Hyde Park. The last time we visited her was July 1961.

I recall that she spoke of the urgency of promoting public dis-
cussions of crucial world issues. She praised the freedom riders
and voiced her opposition to the resumption of nuclear weapons
testing."

Then Miss Kopolov took me to the editorial offices of *The Advance,* the Amalgamated's newspaper, and showed me how to
find the back issues where I was bound to find many items on
Eleanor Roosevelt.

Hilbert Elson, the managing editor, made my work easier for
me. He brought me a page of memories about Eleanor Roosevelt
at the time of her death.

"Let us make the dream world that all of us want, not a dream
world, but a reality, a practical reality brought about by a nation
that understands what living Democracy means," she said in
May 1944, while World War II was still raging. She also com-
mended the Amalgamated for its stand on Civil Rights, and said
she hoped it soon would be shared by all of labor. "I think it is
essential to our nation's leadership that we convince the peoples
of the world that color and race have nothing to do with our
interest in the family of man," Eleanor Roosevelt declared.

In accepting the Sidney Hillman Foundation Award for meri-
torious public service in January 1957, Mrs. Roosevelt, the eighth
recipient of the award, said:

"Sidney Hillman's standards and his values meant a great deal
to the labor movement; and perhaps the greatest thing he emphasized was the fact that no one can be just one thing. You are
not just a great labor leader; you are always, too, a citizen of your
country as well as to whatever work you may be fulfilling in the
world. In accepting this award," she added, "I would like to pledge
to you that—I will try to work with you who want to go forward
in Sidney Hillman's tradition to make our country something
of which we can be proud."

Sidney Hillman was the first President of the Amalgamated
Clothing Workers Union. In the three decades he served as president, his leadership was distinguished by a wide-ranging idealism
and a desire to correct injustice wherever it existed—as well as by a

pragmatic and realistic approach to solving problems, one step at a time. He not only won the affection of his union members, but also the trust of the employers he dealt with and, in time, the respect of the nation's highest leaders. There was a story making the rounds in the Roosevelt years that, whenever a big political issue was about to be settled, FDR would say, "Clear it first with Sidney."

Under Sidney Hillman's leadership, the Union pioneered in building the first cooperative housing projects in the United States. They also started a union bank where workers without "securities" could get a loan, founded health centers and began their own unemployment insurance program.

Eleanor Roosevelt was aware of the importance of the unions as early as 1934. Sidney Benton, a member of the millinery union, recalled a giant parade to commemorate the National Recovery Act. The march of the unions started at ten o'clock in the morning. On the reviewing stand in front of the library on Fifth Avenue were many dignitaries, among them Mayor La Guardia, Governor Lehman, and Eleanor Roosevelt. The millinery union arrived at the receiving stand at ten o'clock in the evening. Eleanor Roosevelt was still there. The newspapers reported the next day that most of the others had come and gone all through the day. Mrs. Roosevelt had not left her place once. "If the industries can march for twelve hours," she declared, "I will be here to greet them."

At the Amalgamated I was given the opportunity to see its fiftieth-anniversary film *The Inheritance*.

It starts with a boat whistle and the sound of sea gulls. "Turn of the Century," says a voice, "Spring 1901. A running river of immigrants pouring toward Ellis Island. A woman begins to sing in a foreign tongue, a man in another one. A baby cries. "Today is born out of yesterday," the first voice says. "And there is no birth without pain." "In the old country I worked like an animal," says a man with a hard Slavic accent. "Even before my children were born the mark was on them. Animal. Before God I swear that my children shall not live as I did." "And then comes a voice singing a song which I won't ever forget. It is called "Pass It On."

Just about the time when I was working on this particular chapter, I attended a dinner party given in the lovely garden of a home in a beautiful suburb of New York. The air was soft, the swimming pool lighted, uniformed maids served a delicious meal of stuffed squabs with wild rice, the tables beneath the trees were candlelit and the linen gleaming. The conversation at my particular table turned to politics. "Things in this country today are really terrible," said an elderly lady in a costly gown, with gray hair carefully arranged. "It's all the fault of the labor unions. They have become far too powerful." Her diamonds sparkled as she raised the demitasse to her lips. "The labor unions in this country should be made as responsible as employers. The union leaders are so irresponsible that you can't really much trust in what they tell you. Their arrogance is outrageous!"

I looked at her in the dim light of the flickering candle and before me rose the film I had seen, the boat, the masses of refugees arriving in steerage. These men, women, and children who had worked for a pittance in the factory sweatshops which had signs that said, "If you don't come in Sunday, don't bother to come in on Monday." I thought of the girls who had worked at the sweatshop of the Triangle Shirtwaist Company and finally leaped to their deaths in that fire, women who had to pay for the thread they needed in their work by selling their young bodies. I thought of the many rural parts of the United States where conditions similar to these still exist in 1968, and where the unions still have to struggle to gain a foothold.

And finally I thought of Eleanor Roosevelt sitting at the reviewing stand on Fifth Avenue in front of the Library from ten o'clock in the morning until ten o'clock at night without leaving her place once, declaring: "If the Union members can march for twelve long hours, I will be there to greet them."

And then I looked around the lovely garden of the Westchester home again, the tablecloths that were a little messy now, the candles that had burnt low, the people in evening clothes sitting back, satiated and relaxed, sipping after-dinner brandies.

"I have heard a song recently," I said to the lady at my table. It is the theme song of a film * made by the Amalgamated Clothing Workers Union. The music is so stirring that I wish I could sing it for you. I can't. But I do remember every word of it. It goes like this:

> "Freedom doesn't come like a bird on the wing,
> Doesn't come down like summer rain,
> Freedom, freedom is a hard-won thing,
> You've got to work for it,
> Fight for it,
> Day and night for it,
> And every generation's got to win it again.
> Pass it on to your children, mother,
> Pass it on to your children, brother,
> They've got to work for it,
> Fight for it,
> Day and night for it,
> Pass it on to your children,
> Pass it on!"

---

* From the fiftieth-anniversary film, *The Inheritance,* of the Amalgamated Clothing Workers of America, AFL-CIO. Lyrics of the theme song, "Pass It On," by Millard Lampell.

Chapter Seventeen

Her Critics

"WE PITY YOU," Margaret S. Ernst, wife of the distinguished lawyer and writer Morris L. Ernst, used to say to the Roosevelt-haters, a species she called bitter and unpersuadable. "We pity you because you are missing so much—living in these days without affection for President and Mrs. Roosevelt."

Much in the same vein, George R. Spota, Executive Vice President of a television production company, challenged the "Roosevelt haters" to search their own hearts as to why, in their clubhouses they broke into raucous laughter when they made fun of "that cripple in the White House," and "that shrill woman with her awful taste in clothes."

"When I graduated from the University of Maryland," wrote Jack L. Gordon from Rockville, Maryland, "Mrs. Roosevelt gave the commencement address. She talked about her recent visit to West Virginia, told of the hard-working mountain people in the mine areas she had met and how they had to walk some distances for a bucket of water from a spring. Soap cost money, of which they had very little, she said, and went on to speak about their lack of work, low wages, ill health and low educational level. All around me I could hear people snicker and whisper remarks about Eleanor Roosevelt's protruding teeth, her low-heeled shoes, the simplicity of her dress, and the way she combed her hair. 'Don't they listen to *what* she is saying?' I recall whispering to my mother. 'Don't they hear her at all?' "

"I met Mrs. Roosevelt at a parents' meeting at a school on West Eleventh Street," an elderly lady reported to me. "Margaret Mead introduced her. It was shortly after FDR's death and Eleanor Roosevelt wore an unbecoming black dress, black woolen stockings, and high button shoes. Her hair was done in her usual nondescript fashion and her complexion was sallow. I was sitting in the first row and still remember that I thought to myself what a terribly homely woman Mrs. Roosevelt was, so tall and gawky and poorly dressed. Not even my maid would appear like that in public, I thought. I no longer remember the topic of Mrs. Roosevelt's talk. But afterward there was a question period. One woman in the audience directed an incredibly rude and insolent question at her: something, I think, about the divorces of her children. The audience gasped. But Mrs. Roosevelt turned to the questioner with perfect courtesy and poise, replied to the question calmly as though speaking to someone of equal education and social level. The woman who had posed the question reddened and silently sat down. Only someone of real greatness could have behaved as Eleanor Roosevelt did that night. Her clothes and appearance no longer were important to me. This, I realized, was a beautiful woman.'

Among the people who disliked and feared Eleanor Roosevelt were some of those who were involved in "big business."

"In the fall of 1958, on the spur of the moment, I wrote to Mrs. Roosevelt and asked her if she would come and speak under the auspices of my Temple Sisterhood," wrote Elizabeth Sondheimer from Lima, Ohio. "I told her candidly that our town was conservative, almost reactionary, and that I felt her voice should be heard there. To my great surprise and joy, Mrs. Roosevelt at once accepted my invitation.

"I was born and raised in Stuttgart, Germany, and came to this country as a refugee at the time of Hitler. Although I was well aware of the political climate of my new hometown, Lima, it never seriously occurred to me that anyone could not love and admire Eleanor Roosevelt. Accordingly, I was completely aghast when I was made to realize that some people in our town actually hated this wonderful woman. At that time a controversy was raging in the country about the Right to Work Law, which was to permit people to work in union shops without being union members. Many fair-minded people, Mrs. Roosevelt prominent among them, were strongly opposed to this law. (It was finally defeated in Ohio.)

"When I made public the forthcoming visit of Mrs. Roosevelt and began to send out invitations and tickets for the event, I instantly was bombarded with insulting letters, threats, obscene and hateful telephone calls. The president of a bank offered me one thousand dollars if I canceled Mrs. Roosevelt's visit. The president of a large steel company wrote coldly as he returned the tickets that 'at any other time we will be glad to make a contribution to your sisterhood. But we believe that the anti-business feeling, expressed over the years by both President and Mrs. Roosevelt, was a great detriment to industry and business in our country. Therefore, we do not feel we should support any appearance of Mrs. Roosevelt.'

"The manager of another large business corporation returned the tickets with the words 'so far as Mrs. Roosevelt is concerned, her views on communism or any other subjects are of no possible interest to us. We feel quite strongly opposed to her philosophy and therefore cannot in any way assist in dissemination of her views.'

"In spite of all this," continued Mrs. Sondheimer, "I did sell all the tickets. It took a long time but I never was happier than when I could tell those who had waited until the last moment that *we were completely sold out!*

"When Mrs. Roosevelt arrived, we did have to tell her that we were forced to call the FBI for her protection. She just smiled."

"It was a cold and gray afternoon," a local newspaper reported later, "but as Mrs. Roosevelt stepped from the train, it was as though the clouds broke and the light from her eyes radiated warmth and sunshine. She came alone, carrying a small suitcase.

Wrinkle-free clothes were more practical than heavy luggage, she explained to the women who had gathered to greet her at the station."

"She came to our simple home," Elizabeth Sondheimer continued. "We asked her whether she would like to rest in the room we had prepared for her, but Mrs. Roosevelt said no, she would rather stay with us. If she got tired she would just turn off her hearing aid. I was dreadfully embarrassed when my husband told Mrs. Roosevelt that he is a Republican. I, of course, am a Democrat! Again, Mrs. Roosevelt just smiled and said that her son John was a Republican also. Later, she asked to see the slum area of Lima and, as we drove her around, she made many constructive suggestions. The Chief of Police and a sergeant served as personal guards for Mrs. Roosevelt from the moment she got off the train, but I had not realized they would be with us for meals also. Our dining room table was not large enough for everyone and we had to put up a card table.

"We had prepared for Mrs. Roosevelt all the delicacies we could think of. All the women of the Sisterhood had baked and cooked for days. But we did not have the only thing she wanted. Sanka Coffee! Someone dashed out to get it.

"Before her talk at Memorial Hall I spent a few moments alone with Mrs. Roosevelt," she went on. "I was to introduce her and I showed her the speech that I had written down.

"Mrs. Roosevelt looked at it and shook her head. 'I never have a note,' she declared and chuckled. 'Even now at seventy-four! If you have your subject at heart, you will be so involved that you know what you want to say at all times!'

"The auditorium was overflowing when Mrs. Roosevelt arrived. She was greeted with much enthusiasm. She spoke of how she felt the United States could best influence the world against Communism.

" 'We in America seem to have almost forgotten what it means to do a selling job for Democracy,' she began. 'Not so in Russia. They plan on a complete coverage of everything they do. We seem to forget we educate our young people for a different purpose. The Soviets want a completely disciplined people while we want good citizens for a Democracy. I am constantly impressed with how much we need to learn,' Mrs. Roosevelt went on. 'In order to lead as we want to do, we must learn about other people and take the trouble to understand them. We seem to have lost respect for learning as learning and we are not fond of new thinking!'

"About Foreign Aid, Eleanor Roosevelt said, 'We are the most productive nation in the world. Why can't we share our food? Learning how properly to distribute what we have would bring us many friends. Instead, when we occasionally give, we somehow complicate the gift until the persons receiving it are resentful.'

"She criticized American narrow-mindedness in these words: 'When we Americans find something we don't like or understand, we either immediately brand it as communism or we discard it. This is no solution.'

"In the question period afterward someone asked, 'Why did Pasternak reject the Nobel Prize for literature?'

"Eleanor Roosevelt's face broke into a wide smile.

" 'Why, I should think the poor man wanted to live,' she replied with a chuckle.

"As we left the lecture hall," Elizabeth Sondheimer recalled, "a man with his fists clenched tried to run up to her. The FBI held him back. If Mrs. Roosevelt had noticed him, she gave no indication of it. She shook hands good-bye. 'I have enjoyed my visit so much,' she said. 'How very kind it was of you to ask me to come. How very thoughtful all of you were to me.' "

A few days later, Elizabeth Sondheimer received a letter from New York.

"I just want to put into writing my very warm thanks for all you did for me during my visit to Lima. It was more than good of you and Mr. Sondheimer to take me in under such difficult circumstances and I cannot tell you how much I appreciate your loyalty. It takes strength and courage to withstand the kind of opposition you encountered, and I am proud of the way you acted and of the opportunity I had to meet you. With gratitude and every good wish . . ."

Four years later, in November 1962, an editorial written by Mrs. Hope Strong, appeared in *The Lima News*.

"A great lady is to be laid to rest today," it said. "Eleanor Roosevelt was perhaps our most famous First Lady; but she was more. To much of the world she became a symbol of American

Humanitarianism. To much of America she became an example
of the increasingly important role of women in our nation. She
was outstanding even at a time when many women were rising
to new heights of acclaim never before achieved by her sex.
Mrs. Roosevelt was controversial. But she was respected by everyone. Even by those, as we realized on the occasion of her visit to
our town four years ago, who disliked her."

Others who criticized Eleanor Roosevelt misinterpreted her
deep concern for the poor and the underprivileged and called her
a communist.

"I vividly remember a night during the last week of July
1962," wrote Ellis L. Bert, of Syracuse, New York. "I was a candidate for the Reform Democratic Movement of the Sixth Assembly District of Queens. We had an outdoor street rally and
a large crowd had gathered in anticipation of Mrs. Roosevelt's
appearance. Nearest to the platform were some teen-agers wearing buttons of the newly formed Conservative Party. Mrs. Roosevelt arrived about 8:30 P.M. and was greeted with a tumultuous
ovation. She was wearing a light blue, print summer dress but
her face was pale and she appeared to be quite ill. As she stepped
onto the platform to begin her speech, the teen-agers started to
chant, 'Communist, go back to Russia!' Eleanor Roosevelt ignored them. She very forcefully urged the people to vote for the
reform ticket and spoke for about fifteen minutes. When she
had finished, the boys started their chant again. Mrs. Roosevelt
stepped down, went through the crowd to shake hands. Then she
murmured, 'I don't feel very well.' It was her last public appearance."

In 1960, at the time of Mr. Khrushchev's visit to the United
Nations in New York, a man wrote to Mrs. Roosevelt, taking
her to task for a newspaper column in which she had criticized
the way that visit was handled. Mrs. Roosevelt took time out to
explain to her critic what she had meant.

"I think you may have misunderstood my statement," she
began her letter. "It is not the security measure as such which
I think is silly. It is the way in which we handed Mr. Khrushchev
something critical to say about these measures of security. If
instead of announcing that we were curtailing Mr. Khrushchev's

movements while here to this island of Manhattan, we had explained unofficially through our Ambassador that his safety depended on his staying in Manhattan Island where he could be adequately guarded and said nothing publicly, he would not have been able to make the statements about the fact that we are as much a police state as they are. It is the stupidity with which we hand things to our enemies which they can use which I think is silly—not the fact that we have to guard people and hope they are safe while they are here."

To that same critic's question as to why Mrs. Roosevelt was supporting John F. Kennedy, a Catholic, for the Presidency of the United States, Eleanor Roosevelt added a postscript. "As a Democrat I am supporting Mr. Kennedy because I think he will make a good and liberal president," she wrote. "Our constitution grants freedom of religion and equality of opportunity to all. After all, a candidate should be judged on his abilities to fill the highest office in our country and not on his religious affiliations."

Among the hundreds of letters I received, there were about three or four which were filled with hatred and venom. The grammar and spelling in them were poor; none of the writers signed his name. They accused Eleanor Roosevelt of being associated with "sixty Communist organizations," of a "plot against Christianity," of "trying to smuggle a ring into this country," of "trying to cheat the tax department."

Curiously, the same mail which brought me this last letter, also brought me a newspaper clipping of an article by Carl T. Rowan, which appeared in *The Boston Globe* in 1962. It was titled "She Gave Away Millions."

"Actually," it said, "Mrs. Roosevelt hasn't the remotest idea how much money she has given away. Wiltwyck School and the American Association for the United Nations are two of the biggest recipients from a charity fund to which all her lecture income goes. It is estimated that annually she gives away $30,000 from this one source. During her early years in the White House she received $3,000 per radio broadcast, stipulating that the money was to be paid directly to the American Friends Service Committee. This amounted to $72,000 in one year alone. Between 1933 and 1940 she earned and gave away about $500,000. After congressional protests that Mrs. Roosevelt was short-changing the government by having her radio broadcast money paid directly to charity, income officials ruled that it was within the law to do so. Nevertheless, from then on, Mrs. Roosevelt did change the procedure. She took the money, first paid taxes on it and then gave it to charity. Actually, Mrs. Roosevelt left the White House with less money than when she entered it."

The ring which Mrs. Roosevelt was accused of "smuggling into the country," was an enormous aquamarine which was given to her by the President and Senhora Vargas of Brazil; it is now on display in the Franklin D. Roosevelt Library at Hyde Park.

In the early days of the Roosevelt Administration, a reporter berated Eleanor Roosevelt for going without a hat and wearing a sleeveless dress. "If she only knew," commented the President's wife, "I had no stockings on either."

But deadly serious and even venomous was the criticism directed at Eleanor Roosevelt by the most passionate and persistent of her attackers, Westbrook Pegler. Westbrook Pegler earned his living by writing an ofttimes libelous and calumnious syndicated column for the Hearst newspapers. For some reason, he chose Eleanor Roosevelt as his special target.

In August 1940, he attacked Mrs. Roosevelt most viciously in his columns. At that time the American Newspaper Guild was accused of being Communist dominated. Because of these accusations, some newsmen were publicly resigning. Not so Eleanor Roosevelt, who was also a member. "I am going to be more active in the Guild from now on," she stated publicly. "I believe that until you have done your very best to make an organization useful, you have no right to leave it."

"Eleanor Roosevelt is no more eligible for Guild membership than for membership in the D.A.R.—from which she had resigned," retorted Westbrook Pegler in furious rage in his column. "Membership in the American Newspaper Guild requires for the individual to be gainfully employed as a journalist," he informed his readers. "In the case of Eleanor Roosevelt she was only *gainfully employed* because she was the wife of the President." Then he continued that the first step toward rehabilitating the guild would be to get rid of those who did not belong, starting with Mrs. Roosevelt.

"How long will you permit Mr. Pegler to go on with his scurrilous campaign?" many readers of her column wrote to Mrs. Roosevelt.

"I have learned that the only way to cope with unfair critics is to ignore them and not to lower oneself by answering back," Mrs. Roosevelt replied calmly.

The constant attacks on Mrs. Roosevelt finally became boring even to the readers of Mr. Pegler's column. William Randolph Heart himself became annoyed with the way Westbrook Pegler "smeared" the wife of the President. Mr. Hearst repeatedly instructed the columnist to stop, but after each request by Mr. Hearst, Pegler's columns became even more vitriolic.

"So we decided to move him off page three and put him back where he belonged," William Randolph Hearst finally announced. "I never read his stuff any more."

"After a dinner party at the White House, the guests were sitting around the fireplace in the living room," wrote Mr. Newcomb, a Professor of Art at the University of Michigan. "Someone asked Mrs. Roosevelt if she would care to make any comments about Westbrook Pegler. 'I am sorry,' Eleaner Roosevelt replied without hesitation, 'I just don't know Mr. Pegler well enough to say anything at all about him. You see, I have never met him except twice, when he was a guest in my home.'"

"Just before Pearl Harbor, when Mrs. Roosevelt invited me to come to Washington to help in the Office of Civilian Defense, she was under terrible attacks from many sides," wrote Judge Justine Wise Polier. "I have never forgotten how she met friend and foe alike, apparently unperturbed by what people had said or done to her personally. One day I asked her how it was possible for her to react so calmly to all her enemies. She replied by telling me that she had all adverse clippings put on her bed at night because she felt she should know what people were saying against her. But, she added, once having read them she forgot them and turned to other things. Thus she was able to go on with her life without friction, unruffled and unembittered by what would have interfered with the functioning of a lesser person."

Chapter Eighteen

Some People

Who Worked for Her

THE UNITED NATIONS HAD ASSIGNED CLAUDIO LATTANZI as a chauffeur to Mrs. Roosevelt. He drove her for one year.

On a Sunday afternoon, Claudio and his girl friend came to visit me and we had coffee togther. Claudio was tall and dark with flashing white teeth; as he talked he gestured widely in Italian fashion. His girl friend never took her eyes off him. "I loved Mrs. Roosevelt like a mother," he said as he took a sip of his coffee. "I was a school dropout and when I got out of the army the government would have paid for my education. Mrs. Roosevelt urged me to go back to school. But I only went to beautician school. I thought I would meet a lot of pretty girls that way!" He gave his girl a dazzling smile.

"What did you talk about with Mrs. Roosevelt while you drove her?" I inquired.

"Not too much," Claudio admitted. "After she gave up urging me to go back to school, she mostly sat silently in the back of the car. Often, when she returned home from a United Nations meeting she seemed very tired and dozed a little. But even when

I took her on longer rides, say to Hyde Park, she did not talk much either."

I looked at his lively Italian features, the gesturing hands. "I can't imagine *you* being silent for very long," I said.

"Well," Claudio said with a sudden shy grin, "Mrs. Roosevelt was not a person whom you addressed. You waited until she spoke to you first. Still," he added fervently while he gave his girl an apologetic glance, "Mrs. Roosevelt was the most wonderful woman I have ever known. I feel a monument should be built to Eleanor Roosevelt in every city of the world!"

Anna Polenz worked as Mrs. Roosevelt's maid for thirteen years; she was with her until her death. Yet, when I phoned her, she was very reluctant to talk to me.

"What could I, a simple woman, possibly tell you?" she asked. However, after some urging on my part, she agreed to visit me the following week.

Anna Polenz was a pleasant Austrian woman in her forties. She was shy when I opened the door for her, shy and yet somehow very dignified. I took her to my workroom where we had tea, and, as soon as she saw Mrs. Roosevelt's picture on the wall, she began to smile. Two deep dimples appeared in her cheeks. She told me that she had come to the United States when she was seventeen years old and had worked in homes ever since. "It is the nearest to what I do in my own home," she told me. She has a husband, a twenty-two-year-old son, and twin daughters.

Mrs. Polenz talked freely about her family, but, as soon as I brought up the topic of Mrs. Roosevelt, a guarded look came into her eyes. Perhaps she didn't really like her, I found myself thinking. It was, after all, possible that even Eleanor Roosevelt could be different at home, different from her public image.

"Was it hard to work for Mrs. Roosevelt?" I finally asked. "She was so busy. So many people came to see her all the time . . ."

"Oh, no!" Anna Polenz protested at once. "It was not hard at all," she said and finally continued talking. "You know when one cooks dinner for company one expects to answer the door and take the coats when the guests arrive, hoping that one is not detained too long because there are always things still to do in the kitchen. Mrs. Roosevelt was aware of this. She used to tell me to go back to my other work while she herself opened the door and took the coats." The dimples appeared once again in her cheeks. "All of us worried so about her when we left her alone in her apartment at night. We thought she might go out and forget her keys and not be able to get back in, or that there might be a fire, or that she would get sick at night—"

"Was it very bad at the end?" I asked. "Did she suffer much?"

"We did not know," Anna Polenz said. "She never complained."

We sat quietly for a while. "It must have been very hard for you," I finally said.

"Sometimes I helped the nurse to freshen up the bed," she said. "And then I wanted to hold on tightly to Mrs. Roosevelt's arm. So tightly that she could not go away." Her eyes filled with tears.

"When we began to talk, for a moment or so I wondered whether you perhaps did not like Mrs. Roosevelt," I said. "You seemed so hesitant to speak."

"I was only afraid that I might say something that you would misunderstand," Anna Polenz said, while the tears rolled down her cheeks. "And then there would be something published that I would not want people to read, something that I never said at all."

Anna Polenz and I shook hands for a long while as we were standing at the door. "I hope I didn't say anything wrong. God will see to it that it comes out all right."

After she left me, I experienced a sudden sense of loneliness. It had been a comforting experience to spend an hour in the presence of a woman who had shared the very last days of Eleanor Roosevelt on this earth.

Another person who had worked for Mrs. Roosevelt the last twelve years of her life was her private secretary Maureen Corr. Miss Corr now works for the U.S. Mission to the United Nations and is assigned to the United States Ambassador to the United Nations. We had a date to have dinner together and I picked her up at the United States Embassy at the Waldorf Towers. Ambassador Goldberg had just left his post and the new Ambassador, George Ball, had not yet moved in. Maureen Corr showed me around the lovely suite of rooms which the American Government provides for its Ambassador to the United Nations. I admired the sweeping view of the East River from the forty-second floor, the modern paintings, the thick white rugs, the exhibit of exquisite glassware. Then we went down to a pleasant summer-empty restaurant for a leisurely dinner and a long talk.

Maureen Corr was born in Armagh, Northern Ireland. She is tall and slim, her hair is auburn, she has large expressive eyes. Maureen graduated from Hunter College and afterward took education courses at Columbia Teachers College. "I had hoped to become a teacher," she said, "but there just was not enough time." Instead, she became secretary to an eye specialist at Columbia Presbyterian Medical Center. "I was not happy in that job," she said, while her large, honest eyes clouded a little. "A nurse in the office was not cooperative and I simply cannot work with individuals with whom I am not compatible."

And so she consulted an agency and registered for any suitable position that might come up. At once, she was told to report for an interview.

On leaving the agency she glanced at the name and gasped. Assistant secretary to Eleanor Roosevelt? But that was impossible, she thought. Surely, in order to qualify for a position with Mrs. Roosevelt you would have to have connections, social recommendations, not just an application with an agency.

What an adventure this is, Maureen Corr thought to herself on the way. To apply for a job with Mrs. Roosevelt! Of course she wouldn't get the position, she laughed to herself. But—what fun just to go for the interview.

It was not Eleanor Roosevelt but Malvina Thompson, Mrs. Roosevelt's secretary, who interviewed Maureen. She explained that she was to be her assistant.

Maureen Corr started her new job on November 1, 1950. Mrs. Roosevelt was out of town at that time, and Maureen worked at the office at the Park Sheraton Hotel for a week; then, one morning, Eleanor Roosevelt strode into the room.

Her lively eyes focused on Maureen behind her typewriter. "Good morning," she said and smiled radiantly as she stepped forward holding out a welcoming hand. "I am Eleanor Roosevelt. How do you do?"

"The naturalness of her greeting made it seem as though she really was happy to meet me," said Maureen as she recalled that first meeting. "But then Mrs. Roosevelt went on to her own work and I did not see very much of her in the months to come. She was traveling and Malvina Thompson usually accompanied her.

"In Paris Miss Thompson became ill," Maureen continued, "and at the end of 1951, to my utter astonishment, Mrs. Roosevelt asked me to go with her to Europe on her next trip. She was going to the General Assembly meeting of the United Nations in Paris. Mrs. Roosevelt said that it would end early in 1952. She had received a number of invitations to visit various countries, one of them was extended by Prime Minister Nehru. Mrs. Roosevelt also long had wanted to visit Israel and she told me that, instead of going back to New York as usual, we would go home the long way—around the world!

"We took the midnight flight out of Idlewild Airport to Paris on December 31, 1951. Everyone on the plane greeted Mrs. Roosevelt and she introduced me around. Then she wrapped herself in a large blanket and settled down for a night's sleep. She was given two seats so that she could stretch out. I was seated across the aisle from her. Since it was New Year's Eve, everyone on the flight was in high spirits. There were many interesting people aboard including the two people seated behind me who invited me to join in a toast to the New Year. While I drank the champagne, I caught a glance from Mrs. Roosevelt across the aisle. She had her blanket pulled up to the tip of her nose and all that I could see were her eyes. By their expression I felt she must be thinking. Oh, dear, I do hope that it wasn't a mistake to take this flighty young thing along on the trip!

"I got a little worried," said Maureen. "I remembered my first trip home to Ireland when, because of the change in time and the excitement of the flight, I could not sleep for several nights. When I got home, the lack of sleep and the excitement caused me to be slightly hysterical. I did not want that to happen on this trip, so I swallowed a sleeping pill with which I had armed myself. That was neither a good nor a sensible idea. The sleeping pill and the champagne reacted in such a way that when we arrived in Paris at seven o'clock in the morning, I was completely exhausted.

"We went straight to the Crillon Hotel where I had a lovely room with a big bed and a golden satin quilt. It looked ever so inviting. But Mrs. Roosevelt said we would immediately have a conference with some members of the U.S. Mission, lunch with some friends, and take a drive in the Bois de Boulogne followed by tea with her granddaughter Sistie, her husband, and children. In the meantime, I was asked to order lunch for so many, and tea for a few more and then dinner, and so on and on.

"I kept nodding my head and murmuring, 'Yes, yes, of course, Mrs. Roosevelt,' and all the while I was just thinking of that lovely bed with its golden quilt. All that day we kept on the go and there was no time for a rest or a brief nap. When midnight came I was barely conscious. I thought that this routine was impossible and that I simply would not have the physical strength to keep up with Mrs. Roosevelt. Just as I was about to say good night to her, Mrs. Roosevelt sat herself down and announced, 'Now we will do my column and a few notes on the trip so far.'

"All those years I worked for Mrs. Roosevelt," Maureen Corr continued, "at midnight each day, no matter where we were, Mrs. Roosevelt would dictate her column, 'My Day.' I took out my pad and pencil, but my brain was tired. Somehow I managed to type out the column. Every now and then I could sense a questioning glance. 'All right,' she said at long last, 'this will be all for today. There are still some letters to write but that I can do myself.'

"I murmured a tired 'thank you,' " said Maureen, "and went tottering to my room. I thought I would not be able to undress. Before I could undress, however, there was a knock at the door and Mrs. Roosevelt came into the room in her dressing gown, her hair neatly tied in a blue ribbon.

" 'It has been a long day. You must be tired,' She put her arm around my shoulder. 'Everything will be all right and we will manage beautifully.' Then she kissed me lightly on the cheek and bade me a cheery good night.

"I was so disarmed," said Maureen Corr, "I think had she asked me to work around the clock, I would have gladly done it. As it was, we nearly did work around the clock. There were those thousands and thousands of letters which we wrote in answer to calls for help, the endless journeys, the hours and hours of traveling. But in spite of all the work, whenever we passed through Europe, Mrs. Roosevelt would always make arrangements for me to spend a few days in Ireland with my family. She even wanted to pay for this extra leg of the trip which I, of course, would not accept."

We finished our dinner. "From all the mail that I am receiving," I told Maureen, "it really seems that not one call for help directed to Mrs. Roosevelt remained unanswered!"

"Of course not," Maureen said gaily. "I just told you of the thousands and thousands of letters we wrote. Mrs. Roosevelt tried to help with each problem. And you know," she added almost as an afterthought. "we almost never got a thank you note."

I stared at her. "Never?"

"Very rarely," said Maureen.

"How did Mrs. Roosevelt react to this?" I asked.

"Oh," said Maureen, "I don't think she noticed it. She went on doing all she could for the pleasure of the doing, not in anticipation of any reward."

"Perhaps people were shy," I said. "Perhaps they did not want to bother her." I told Maureen of that one woman whose mother Mrs. Roosevelt had saved from the Nazis and who, ever since then, sold UNICEF cards for Christmas each year and gave her commission to the Eleanor Roosevelt Foundation, as *her* expression of thanks. And yet—I also remembered that first letter which I had received from Mrs. Roosevelt, in which she had said that my report had made up for much time she had thought wasted.

"The people should have taken the trouble to thank Mrs. Roosevelt for what she had done for them," I said to Maureen as we left the restaurant. "This is one thing that I have learned doing this book. Everyone likes to be told that he is appreciated. Even the 'big people' of this world."

Chapter Nineteen

Her Friends in Hyde Park

"WELCOME TO HYDE PARK!" * says a sign on Route Nine in New York, and there is the profile of FDR, with his long cigarette holder at the famous jaunty angle.

I finally traveled down that road, past a thick hedge that enclosed the Vanderbilt estate on the right, the new Hyde Park Post Office on the left. Then I came to the Roosevelt Estate. At the entrance it said in big letters: THE FRANKLIN D. ROOSEVELT LIBRARY.

The sun was shining the day of my arrival in Hyde Park and the large old trees and the beautifully kept lawns had a specially rich green hue. I crossed the road and entered the Roosevelt estate. A wide path led to the parking area and all around were trees heavy with red-cheeked apples. On the left was the Franklin D. Roosevelt Library.

---

* The home of Franklin D. Roosevelt was designated a National Historic Site, January 15, 1944. The site, a gift of President Roosevelt, then consisted of 33.23 acres surrounding the house, adjacent outbuildings and the gravesite. After the death of the President, Mrs. Roosevelt and her children waived their life interest, and the Secretary of the Interior accepted full title to the area. The site now contains 187 acres. The Home was formerly opened to visitors with the dedication ceremonies on April 12, 1946, the first anniversary of the President's death.

President Roosevelt was the first President to give his Presidential papers, as well as all his other papers, to the Government. The Library was established as a Federal agency on July 18, 1939. It was built and equipped without cost to the Government from funds donated by thousands of the President's admirers. Mr. Roosevelt himself laid the cornerstone on November 19, 1939; it was opened to the public in 1941. Materials given to the Library by President Roosevelt, aside from the Presidential papers and correspondence, relate to his private life, family background, and special interests—the history of the United States Navy and the history of Dutchess County and the Hudson River Valley.

Mrs. Roosevelt was the greatest and most beloved friend of the library. After Franklin D. Roosevelt's death in 1945, she was deeply interested in carrying out her husband's wishes. In her column, "My Day," on April 12, 1949, the fourth anniversary of the President's death, Mrs. Roosevelt wrote: "The Library was of such great interest to my husband that I am always grateful when his friends take an interest in it. Someday I hope there can be an additional wing added to the Library where the things given by foreign countries can be permanently on exhibition. We need to be reminded of the good will that can exist in the world, and these gifts always remind me of the good will my husband felt for all the people of the world."

In addition to all the material, President Roosevelt has given to the nation sixteen acres of land for the building. The need for additional space for the library became more evident with the passing years. Now that Mrs. Roosevelt is no longer alive, there could be no more fitting and suitable tribute to her memory than the construction of an addition to the Library that she so long desired. In an Eleanor Roosevelt Memorial Addition, it will be possible to depict her life and accomplishments along with those of her husband. No better place could be selected because the library already has so much of her spirit and inspiration.

I myself discovered this as soon as I passed the bust of President Roosevelt at the entrance of the building. It was donated in 1947 by the International Ladies Garment Workers Union.

A guard inside the door of the museum asked if he could help me and asked for my ticket of admission. I told him that I would be doing some research there for a few days and asked whether

I would have to buy a ticket each day. He replied that people doing research at the library never need a ticket and then asked pleasantly whether I had written that I was coming. I explained about my book of stories and anecdotes about Eleanor Roosevelt and also told him that the director of the library, Dr. Elizabeth B. Drewry, and I had had a long and very friendly correspondence. I showed him her last letter in which she wrote, "I am so glad to hear that you are planning a trip to Hyde Park at last."

"Just a moment," the guard said and left to make a call. "Follow me," he said as he came back and led the way to the Administration wing.

And there behind her desk was Elizabeth Drewry.

"Here you are at long last," she said with a lovely smile and held out her hand.

I sat down and we talked. I told her how the book was coming along, some of the stories that had come my way. Her eyes turned moist. My own eyes were drawn again and again to a photograph on the wall next to Miss Drewry's desk. It was a photograph of hands. Eleanor Roosevelt's hands; praying, reposed, holding a pencil.

"I am happy you are doing this book," she said. "I was afraid that Mrs. Roosevelt was beginning to turn into a noble statue; that all her humanness and humor would be lost to the next generation. Come, I will take you to the research room. Our librarian, Mr. Joseph Marshall, will try to find for you all the material you are looking for."

On our way to the research room, we walked through the FDR Museum. Of course it would take many days or even weeks to see everything on display there. But I glimpsed a large pen-and-ink drawing made by the Japanese artist Tobun Hayashi, a portrait of the President's mother, Sarah Delano Roosevelt, and the Roosevelt family Bible in Dutch on which Mr. Roosevelt took his oath of office as Governor of New York and as President. There was a gold filigree tiara and bracelets presented to Mrs. Roosevelt by the Sultan of Morocco, and a large aquamarine given to her in 1936 by President and Senhora Vargas of Brazil. Elizabeth Drewry stopped before a glass case. "Here is Eleanor Roosevelt's wallet," she said. It was red, with her name stamped on it in gold letters. It was well worn. Very well worn. Displayed around it were all the items that had been in it at the time of Mrs. Roosevelt's death: her driver's license, a credit card, another card which stated that she had donated her eyes to the eye bank. Also, a typewritten piece of paper. It was Eleanor Roosevelt's favorite prayer:

> Our Father, who has set a restlessness in our hearts and made us all seekers after that which we can never fully find, forbid us to be satisfied with what we made of life. Draw us from base content, and set our eyes on far-off goals. Keep us at tasks too hard for us, that we may be driven to Thee for strength. Deliver us from fretfulness and self-pitying; make us sure of the good we cannot see and of the hidden Good in the world. Open our eyes to simple beauty all around us and our hearts to the loveliness men hide from us because we do not try to understand them. Save us from ourselves and show us a vision of the world made new. May Thy spirit of peace and illumination so enlighten our minds that all life shall glow with new meaning and new purposes.

We entered the research room. It was very quiet there. Several people were studying large volumes on individual desks. Miss Drewry introduced me to the librarian, Mr. Joseph Marshall. Mr. Marshall was a tall, courteous man. He had come to the Roosevelt Library in 1959 from Washington, D.C., where he had been with libraries of the District of Columbia government and the Department of Navy. "Shortly after my arrival here I was introduced to Mrs. Roosevelt," he said. "In the course of the usual pleasantries I said something about my hope of being able to do my work here well. She said that she was glad I was here and that she was sure I would do a good job. I was pleased, of course, to begin my work here under those circumstances. In watching Mrs. Roosevelt at the library with various groups, and at her home when the staff, the Roosevelt Home Club, and friends were invited on special occasions, I could readily see the graciousness and kindness about which I had heard so much. And as I became more acquainted with her life and her activities through working with the materials at the library, my respect for her grew. Eleanor Roosevelt had that most beautiful of virtues, a genuine concern for others, and the will to put that concern into action."

I gave Mr. Marshall a list of the material I hoped to find. He assigned me a desk. Then he placed before me a file of Mrs. Roosevelt's column, "My Day." When I returned the next morning, another file of Eleanor Roosevelt material was waiting for me at that same desk. I had told Mr. Marshall that I needed one particular newspaper clipping for one of my stories. He promised to look for it. I think it took him an entire day to search for it. But at long last, without any comment, he placed it before me.

Miss Drewry took me for lunch. I told her more of my Eleanor Roosevelt stories and, as always when I talked with people about her, we smiled a lot and we wept a little.

"The personal correspondence of Mrs. Roosevelt is not yet open for research," Elizabeth Drewry said as we went back to the Library. "However, I would like to give you just a glimpse of the size of it." We took the elevator to the archives. The room was filled with rows and rows of metal cabinets. They reached from floor to ceiling. There was no end to them. Miss Drewry introduced me to Mr. Jerome V. Deyo, the archivist. He was a tall, slender, somewhat reserved man. Miss Drewry told him about my book of stories and anecdotes about Eleanor Roosevelt. His face softened. "I have an Eleanor Roosevelt story," he said in his calm way. "I shall type it up for you."

The next morning when I returned to my desk, I found the following report:

"I have been associated with the Franklin D. Roosevelt Library since September 1951. After service in World War II, I resumed my education and earned a Master's degree in education at Syracuse University. After a year of teaching in Ithaca, New York, where my first son was born, I came to the Library. Often I was invited, along with the rest of the staff, to Mrs. Roosevelt's annual 'teas' for the workers here, usually at Christmastime and on Memorial Day. Of course I also saw her whenever she came to the Library, usually surrounded by foreign students, members of the U.N. Secretariat or very important personages such as Khrushchev, Adlai Stevenson, and Averell Harriman, among others. Although she was most approachable and the very spirit of hospitality in her home, I cannot say that I got to know her well. But I, my wife, and my entire family owe her a great debt—a debt that I was never able to repay, and a debt that she never even knew we owed her.

"In January 1954, my second son was born. We named him Kipp. For several months we suspected that something was wrong with his development, and finally the blow fell. We learned that Kipp was severely mentally retarded. Furthermore, he became epileptic as he grew older so that increasingly heavy doses of drugs were administered to him to ward off grand mal seizures. Nevertheless, he went to school—a small local school for the mentally retarded—which could offer only a four-hour school day. This was insufficient for his needs and was totally inadequate for his mother, who became increasingly tense and worn with the constant care that his precarious health necessitated. As Kipp grew older, it became evident that some residential school would be best for him and the rest of the family as well. Because of his epilepsy many otherwise promising schools turned us away. By the end of 1962, we had nearly reached the end of what seemed to be a hopeless search. It was upon our return from the Kennedy Clinic in Boston, after yet another discouraging interview, that we happened to see Mrs. Roosevelt's column of July 13, 1962, in which she mentioned the Camphill Special School at Copake, New York. We wrote the school immediately for an interview that was granted. What we found there bore out Mrs. Roosevelt's impression as reported in her column. We placed Kipp on the waiting list and in one year he was admitted. He has since thrived in this kindly atmosphere.

"Of course my wife and I wanted to speak to Mrs. Roosevelt about our experience at Copake. But we did not see her any more at the Library. Before we had a chance to tell her what she had done for us, Eleanor Roosevelt had died."

Before I went to Hyde Park, my friend Beth Vardon, a high school English teacher in Babylon, Long Island, told me she knew some people who ran a small pottery shop there where Mrs. Roosevelt used to buy gifts. It is called the Bantam Roost, and the Hesselbarths own it. "You'll find it right behind St. James' Church," Beth told me.

I drove there one morning, but behind the church there was nothing; just empty fields, trees and bushes, and a dirt road that seemed to lead nowhere. Finally, buried beneath willow trees, there was something blue. It turned out to be a swimming pool. A young girl in a bathing suit stepped forward as I stopped the car. "Is this where Mrs. Hesselbarth lives?" I inquired. The girl nodded. "Ma!" she called out, "Someone to see you!"

A woman came from a small building a short distance away. I apologized for intruding and explained about my book on Mrs. Roosevelt. She broke into a smile. "I am Suzanne Hesselbarth," she said and extended her hand. "Come right in!"

"This used to be a chicken coop," Suzanne Hesselbarth explained as we entered. "We used to live in Chicago but then my husband became ill with a lung ailment. His doctor said he had to have country air. So we came here and bought this property from the Vanderbilt estate. We fixed the place up into a home all by ourselves!" She showed me around a vast pleasant living room, the sleeping quarters, and a large kitchen. "My husband is out in the shop firing today," she said. "It's always a big moment with much excitement. We have built up a nice little business with our pottery."

I looked at the brightly colored ash trays, jugs, lamps, and vases that were everywhere. "Is it true," I asked, "that Mrs. Roosevelt used to come here often to shop?"

Suzanne Hesselbarth nodded, then laughed. "The first time she came I didn't even realize who she was. It was right after we had finished the place. Very early one morning a car drove up and a tall woman got out. I went outside and asked whether I could help her, thinking she had lost her way or something. She said that she had heard about us and what we had done with the Vanderbilt's chicken coop and would be much interested in seeing the place if it was not too much trouble. I said of course not, and showed her around. She also wanted to see the shop and bought several pieces of pottery.

" 'Gee,' I said to my husband after she had left, 'that woman looked awfully familiar, didn't she?' He just looked at me. 'That was Eleanor Roosevelt,' he said. 'Didn't you know?' 'How could I?' I exclaimed. 'She never said so!' I began to worry then because I realized suddenly that my beds had not been made.

"After that incident, she came often, always early in the morning and always in a great rush. She liked to do her shopping before early Mass at St. James's. Once she admired our large wooden table which we had made ourselves. 'I love wood,' she commented and ever after, as soon as I heard her car driving up, I rushed to give it a quick polish. The beds were never made when she came but she did not seem to notice. Sometimes she would bring friends from the United Nations and, whenever someone would handle an ash tray or a jug, apparently liking it, Mrs. Roosevelt would quickly buy it when the person's back was turned. Often she was accompanied by a group of children. She was such a tall woman," Suzanne Hesselbarth said thoughtfully, "I can still see her striding through the fields toward our house, always in a hurry," Suzanne Hesselbarth repeated, "always in a hurry! It was as if she felt that there was not enough time for all she wanted to do."

I thanked Suzanne Hesselbarth, said good-bye to her, and went back to the research room at the library.

While I was working there, Miss Drewry would drop by to say hello. "One of our guards used to be very friendly with Mrs. Roosevelt," she said. "His name is Harold Farley. Try to talk with him, he might have a story for your book. Also look for Tubby. He used to be Mrs. Roosevelt's chauffeur. She was very fond of him. He now works for the Park Department here. He is usually all over the place. And before you leave you might contact the Entrups. They are a couple who used to work for Mrs. Roosevelt the last eight or nine years. They now have a luncheonette at the Haviland Shopping Center. It's quite close to Val-Kill, Mrs. Roosevelt's private residence where she lived after the President died. And, finally, there is Arthur E. Smith. He used to be the postmaster here. He does not always agree to talk with writers but you might try him anyway . . ."

I jotted down the names of all these people. Harold Farley, the guard, was closest to me at the moment, and whenever I passed through the museum I asked one of the guards for him. But Harold Farley had always just left, or was out on the grounds, or somewhere around a corner. "Look for a fellow with a golden badge," one of the other guards told me. "He is the sergeant and really our boss."

Finally, on my third day in Hyde Park, I glimpsed a gold badge in the small office of the guards. I stuck my head in. "You must be Harold Farley!" I said.

"Yes," he said calmly, "I heard about you and what you are doing." He sounded extremely reserved, as though he were holding me off at arm's length. "But I don't really think that I have anything that I could tell you. I have known the Roosevelts all my life. Mrs. Roosevelt is different from any other person in the world."

"In what way?" I asked.

"Most people only really *look* at another person when they want something. But Eleanor Roosevelt would look at everyone anyway. Without ever wanting anything."

"Oh," I protested, "I don't believe that most people are that way!"

Harold Farley looked at me again with his calm gaze.

"Not that I want to become personal," he said slowly," but— you have been here at the Library about three days. I saw you. You passed me at least a dozen times. Well . . ." He didn't say anything else nor did he have to do so.

I felt my face turning warm. "You know," I said, "you just taught me a lesson. A very important one."

"How long will you remember it?" he asked.

"I don't know," I said. "But I will try to remember it. I know that if I do, my life will be the richer for it."

At long last, Harold Farley's face broke into a smile. "It is true with Mrs. Roosevelt," he said. "She always talks to you and wants to know all about you without ever wanting anything from you. If you like"—his voice now was friendly—"I'll take you on a private tour of the house on Saturday morning. It'll give us a chance to talk."

I left the library and drove to the Haviland Shopping Center to look for the Entrups. When I got to the luncheonette it was closed for the day. So I went on to look for Val-Kill, Mrs. Roosevelt's cottage about which I had heard so much. I found a small road that had a sign which said, "Private." I turned into it anyway. It led up a small hill with large, shady trees and there was not a soul around whom I could ask for directions. At last I arrived in front of a fairly large house with a swimming pool, but there was a closed gate and no people. So I turned back.

As I drove back down the road, a blue truck appeared. I

stopped and leaned out. The man who was driving the truck was big and blond; his eyes matched the color of the truck.

"Excuse me," I called out, "Is this Val-Kill?"

"Yup."

"Do you live here?" I continued, somewhat intimidated.

"Yup."

"Have you been living here long?"

"Yup." He paused. "All my life."

"Oh! You see, I am writing a book about Mrs. Roosevelt—"

"That so?" An interested gleam appeared in the blue eyes.

"Did you perhaps know Mrs. Roosevelt?"

He got off his truck, took a few steps closer to me and put his large hands on his hips. "Did *I* know Mrs. Roosevelt? Why, I have been working for her for thirty-eight years!"

"Would you talk to me about her?" I asked as I hurriedly got out of my own car.

The blue eyes looked at me long and probingly.

"Sure," he said at last. "I'll be glad to. My house is at the end of that road. Come and see us tomorrow afternoon. My wife will be happy to meet you too. We have all kind of pictures of Mrs. Roosevelt. And books too. She autographed them all for me. I am Charles Curnan. Everyone around here calls me Charlie."

The next day, after I finished my work in the research room of the library, I drove back to the Haviland Shopping Center. This time the Entrup luncheonette was open. A pretty young woman worked behind the counter. I asked her for Mrs. Entrup. "Oh, she isn't here," the young woman said. "She is very very ill. I am her daughter Barbara. Is there anything I can do?"

"I am working on a book about Mrs. Roosevelt," I said. "I should have liked to talk with either your mother or your father."

"My father will be here around four o'clock," she said, as she scrambled some eggs for me.

"You too must remember Mrs. Roosevelt," I suggested.

"Oh, of course," Barbara said with a quick smile. "When we first came here I was quite ill. Mrs. Roosevelt was so kind to me! She sent me to her own doctor in New York at her own expense. Do come back later. I know my father will be happy to talk to you."

"I will," I said. "Just now I am on my way to see Charlie Curnan at Val-Kill. Do you know him?"

"Charlie?" exclaimed Barbara. "He is my brother-in-law. He and my husband and my father were pallbearers at Mrs. Roosevelt's funeral."

"They were? How was that?"

"Oh, Mrs. Roosevelt specified this in her will. I suppose she knew that her sons would be busy greeting all the important dignitaries . . ."

When I drove back the private road to Val-Kill, rain was coming down in sheets, but Charlie was waiting for me in the open door of his garage. "Didn't think that you would make it in this weather," he said.

"You don't think that a little rain would stop me?" I said as I scrambled out of my car. He led me up the staircase leading to his house. It was square and solid, much like Charlie himself, and made entirely of beautiful knotty pine.

"Built it myself!" Charlie pronounced proudly.

"It is lovely!" I exclaimed as I look around the large living room with picture windows facing the woods and a huge fireplace, shelves filled with books, and many photographs on the walls. Most of them were of Eleanor Roosevelt. But there also were some of Harry Truman with his chin jutting out stubbornly, of John F. Kennedy, and also of General Eisenhower and Mamie. All the pictures were autographed to Charlie Curnan.

Mrs. Curnan came out to greet me. She was a tall, pleasant woman with a gay laugh, and offered to show me the rest of the house. The neat bedrooms with the handmade spreads, the pictures of the daughters and nine grandchildren, finally the large kitchen. "This is a working kitchen," Charlie said proudly. "I do all the cooking around here. Did it for Mrs. Roosevelt, too. You know, we grew everything here on the farm and I did all the pickling and preserving for her. At some time I thought I would write a cookbook and give all the recipes I used when I worked for Mrs. Roosevelt."

"That could be a very nice idea," I said. "You could call it 'What Charlie Cooked for Eleanor.'"

Charlie grinned. "Yeah," he said, "that would sound real nice. But the trouble is that I am not so exact with the measurements. Just take a handful of this and a handful of that. Sometime I would dream up a recipe for her. Like the time when Khrushchev came to visit. Mrs. Roosevelt insisted that we have borscht for him. So I used the red beets and the sour cream and all that stuff and we made a real big spread for him and his party. And you know what happened? When he came he just had five minutes to stay and just grabbed a roll from the table to eat on his way back."

"That was the only time I saw Mrs. Roosevelt a little peeved," said Mrs. Curnan. "We didn't know what to do with all that stuff and finally had to give it all away.

"That summer before Mrs. Roosevelt died, she made a big surprise party for Charlie. She was the one who dreamed it up but her daughter Anna was in on it too and I, of course, also knew. The only one who was completely unware of what was going on was Charlie. He even helped preparing the food for the party. And then when he appeared everybody started singing, 'He's a jolly good fellow!' and Charlie sang right along with them and he kept looking around to see for whom all this celebrating was." She laughed and Charlie joined her. "They really caught me by surprise," he said.

"When did you find out that it was for you?" I asked.

"When they gave him this," Charlie's wife answered for him and showed me a lovely large silver platter. Engraved on it were these words: "Presented to Charles Curnan in grateful appreciation of continued association with Mrs. James Roosevelt, President and Mrs. Franklin D. Roosevelt, Mr. and Mrs. John Roosevelt. 1931–July 28, 1962."

"But I received something more important that day too," Charlie said as he led me to the bookcase. "I had always told Mrs. Roosevelt that I would like a set of the books she had written, autographed to me. Here they are!"

"It was just three months before she died," I said as I looked at the date on the silver platter.

"Yes," Charlie said. "She didn't look good. It almost seemed as though she knew that her time was up and she went around in Hyde Park sort of winding up her affairs."

"Every year at about Christmastime," said Mrs. Curnan, "Mrs. Roosevelt would give a Christmas party for all the help and their families and children. The children always got beautiful presents, books and dolls from all different countries. After dinner she would sit down before the tree and tell the children stories about her travels during the year that had just passed. And the children would sit around her, quiet as little mice, with their mouths hanging wide open."

"There is a fellow whose name is Tubby and whom I am supposed to see," I said to Charlie. "Do you happen to know him?"

"Tubby is my brother," said Charlie. "He is a big fellow. Works on the Roosevelt grounds for the Park Department."

"Yes," I said, "I know. Could you perhaps call him for me?"

"Tubby is a bachelor," Charlie said. "He lives alone and I never know where to find him. But I could try to talk to his girl friend, Paulina." He made a call. "Listen," I heard him saying, "I have a woman here who would like to talk with you about Mrs. Roosevelt . . ." It sounded as though there was some reluctance on the other end of the wire. Charlie kept saying. "No, no, it's okay. You go ahead and talk to that gal. She is all right!" Paulina seemed to take his word for it, for when Charlie hung up he promised that Tubby and Paulina would visit me at my motel at six o'clock.

"Would you like to see the place where Mrs. Roosevelt lived?" Charlie asked.

"Oh yes! I would like that very much."

"Come on then," he said and took me to his blue truck. "You know they made apartments out of the place and they are rented now," he explained while we drove through the countryside, "but it still will give you an idea."

Since it was such a gray day, the house seemed rather gloomy.

"See the porch up there on the second floor," Charlie said, "Mrs. Roosevelt loved to sleep there. We always had a lot of trouble to convince her to sleep inside when it got cold."

We walked around the grounds, there was a small lake and the lawn on which the boys from Wiltwyck used to have their picnics. Over the cold fireplace was a sculpture of a boy in blue jeans eating an ear of corn. The eyes seemed strange. Charlie explained that a blind man had done the sculpture for Mrs. Roosevelt.

A car drove up and a young couple got out.

"Those are the people who are living in Mrs. Roosevelt's place now," Charlie said. "I'll ask them whether they will let you look inside."

He introduced me to Mr. and Mrs. Shein.

"We have heard Charlie talking about you," said Mrs. Shein. "My name is Barbara. I'll be happy to show you around."

We entered the house.

"This is Mrs. Roosevelt's living room," Barbara explained as she motioned about the large but unpretentious room.

"It's yours now," I said, "isn't it?"

Barbara Shein laughed. "We have been living here for a year, but I still keep thinking of it as Mrs. Roosevelt's place."

"Tell me," I said as we looked at the rest of the place, "does Mrs. Roosevelt's ghost ever bother you?"

"Well . . ." said Barbara with a quick laugh, "there are some doors that keep opening and closing all the time. But I always tell my husband that it couldn't possibly be Mrs. Roosevelt. She would never impose herself on anyone!"

When Charlie and I returned to his house, Mrs. Curnan had a worried frown on her face. "Marge Entrup has taken a turn for the worse," she said to her husband. "They are trying to get her to a hospital in Boston."

"You have problems," I said, "and I had better leave you for now."

"Don't forget to come back now," said Charlie as we shook hands. "We'll talk about those recipes," he added with a grin.

As I drove down the road I decided to look in at the Entrup luncheonette and tell them that I would come back at a more convenient time. But as soon as I entered the door, a dark-haired little girl of about nine ran into the kitchen and called, "Grandpa, that lady who wants to talk to you about Mrs. Roosevelt is here. You talked to my mother when you had lunch here today," said the child. "I listened to every word you said."

Mr. Entrup emerged from the kitchen. He was a tall, slender man; his face was lined with the problems of life.

"Mr. Entrup," I said, "I do not want to bother you at a time like this. I will come back some other day."

"No, no," he said calmly, "when it comes to talking about Mrs. Roosevelt, no time is ever inconvenient."

"I am so sorry about your wife," I said.

"Yes," he said wearily as we sat down on the stools in front of the counter, "Marge is quite ill. Her asthma is so bad she can hardly breathe at all. And then this afternoon . . . it seemed to get so much worse." He took a deep breath. "Well, as soon as she feels a little better we'll try to get her to the hospital in Boston. But you want to know about Mrs. Roosevelt."

"Well, we met her when Barbara married the brother of Charlie Curnan. Then we just helped out with some cooking for one weekend and she asked us to stay on. No one ever could say No! to Eleanor Roosevelt. But we never regretted that we stayed. Whenever Mrs. Roosevelt had company, even very important personages, she would always bring them into the kitchen and introduce them to us. 'This is Les and Marge,' she would say, 'they are my dear friends and they have made life worth living for me these past years. She even brought President John F. Kennedy into our kitchen. He was so tall, his head almost touched the ceiling. Once, one of her other famous visitors complimented Mrs. Roosevelt on her wonderful servants. 'Marge and Les are not my servants!' she replied quite indignantly. 'They are my good friends.' "

"We never did wear a uniform at that," Mr. Entrup said. "I still remember after we had cooked the first meal for her, Mrs. Roosevelt came into the kitchen and thanked Marge for it. 'Now, Marge,' she said, 'this was a wonderful meal!'

"My wife looked straight at her," Mr. Entrup said, and replied, 'Now, Mrs. Roosevelt, I hope you won't hold it against me when I differ with you. I think the meal was terrible. Just awful!'

"I was so embarrassed," said Mr. Entrup. "I didn't think it was my wife's place to speak up like that to Mrs. Roosevelt. But Mrs. Roosevelt looked at Marge with great interest and surprise and asked her to please explain why she thought the meal had been so bad.

" 'Now you had all ladies who are watching their diets, Mrs. Roosevelt,' Marge said. 'And you made up a menu not only of creamed chicken, but also of potatoes *and* macaroni. And on top of that you gave them a dessert of maple syrup pancakes, and between each pancake was another layer of crushed maple sugar. Now those ladies must have been horrified at all those calories!'

"I thought Mrs. Roosevelt would surely put Marge in her place. After all, she was the wife of the President and she always had made up the menus. But as Mrs. Roosevelt listened carefully, a twinkle appeared in her blue eyes.

" 'You know what, Marge, from now on *you* are going to make up the menus.' And from that day on she left it all to Marge. Whenever she arrived home for dinner, with or without guests, she always said, 'Now, Marge, what are we going to have?' "

At this point, Garret Entrup, Mr. Entrup's son, came into the luncheonette. He was a tall young man with a friendly smile. "We had so much fun with Mrs. Roosevelt when she was alive," said Garret as he poured me a cup of coffee. "I'll never forget a story she told us about some very wealthy shah who visited her after he had gone on a shopping trip to Macy's. One of the American aides who had accompanied him told Mrs. Roosevelt that the shah had bought thirty toilet seats in all different colors. Mrs. Roosevelt was very interested as to why the shah should make such an unusual purchase. But she was too polite to ask him. Several years later, however, she told us, she visited the shah in his palace in Iran and there she found the thirty toilet seats displayed like pictures on the walls of a courtyard.

"I also remember the time I did some housepainting for Mrs. Roosevelt," Garret continued with a wide grin. "When I finished she wanted to pay me. But I would not take the money and told her that I was only too happy to do the job for her. Several days later, I came home and there was a package waiting for me that had been sent by Mrs. Roosevelt. I opened it and found that she had given me her gun."

"Mrs. Roosevelt had a gun?" I asked, incredulous.

"Well," Garret said, "when her husband became President, Mrs. Roosevelt insisted on driving her own car and refused to have a Secret Service agent following her. The head of Secret Service was very unhappy about that and finally brought her a revolver. 'At least carry this in your car,' he said. Mrs. Roosevelt carried it with her religiously. She told us that one summer she took some lessons in target shooting and, after considerable practice, she did learn to hit a target. 'But I never would have used it on a human being, of course,' she told us as she showed us the gun. I admired it at the time," Garret said, "and when she gave it to me as a gift, it seemed as though she was glad to get rid of it."

The older Mr. Entrup smiled. "I just remembered a time when two poor farm women insisted that they had to see Mrs. Roosevelt. When she did speak with them they asked her to give them the money which they owed the government for taxes. Mrs. Roosevelt replied that she could not possibly do that. Then the women asked if she would buy some of their chickens. That was another matter, Mrs. Roosevelt replied, and called me from the kitchen. 'Now, Les,' she said, 'do you think we could use some chickens? Say, about a hundred?' I said that yes, of course we could always put them into our freezer. Mrs. Roosevelt gave the two farm women the order. They left happy.

"When the chickens arrived," said Les Entrup, they were pretty puny looking and I could have bought that quality for half the price at the A & P. Then I counted them, and counted them once again. "Mrs. Roosevelt,' I said when I finally went to her, 'we have been cheated. They sent us only ninety chickens instead of the hundred we ordered.' Mrs. Roosevelt laughed. 'Well,' she said, 'these poor women will be able to sell the other ten to someone else and will have more money to pay their taxes.' "

Mr. Entrup walked me to my car. "You know," he said, "all of my life I had been an active Republican. From Mrs. Roosevelt I learned that I was wrong. The Democrats are the ones who look out for the poor people of this country. What would we all do today without Social Security, for instance?"

We shook hands good-bye. I thanked Mr. Entrup for his kindness, his time, and patience. "That's quite all right," he said and patted me on the shoulder. "I was happy to do it." Then he went back to his ill wife.

Soon after I returned to my motel room, a car drove up and a very big man and a very small woman got out. She had blonde hair and pretty blue eyes. In her hands she carried a large brown envelope.

"Please tell me your real name," I said to the big fellow as we greeted each other. "I do not know you and I couldn't possibly call you 'Tubby.' "

"Now take a good look at me," he said cheerfully as he pointed to his enormous baggy trousers and dark sweat shirt. "What else could you call me? Besides, it was good enough for Mrs. Roosevelt. Whenever I picked her up at an airport, I could hear her calling from far away, 'Over here, Tubby. Here I am.' "

We all laughed and I invited Paulina and Tubby to sit down. Paulina of course had no problem, but for Tubby the motel chairs were not quite wide enough.

"When did you start working for Mrs. Roosevelt?"

"I used to be a truck driver," he said. "And then I filled in driving for Mrs. Roosevelt one Memorial Day. She liked my driving and asked me to stay on."

"Tubby is an excellent driver," said Paulina.

"Mrs. Roosevelt never called me her chauffeur. She would always be telling people that I was just driving her."

"Well," said Paulina, "Tubby hardly ever wore a uniform. He mostly drove her dressed as you see him now. He often helped out at the house with the serving and things, just like this, too. There were always some people complaining in the newspapers that Mrs. Roosevelt did not even have a decent butler and maid. She would get a little angry when she heard about this. 'Now, I don't think it is nice to talk about someone after you were a guest in his house,' she used to say.

"Sometimes, when we were going to some important function," Paulina continued, "I would tell Tubby to put a hat on. But Mrs. Roosevelt protested immediately. "No, he does not have to wear a hat,' she would say. 'It's much too hot for him to wear one.' "

"Tell her the story about Florida," Tubby said to Paulina.

"Mrs. Roosevelt had flown to Miami to the Fontainebleau Hotel to give a speech for something or other," she said. "I think it was the United Jewish Appeal. She wanted Tubby to drive down so she would have a car. But since she knew that I had relatives in Florida she said, 'Now there is no reason that Paulina could not go along!' So the three of us—Tubby, Helen Curnan, who is Tubby's sister and was Mrs. Roosevelt's secretary at the time, and myself—drove down to Florida. We had such a good time, choosing all the motels where we would stay from the AAA book. When we arrived in Miami, Mrs. Roosevelt at once inquired about our trip. We told her of the motels and she sighed and said she wished that she once could stay in a motel too. Besides, she said, she thought it was absolutely ridiculous to pay fifty dollars to sleep at a hotel for one night.

"While we were in Florida, she insisted upon showing us the aquarium. So, on a very hot day, we drove all those miles just because she wanted us to see it. And when we got there it was closed. She was so disappointed. But we had dinner in a very nice place. Mrs. Roosevelt went in first to look at the restaurant, and she came out and said it seemed real nice and the table-clothes were very neat and clean. And so we had dinner there. But on the way out, people recognized her and came running for autographs. Mrs. Roosevelt was always very gracious about autographs, but the only thing that worried her was that Tubby's schedule would be upset and she always apologized for keeping him waiting."

"She never asked me to go slower or faster," Tubby volunteered. "But whenever we went someplace she would ask how long the trip would take. And then she would look on the map to see where we were going. Often while we were traveling, I thought she was napping in the back, but suddenly she would look up, glance at her watch and say, 'Tubby, we are two minutes behind schedule!' She was so fast even in her old age that I never could keep up with her. I was always huffing and puffing, trying to run after her up and down the stairs everywhere.

"I will never forget that day when her granddaughter Sallie died," Tubby said then. "While Mrs. Roosevelt was having dinner guests at Val-Kill, she got the message that the sixteen-year-old girl had fallen from a horse. Someone from the house called to tell me to have the car ready as soon as the guests had left. Mrs. Roosevelt did not mention what had happened to any of her guests and did not leave before she had said good-bye to every one of them."

"We finally did get Mrs. Roosevelt to a motel in Georgia in 1958," said Paulina. "We stopped on the road and Helen Curnan and I went to ask the manager for three rooms. One for Helen and me, one for Tubby, and one for a lady who was waiting in the car. The manager said that he could fix us up very nicely. He had one room for the gentleman, and another one for Helen and me. It was a very large room, he told us, and it would be absolutely no trouble to put up a cot in there for the lady who was waiting in the car. Helen said that this would not do. But the manager was very persistent. He insisted that there was nothing wrong with three ladies sleeping in one room as large as the one he had available. It seemed that those were the last vacant rooms and once he had rented them he could go to sleep. He simply would not let us go. Finally, in desperation, Helen said that the lady in the car had to have her own room because it was Mrs. Roosevelt. As soon as he heard the name, he dashed past us and out the door, ran to the car and grabbed Mrs. Roosevelt's hand. "I have always admired you and your husband so terribly much." He simply would not let go of her hand. When Tubby finally drove off, he practically had to drag the man along a few yards before he released Mrs. Roosevelt.

"It was always a problem when we drove and had to stop for food or to use the bathroom," continued Paulina. "People would be so determined to shake her hand and to have her autograph that they followed her even into the bathroom. There were times when I had to hold them off bodily.

"Mrs. Roosevelt never ceased to be surprised that the people always recognized her."

"Don't you remember the time when you told her to shut up?" Tubby asked Paulina.

"I did no such thing," Paulina protested, while her pretty face turned a little pink. "But we had to get out to use the bathroom and, as it happened, we were late with our schedule. 'Oh, dear,' Mrs. Roosevelt said. 'This stop will delay us if people should recognize us.'

"So I suggested," said Paulina, "that if Mrs. Roosevelt put on my dark glasses and refrained from talking—people always recognized her voice—we might get to the car without being recognized. It really worked and Mrs. Roosevelt was very pleased. 'I must try not to speak up more often,' she said."

"Well, it was just as I said," Tubby commented dryly. "Paulina told Mrs. Roosevelt to shut up!"

Paulina's face turned a deeper shade of pink and she hastily changed the subject. "Tubby and I started the Tiyogy Bowman

Archery Club," she explained as she took some photographs from the brown envelope she had been carrying. The name came from a cougar pup I once owned. Mrs. Roosevelt was very interested in all sports and she thought our archery club was a fine idea. She even donated the Roosevelt Trophy for it. But only under the condition that anyone could win it, which meant that it was judged by individual handicaps. Whenever Mrs. Roosevelt had guests she would bring them to our archery club. Here"—Paulina took some photographs from the brown envelope and handed them to me. There was Harry Belafonte dressed in a casual jacket, holding a poised bow and arrow.

I could have listened for many more hours to Tubby and his girl friend, but they knew that I had another appointment at eight o'clock to see the retired postmaster, Arthur E. Smith. So they took their leave. "It made me feel good to talk with you about Mrs. Roosevelt," said Paulina, her big blue eyes filled with tears. "It brought her back to us just a little."

Postmaster Smith had been most reluctant when I phoned him the previous morning. "I don't talk to writers out of principle," he declared somewhat crustily. "First you talk with them and then they turn around every word you have said. First thing you know is that something appears in print that you had never said, nor meant, and don't like one bit."

"Mr. Smith," I said, "whatever I would write about you and your friendship with Mrs. Roosevelt would not go into print without your approval. I would get a Xeroxed copy to you before publication. But if you really don't want to talk to me about Mrs. Roosevelt, that is your decision. However, this particular chapter is about Mrs. Roosevelt's friends in Hyde Park. I feel you should be among them."

"Well . . . maybe it would be fun talking with you. How about tomorrow evening around eight?"

It was pitch black in Hyde Park when I searched for the house on the corner of Post Road where Arthur E. Smith lives with his wife. There is a dentist's office on the main floor and I climbed up the steep staircase to the apartment above.

Arthur E. Smith had a whole stack of old photographs prepared for me. "I knew Mrs. Roosevelt almost all of my life," he said. "My father was Moses Smith, and I don't want to shock you by repeating some of the language he used. He was a real Will Rogers type. He was the caretaker of the farm at the Roosevelt estate and I remember him as referring to Franklin D. Roosevelt as 'that young fellow.' I recall that I was about ten years old when Mr. Roosevelt came to visit us. My mother offered him some home-baked doughnuts and he liked them so much that he said he must bring his 'Missus' to taste them and to get the recipe. I still remember the suit Mrs. Roosevelt wore when I saw her for the first time. It was purple. I hated that color. I also thought that she was quite gawky and that her voice was shrill when she thanked my mother for the 'wonderful doughnuts.' But then she looked at me and said that she would take me to a hospital in New York. Perhaps those doctors there would be able to do something about my back."

"What was wrong with your back?" I asked.

"Haven't you noticed?" asked Mr. Smith.

"Have I noticed what?" I said.

He stood up. Only then did I see the slight curve which at first I had thought to be just a slightly stooped posture.

"Mrs. Roosevelt took me to the best hospital in New York," Arthur Smith recalled. "They took all my records and then asked me what the E. in my name stood for. Now I absolutely detest my middle name," he said. "It's so awful that I won't even tell it to you. And I certainly was not going to tell it to those doctors in New York. So I quickly glanced at Mrs. Roosevelt and hastily said that the E stood for Elliott. She never said a word to contradict me.

"But, in spite of her kindness, the doctor's diagnosis only confirmed what I had known all along. I had been born with my back that way and I darn well was going to die with it.

"But from that time on I became very devoted to the Roosevelts. I was appointed Postmaster of Hyde Park and I soon started the "Roosevelt Home Club," a so-called nonpartisan political club supporting our own Franklin D. Roosevelt. You know, of course, that we have a lot of Republicans around here and that Franklin never carried his home district. After the death of FDR in 1945, the club started holding memorial services in his honor. We still have these services each year on May Thirtieth. The membership fee was only one dollar a year, but after a while people lost interest in the entire matter. There was a time when we had only ten members left. I did not have the heart to tell Mrs. Roosevelt, so, when the time of the services came around, I got an especially important speaker and sent out five hundred invitations. Three hundred people came and Mrs. Roosevelt was very happy to see that the club was still flourishing. Now, in 1968, we again have about one hundred members."

I hastily paid my dues of one dollar and became the proud one hundred-and-first member of the Roosevelt Home Club.

"It always was a lot of fun to be with Mrs. Roosevelt," Arthur E. Smith recalled. "I remember one time when I drove with her in her son John's car. Now, John is the sole Republican of the family. He had to get out of the car to do some shopping, and Mrs. Roosevelt noticed that there was a Democratic headquarters still open. She sent me to get as many Democratic stickers as I could find and, before John returned from his shopping, Mrs. Roosevelt and I had the entire car plastered with the stickers. You should have seen John's face! Mrs. Roosevelt just sat there and grinned."

"Tell her the story about Princess Martha from Denmark," Mrs. Smith prodded her husband.

He laughed. "Well, we had the annual Home Town Reception for the Roosevelt Home Club at my father's farm," said Arthur Smith. "FDR was still alive at that time. Princess Martha was the guest of honor, and I was seated next to her. Everything was ready. Everything except that Mrs. Roosevelt had not yet appeared. The West Point Band began to play the National Anthem, everyone stood up, and, when they had finished, there still was no sign of Eleanor Roosevelt. The West Point Band began to play again. When we sat down the second time I finally muttered under my breath, 'Now, where the h— is Mrs. Roosevelt?'

"Princess Martha overheard me and leaned toward me to tell me that Mrs. Roosevelt had said that she and FDR should go ahead. Mrs. Roosevelt would wait for Irene, their beloved cook, who was not quite ready yet."

We all laughed. "Tell me," I said, "how did you cope with all the mail that Mrs. Roosevelt received?"

Arthur E. Smith grinned. "I really shouldn't tell you this, because it puts me in a bad light as a postmaster. But I'll tell you anyway. Our local post office was of course very small. Everyone had just one tiny cubicle for their mail. And of course it could not hold the tons of mail Mrs. Roosevelt was receiving. So, we simply got two huge grocery boxes from the market next door, put them under the table and whatever arrived for Eleanor Roosevelt would be thrown in there. Later we put it all in large bags and someone from the Roosevelt house picked it up. After a while though, we got a very nice post office built in Hyde Park. Mrs. Roosevelt was very proud of it. She always brought her guests to see it, introduced me, and pointed out the murals on the walls which depict the history of Hyde Park and the Hudson Valley in all seasons; covered with snow and ice in the winter, everyone fishing in the spring and summer, and, finally, the fall, when people are busy with the harvest."

On Saturday morning I returned to the Franklin D. Roosevelt Library and Museum as a tourist. Harold Farley was expecting me. "I'll be gone for quite a while," he told the other guards.

We walked first to the rose garden where Franklin D. Roosevelt and Anna Eleanor Roosevelt are buried. The small garden is northeast of the house almost completely surrounded by a century-old hemlock hedge. The site was chosen by FDR himself as his burial place. The rose garden was traditional with the family because the surname Roosevelt was adopted from the Dutch "field of roses." The family coat of arms shows three roses on a shield, surmounted by a casque and three feathers. A white marble tombstone, with a slight trace of color, stands immediately north of the grave. It is from the quarry in Vermont that produced the marble for the Thomas Jefferson Memorial in Washington. President Roosevelt drew up the plans for the tombstone, which is eight feet long, four feet wide, and three feet high. For a while, Harold Farley and I stood there silently in the sunshine. "You must be wondering why the graves are sidewise. You see, the President was a Mason and it is a tradition that Masons must be buried facing the east so that the sun rises each morning facing the grave. Come," said Harold Farley, "since there are no tourists here right now, I can show you something special." We walked down the path to the sundial and there, behind the graves of Franklin and Eleanor, were two more graves. They were very small. One said, "Fala," and the other, "Chief," a German shepherd which had been the dog of Anna, the Roosevelt's daughter.

We left the graveside and walked to the house.

On entering the house, one can rent a small tape recorder with an earphone and be guided on a tour by Mrs. Roosevelt's voice. I had this exciting experience at an earlier visit but for some reason, I wanted Harold Farley's explanation of the house. As we entered, we stopped before a massive oak wardrobe. "The Roosevelt kids usually left all their junk in here, tennis rackets, ice skates, whatever they just had been using. It was too much trouble to carry it all to their rooms. Often they would come in from horseback riding to the dinner table and Mrs. James Roosevelt would sniff a little and say, 'Do I smell horses?' And then the boys would quickly run to wash their hands." We looked at the room which was called "The Snuggery," Mrs. Sarah Delano Roosevelt's writing and sitting room, to the living room, which is spacious and cheerful and where the family met to play, to read, to entertain.

The Dresden Room took its name from the delicately wrought Dresden chandelier and mantel set and the floral draperies and matching upholstery that were hung in 1939, shortly before the King and Queen of England visited there.

It was before that visit, Harold Farley explained, that the President and Mrs. Roosevelt became worried about the set of cartoons out of *Punch,* displayed in the foyer. Mrs. Roosevelt was afraid that the King and Queen would feel offended about them and suggested they should be taken off the wall during the royal visit. But then the President said that this would leave marks on the walls where the pictures had been and that would be even worse. Mrs. Roosevelt suggested that they have the wall painted. But the President said it would be impossible because they would have to paint the entire hallway. And so the cartoons lampooning the British remained on the wall. King George went down every morning to gaze at them for a long while. He said at the end of his visit that those cartoons had added a great deal of enjoyment to his stay in the United States.

Upstairs are the bedrooms. In the President's dressing room, the closet doors stand open. Inside are some of his clothes, the dark cape and famous fedoras he wore during his campaigns, and also his wheelchair.

Harold Farley said that after the death of FDR, they had to establish a first-aid station in the butler's pantry, because so many people would collapse at the sight of it all.

We walked back to the grounds, where there is a sweeping view of the magnificent Hudson River.

"See that house over there on the other side of the river?" Harold Farley said. "It's Father Divine's place. Someone sold it to him, thinking it would annoy President Roosevelt. But whenever the music drifted over, President Roosevelt sat on his balcony up there and listened; he enjoyed every moment of it. From this balcony he also watched the yacht races on the Hudson."

From the lawn we went to the stables. Photographs of all the Roosevelt horses are displayed there.

"Mrs. Roosevelt is quite a horsewoman," he said. "I forgot to show you the path where she goes riding almost every morning."

"Do you realize," I said to Harold Farley, "that whenever you speak of Eleanor Roosevelt you never say 'she was.' You always talk as though she were still alive."

Harold Farley gazed at me with his thoughtful philosopher's eyes. "Didn't you know that?" he asked with gentle surprise. "The people we know and love never really die. They are with us always."

Chapter Twenty

Strangers in All Places Everywhere

ONE OF MY FOLDERS WAS BULGING with letters that refused to be classified into any one category. They came from people who had met Eleanor Roosevelt in the subway, on a plane, at an airport, in a hotel corridor, at a convention, at a tea shop; from people who had shaken her hand once on a receiving line, who had been invited to her home, or, on the spur of the moment, had invited *her* to their homes. All these contacts had been brief and, as the people reported, "nothing really happened." And yet, the Eleanor Roosevelt touch had somehow transformed them.

"In 1946, a few months after I was discharged from the army," wrote Irving Harrison of Merrick, New York, "my wife and I were on the subway one Sunday afternoon, headed for Washington Heights. Suddenly I noticed a lady seated in the next car. She wore a white dress and had a white band in her hair. 'Look, there!' I said to my wife. 'Isn't that Mrs. Roosevelt?'

" 'There is some resemblance,' my wife said. 'But of course it can't be Mrs. Roosevelt. Not on the subway.'

"'I am going to take a closer look,' I insisted and got up. Somewhat nervous I sat down next to the lady in white and said, 'Good afternoon, Mrs. Roosevelt.'

"She looked up from the *Herald Tribune* magazine section which she had been reading. 'Hello, young man,' she said. Then she noticed the veteran's button in my lapel and immediately inquired whether I was having a difficult time finding a place to live. When I said yes, she commented that she had often spoken to her husband about that problem. I apologized for accosting her in this presumptuous manner but she waved away my apology and asked me more questions about my adjustment to civilian life. Of course it was hard to hear each other over the roar of the train, and I am afraid I had to shout while unburdening all my GI gripes. I then told her my solutions to these problems. Mrs. Roosevelt held up her hand and said, 'Let me write all this down.' From her pocketbook she took out a pad and a pen and studiously wrote down all my suggestions to the world's problems. When I had finally finished, she thanked me courteously and assured me that she would bring all this to the attention of President Harry Truman. We shook hands and she left the subway at the Medical Center where, she told me, she was going to visit someone.

"I don't of course know," Mr. Harrison concluded, "whether Mrs. Roosevelt really conveyed my suggestions to the President. However, each time some legislation of social importance was enacted, in the back of my mind persisted the thought that perhaps, through my conversation with a great lady, shouted over the roar of a subway train in New York, someone, somewhere in this country, had benefited!"

"I am old, I am tired, and I am lazy," wrote Charles Bernstein from Front Royal, Virginia. "And yet I think that this little drama illustrative of Mrs. Roosevelt's great heart, her compassion, and thoughtfulness should be saved from oblivion. Ironically, I am the only actor in this drama still alive. If it had not been for Mrs. Roosevelt's intervention, I should have gone to my death in the electric chair on January 11, 1935. I had been convicted for a murder I did not commit. For two years I sat in death row. Then, less than a week before the execution of my sentence, my attorney and I appealed directly to Mrs. Roosevelt. She asked for a summary of the case and stayed awake all night to study it. When she concluded that all the facts had not been revealed, she asked President Roosevelt to give my attorney time to explore the case further. Please note how thoughtful she was," Mr. Bernstein continued his letter. "She said that she could not let me suffer needlessly, so she sent word to me on Sunday, January 6, 1935, that the President would issue a reprieve."

Mr. Bernstein's lawyer and others who believed in his innocence resumed the fight to save him. Four years after the murder had been committed, new evidence was discovered that could not be linked to Mr. Bernstein. This caused President Roosevelt to grant him a conditional pardon. In 1940 he was released. Further evidence of his innocence came to light, and in 1945 Mr. Bernstein was pardoned unconditonally by President Truman.

"I was standing outside the Biltmore Hotel in New York City," wrote Julia Broughton from Saint Louis, Missouri, "when I noticed a young woman waiting for a cab. Then I saw Mrs. Roosevelt emerging from the hotel door, also in search of a cab. When a taxi drew up to the curb the young woman stepped aside and offered it to Mrs. Roosevelt.

" 'Oh, no!' Eleanor Roosevelt replied and emphatically shook her head. 'This one is yours. I shall wait for the next one.' "

"In 1936, Mrs. Roosevelt paid a visit to Camp Grayville, Illinois," wrote Gerald H. Reynalds, former Army Captain of Company 694 there. "Grayville was the home of Mrs. Edith Helm, widow of Admiral Helm, who was part-time social secretary for Mrs. Roosevelt. Since the Roosevelts at that time were on a campaign trip nearby, Mrs. Helm invited Mrs. Roosevelt and her secretary Malvina Thompson for a brief visit. When Mrs. Roosevelt accepted, our little town of seventeen hundred or so inhabitants burst into frenzied activity; everyone wanted to give the First Lady a taste of Southern Illinois hospitality. I arranged for Mrs. Roosevelt to have Sunday dinner at the camp's mess hall with all the personnel present. Mrs. Helm and I checked the facilities before Mrs. Roosevelt's arrival and I particularly asked her to try out the dining arrangements. Mrs. Helm sat down at one of the benches, which were attached to the tables. Since they had been built for tall soldiers, the distance between bench and table was a little too wide for Mrs. Helm. But she said it would be just right for Mrs. Roosevelt because she had long legs. We went over the rest of the camp together and discovered that we had no patients in our little six-bed infirmary. I thought that Mrs. Roosevelt would like to have someone there with whom she could sympathize. After some thought I called back a recent patient and asked him to report as a temporary patient again on the day of the visit.

"Mrs. Roosevelt finally arrived with her two secretaries, and the ladies inspected the camp. The last stop was the infirmary. Our lone 'patient' was the one redhead in the company, we had him all covered up in bed, and, since it was a very hot summer day, his freckled face was perspiring heavily. Mrs. Roosevelt gave him some encouragement and expressed her hope for a speedy recovery. Then we proceeded to the mess hall for dinner. Mrs. Roosevelt was seated at the head of the long table which was facing the door and I sat next to her. Just as the Chaplain finished asking the blessing, I was mortified to see our 'patient' appearing in the doorway. I frantically motioned for him to disappear and was greatly relieved that Mrs. Roosevelt did not seem to notice anything. She remarked that the baked ham we served was excellent and that it was a real pleasure to have something to eat other than chicken which they had eaten practically three times a day on that particular trip.

"A few weeks after that visit I received a thank you letter from the White House," Captain Reynalds concluded his letter. "It said at the end, 'and the best tribute to the healthful condition of Camp Grayville was the lone patient in the hospital.' I could almost see Mrs. Roosevelt's blue eyes twinkle," he wrote, "and in my mind I heard her chuckle and say, *You didn't fool me one bit!*"

A tailor, who had his small shop in Albany during the time Franklin D. Roosevelt was Governor, remembered Mrs. Roosevelt trudging down the hill from the Governor's mansion, her arms loaded with her children's worn-out clothes. She wanted the frayed cuffs and collars repaired before the garments were given away to the needy.

"It was a very cold day toward the end of World War II," said Kathi Rogers, an artist who lives in New York's Greenwich Village. "I stepped into Mrs. O'Leary's Tea Shop on McDougal Street. It was quite quite empty and, as I entered, the room felt especially warm on this snowy afternoon. As I glanced around for a table, I suddenly recognized Mrs. Roosevelt sitting all alone. As I stared at her she began to smile and I haltingly said hello. Her smile became broader and she gestured to the empty chair for me to sit down. We talked as though we were old friends: about politics, Greenwich Village affairs, my work as a painter. I often met her afterward at various art shows around town. 'Why, hello there, Miss Rogers,' she would always say. 'Wasn't that a cold day when we had tea together at Mrs. O'Leary's on Mc-Dougal Street?' "

A woman at the New School told me that she once drove Mrs. Roosevelt to a dinner at which she was the guest of honor. "I am so sorry but we must turn back," Mrs. Roosevelt exclaimed half-way to the hotel where the dinner was to take place. "I forgot something at home." It was late, the woman said, and she hesitated about turning around in the heavy New York traffic. She inquired what it was that Mrs. Roosevelt had forgotten. "My ticket of admission," the guest of honor said embarrassedly. "How silly of me, I left it in my other purse!" It took her driver quite a while to assure Mrs. Roosevelt that it would be all right, that she would be admitted even without her ticket.

Rabbi Judah Cahn of New York, who was National Vice-President of the NAACP, received his life membership in that organization in an unusual way. One day he was to drive Mrs. Roosevelt, whom he had known for a number of years, to Lawrence, Long Island, where she was to give a lecture. On their way out he asked whether she would mind very much if he were to make a brief stop to deliver a gift. He explained that the gift was a baseball bat for a little boy who was dying of leukemia. Mrs. Roosevelt assured him that she would not mind. When he stopped

the car in front of the house where the child lived, she jumped
out before him and announced that she would go along. "The
light which came onto the boy's thin cheeks when he sighted
Mrs. Roosevelt in his sickroom is hard to describe," Rabbi Cahn
said. "She sat down at his bedside, discussed baseball with him
and how he would use the bat in the spring. I think the visit
made the child live six months longer," Rabbi Cahn added
thoughtfully. "And the parents were just overwhelmed. Mrs.
Roosevelt's kindness seemed to give them courage to cope with
that great tragedy in their lives."

With the money that Mrs. Roosevelt received for that particular lecture, she bought a life membership in the NAACP
for Rabbi Cahn.

"At a concert after a White House dinner," wrote Mr. Albert
W. Atwood, who resides in Washington, D.C., "a crippled woman
in a wheelchair came in late. Mrs. Roosevelt, who was in front
with the musicians, discovered her as she hesitated in the rear of
the large room. She rushed back and herself wheeled the crippled
woman up front to the best position."

"I was a student at Oberlin College, in Ohio," wrote Mrs.
Reinhart W. Koch of Rockville, Maryland. "In 1941, or perhaps
it was 1942, Mrs. Roosevelt came to address a meeting of a student
group. After the speech there was a reception with several hundred students. I went through the line at the beginning and
Mrs. Roosevelt spoke with me briefly. Mrs. Roosevelt is the most
charming person I have ever met, I reported to my friends and
said that I wished I could go through the reception line again.
'Why don't you?' one of my friends asked. 'After a hundred or
so people she would never recognize you.' I thought this was a
splendid idea and went back into line. When I arrived before
Mrs. Roosevelt I held out my hand and said, 'How do you do?'
She looked at me for a second with her clear blue eyes, shook
my hand, and said, 'How do you do—again!'"

Joseph S. Blair of Columbus, Ohio, remembered the time,
about 1952, when he was on the staff of a YMCA group at City
College in New York. "There were about fifty students who met

every Thursday noon for a quick sandwich and a short program," he reported. "Once when we were planning further events somebody suggested that we invite Mrs. Roosevelt. The suggestion had been made facetiously. But I thought it was a grand idea. I wrote to Mrs. Roosevelt, telling her about the group, something of its interests and needs, and asked her to speak to us on 'The Christian and World Responsibilities.' Her reply came by return mail. She would come! Since the meeting date was April 1, most of my students thought I was fooling them. They arrived for the meeting with great laughter and guffaws, making it clear to me that they were just humoring me and were not one bit taken in by my little joke. They were stunned when, right on time, Mrs. Roosevelt in person entered our room. She sat down with us, sharing our sandwiches and fruit with that natural humanness everyone who ever met her will always remember. She stayed with us for an hour and a half. By giving each student an opportunity to talk with her, she demonstrated her conviction that each individual is just as important as the world leaders whom she met every day."

"I knew Eleanor Roosevelt when I was a child with polio down at Warm Springs, Georgia," wrote Barbara Rossmore from Upper Montclair, New Jersey. "Mrs. Roosevelt and the President always had Thanksgiving dinner with us patients at the big hall. We drew lots to determine who was to sit at their table and one time *I* won! Mrs. Roosevelt was the head of the Girl Scouts of Warm Springs and she established special rules for us. If we had a disabled hand and could not tie knots we memorized the state capitals; swimming certain distances, some underwater, equaled nature walks for those in wheelchairs; Mrs. Roosevelt also made us recite the scouts' pledge and rules and pinned the pins on us. She had no school there and it was wonderful to have her teach us. She often had a reception for the local farm women who came in in poke bonnets and heavy men's work shoes; they walked all the way from their homes many miles away. They brought presents of the only thing they had—peach marmalade from peach country—and Mrs. Roosevelt carefully wrote each individual name and FDR on the label. Months later the farm women would proudly show around notes from the White House which said, 'This morning the President and I enjoyed your wonderful jelly preserves for breakfast and we want to thank you again for your kindness in presenting it to us.' I was about ten years old then," said Barbara Rossmore, "but even now, some thirty years later, I still remember the great love we all had for Eleanor Roosevelt!"

"I was in Warm Springs with my daughter for two years," Mrs. Laura Miller, Barabara's mother, told me over the telephone. "Of course I did not know Mrs. Roosevelt personally. But she was always there when her husband was, and I saw her almost daily then. She was walking around everywhere simply dressed and she went swimming with the children. When she got out of the water she just braided her long hair and let it hang down. The President was a great inspiration for all the polio victims there. The children felt that if he could do so much in spite of being crippled, then surely they could too. Once at Thanksgiving dinner at the Foundation we were standing in the receiving line waiting to shake hands with Mrs. Roosevelt. Suddenly Mrs. Roosevelt held up the long line and insisted that a woman who had given her a jar of jam and walked on must be called back. I heard her saying, 'Oh, but I could not accept a gift and not know where to send my note of thanks!' The children in Warm Springs always waited for her and when she spoke to them they later would exclaim to their mothers, 'You see, Mrs. Roosevelt knew me!'"

"I met Mrs. Roosevelt sometime in 1960," said Mrs. Emmie Breitbach of Tarrytown, New York. "Ever since I came to this country as a refugee from Nazi Germany in 1938, I wanted so very much to meet this wonderful woman. One day Mrs. Roosevelt was scheduled to give a talk for the Cancer Fund in a hairdresser's salon on West Eighth Street in Greenwich Village. The owner had died of cancer a short time before and Mrs. Roosevelt used to be a customer there. My friend and I arrived at the place well before the time of the speech, as we wanted to make certain that we could get in. It was raining heavily that day and a crowd of women were gathered before the store which had not opened its doors as yet. Everyone was complaining angrily. Next to me stood a woman who did not say a word. Like the rest of us, she was soaking wet. I glanced at her, looked away, then, startled, I took another look. It couldn't be! But it was. 'Mrs. Roosevelt?' I asked, incredulously. She smiled. We shook hands. 'Isn't it awful that they let us wait out here?' I asked. Eleanor Roosevelt admitted that it was a little hard for her also to stand. But this was only because she had hurt her leg in a little accident a few weeks before. Now, finally, the other women noticed her. All complaints stopped. The door of the beauty parlor was opened at the scheduled time."

"In the summer of 1955, I was pregnant with my third child," wrote Rita Lendman of Radburn, New Jersey. "For some reason I felt blue and lonely at that time and probably projected my own feelings onto Mrs. Roosevelt when I saw her on television on the Ed Murrow show. What a lonely woman she seems to be, I found myself thinking and, on the spur of the moment, sat down to write her a letter inviting her into our home. I explained that we were simple people, but that I felt everyone could meet the person he admired if he only made the effort to do something about it. I did not really think I would hear from Mrs. Roosevelt. But she answered at once, thanking me for my letter and invitation, said that she was going to Europe now but would like *us* to visit *her* in Hyde Park when she returned. And really, immediately after her return, she wrote us again and invited us for a specific date. We thought that she would send someone to meet us at the train and I almost fainted when I saw her standing at the station in a simple dress and white sneakers. Driving her small car herself, she took us to her cottage, Val-Kill. We thought that this must be a day when a lot of unimportant visitors were invited. But nobody was there except us. Mrs. Roosevelt's son John joined us for lunch. From their talk I could tell that she was just as busy as always. She took us to the Hyde Park home which now is a museum and she talked a lot about her mother-in-law. My husband wanted to open doors for her but she was much too fast. Probably because I was pregnant, Mrs. Roosevelt kept waiting on *me*! I saw Mrs. Roosevelt many times afterwards," Rita Lendman concluded, "at lectures and at fund-raising dinners. But I never approached her again. I felt that Mrs. Roosevelt had given me so much more than I ever deserved."

"As I was coming out of the United Nations Headquarters in New York," wrote John Maktos, a lawyer in Washington, D.C., "I saw Mrs. Roosevelt standing near the curb. The delegate of a foreign country who was with me saw her, too. He declared that he would help her across the street. He ran up to her, took her arm, and carefully guided her to the other side. I saw her smile at him and shake hands with him when they got there. Then, as I kept watching her, I noticed Mrs. Roosevelt remainig standing there for another few moments. But just as soon as the foreign delegate had disappeared around a corner, she came dashing back to my side of the street where, the next instant, her car drew up with her chauffeur."

"At a Detroit convention of the National Lawyer's Guild in the midst of the Joseph McCarthy tumult in about 1956, I was publicity man for the Guild," wrote Carl Hessler from Detroit, Michigan. "Because of Attorney General Brownell's public vendetta against the Guild, most public figures found it prudent to reject or ignore our invitations to speak at a convention banquet at the Statler Hotel. On the day of the convention we therefore found ourselves without a speaker.

"Just before the banquet, we heard that Eleanor Roosevelt was in town for an Israeli bond drive, and a young reporter told me there was to be a news conference in Mrs. Roosevelt's room. I mingled with the reporters and after they had gone approached Mrs. Roosevelt and invited her to greet the Guild cocktail party at five o'clock. She said it was impossible because she had to dress for dinner at the Israeli affair. I explained our predicament and told her that all the prominent people were afraid to speak to us because of Joseph McCarthy. 'All right, I will come,' she said at once. 'But only for two minutes.' Of course she was received by the people of the Guild with much enthusiasm. She stayed longer than two minutes, spoke in her friendly, gracious way for some time, posed for photographs for the press and thus filled a gap which no other prominent personality had dared to fill."

"During the Joseph McCarthy era I was trying to organize a group, 'American Kinsmen of Service Men,'" wrote Rebecca Susan Haile from Ossining, New York. "Our idea was to give the United Nations a real collective security force to outlaw war and cooperate with world developments. I sent Mrs. Roosevelt some of our literature and she kindly granted me an interview. I took my young co-worker Frances with me because she was a fervent admirer of Mrs. Roosevelt, a great fighter for liberal ideas, and a girl with a high sense of justice. But when we were at Mrs. Roosevelt's home she was so awed that she did not utter a word. On our way home she kept talking about Mrs. Roosevelt, how she never was afraid to take a stand against crooked politicians and always spoke up about what she thought was right. 'I am going to do it, too!' Frances suddenly declared. About that time, a child in the neighborhood had been killed by a car. During an election soon afterward, the promise was made that a huge city-owned block would be torn down to make place for a neighborhood playground. But after the election was over, nothing was heard of this any longer. Instead of the playground, it now was planned to use the territory for a private garage. That night after our visit with Mrs. Roosevelt, Frances wrotes a letter to the local paper, demanding that the pledge for the playground be kept. She, her sister, and another friend and their children formed a committee and took the petition to the editor of the paper. It was printed, the American Legion and the Catholic Church became interested, citizens wrote more angry letters, and soon things began to move. The plans for the garage were abandoned, funds were allotted for the playground, and eventually it was really built. One day the parish priest met Frances on the street and told her how impressed he was by the accomplishment of her committee. 'I would like to come and talk to all of you one day,' he said. Frances looked at him. 'But, Father,' she said, 'there is no committee except me and my sister. It mostly takes just *one* person to start things rolling. I learned this from Mrs. Roosevelt!'"

Gerhard E. Karplus is Viennese. In 1938 he came to the United States as a political refugee. All that he was able to bring along was his talent. Gerhard Karplus is an architect, carrying on a family tradition. His father was one of the most outstanding architects in Austria, a pioneer in the field of modern architecture.

Soon after Gerhard Karplus arrived in his new country, World War II broke out and he was drafted into the army. As an alien, he could have refused. He chose not to. He started as a private, became a first sergeant and as soon as he became an American citizen applied for Officer Candidate School, where he was accepted. Once he was second lieutenant, Gerhard Karplus volunteered for combat in Europe. But his fervent wish to have the opportunity to fight the Nazis was not granted. He was sent to the China-Burma-India Theater of War.

In 1946, after having served four and a half years in the army, Gerhard Karplus came back to the United States with two battle stars and many ribbons. He started to work on his own as an architect in New York, assisted by his wife Gertrude.

It was in March 1958 that Gerhard Karplus received a phone call in his office. Some satisfied customer, he was informed, had recommended him as an architect to Mrs. Eleanor Roosevelt. She had just bought a house on East Seventy-fourth Street and wanted to arrange an appointment the following week, if possible.

After a moment of stunned silence, Gerhard Karplus said, "Of course!"

Would it be possible for him to make the appointment at 8 o'clock in the morning? was the next question.

"Any time!" said Gerhard Karplus.

On the day of the appointment, he stood on the stoop of 55 East Seventy-fourth Street fifteen minutes before eight o'clock.

Five minutes later a taxicab drew up, and a tall lady alighted. "I am Mrs. Roosevelt," she said with a smile, "so kind of you to come, Mr. Karplus."

They walked into the house in which Mrs. Roosevelt was to occupy two floors. "I want everything very simple," she told him as they entered. "Simple and inexpensive. I don't like gimmicks."

In spite of Mr. Karplus's protest, she helped him off with his coat and proceeded to put it on a hanger. The hanger slipped from her hand and even though Gerhard Karplus was a few decades younger than Mrs. Roosevelt, she was faster to bend down and pick it up.

"But, Mrs. Roosevelt," he protested unhappily, "why don't you let me do that?"

"Nonsense," she gaily responded. "Since *I* dropped the hanger, it is only fair that *I* pick it up again."

Again she explained to him that all she wanted was a simple place: a home where she could surround herself with her dearest memorabilia. "My apartment decorations and furniture are of no particular period or style," she explained: a couple of her favorite pictures of Franklin, an oil painting of her son John's house and the pool at Hyde Park, a water color of Washington Square and several water colors of Venice. There was also a black-and-white illustration that was done for the cover of a book called *A Christmas Story,* a few small tables that came from the Val-Kill factory for Early American reproductions, and a Japanese screen about five feet tall and ten feet long.

"I won't need many closets," Mrs. Roosevelt said, "because I do not have many clothes. Just keep it simple. Simple and inexpensive."

"From then on we had many meetings," recalled Gerhard Karplus as he told the story in his lovely bright office on the forty-seventh floor of a building on Park Avenue. "But Mrs. Roosevelt always was in a hurry. Either she was just returning from a trip to the West Coast, or she was about to leave for overseas. Usually we met either very early in the morning, or very late at night. Decisions over which the average customer ponders many days or even weeks, Mrs. Roosevelt settled in two minutes.

"Whenever she inspected something that was done during her absence, she would say, 'Oh, it is lovely, Mr. Karplus. Exactly what I wanted!'

"Her only complaint was that things did not move fast enough. Once, to my horror, I heard that she had written in her column, 'My Day,' that the decorating of her new home was going very slowly and that her architect had said there was nothing he could do about it. Of course, I never heard the end of that story from my friends!

"So the next time we met, I told Mrs. Roosevelt how unhappy I was about her column and that it really was not my fault that things were going so slowly, but the workmen simply could not be pushed.

"So Mrs. Roosevelt promply wrote another column in which she said that things were progressing very satisfactorily in her new home and that her architect—whom she mentioned this time by name—was most efficient.

"When we began discussing the setup of the kitchen," Gerhard Karplus recalled, "Mrs. Roosevelt again declared that she wanted everything very simple. No fancy colors, no gadgets that moved and would need many repairs. 'We'll best discuss the kitchen situation with my cook and she can tell you herself what she wants, said Mrs. Roosevelt."

When Anna, the cook, came in and began to speak with a heavy German accent, Gerhard Karplus suggested that they confer in their native language. Mrs. Roosevelt smiled her wide smile and said, "How very nice. Now we all can talk German together." Her German was not perfect but she could express herself in it.

"One of the difficulties in doing that job was that one of the former tenants of the house delayed his moving out," said Gerhard Karplus. "My wife and I usually took our vacation in September but that year I did not want to go because I was determined that I would personally supervise the entire work.

"However, Gertrude, who works as a gym teacher, had no other possible time to take a vacation. So I finally, rather reluctantly, approached Mrs. Roosevelt and asked her whether we could settle for the beginning of the work in October; by that time surely the old tenant would have moved out. I also explained honestly to Mrs. Roosevelt that I wanted to go on a trip with my wife.

" 'Where do you want to go?' she inquired.

"I told her that we were planning to go to Israel. The moment she heard this her face lit up. 'Oh, of course you must take your vacation then!' she exclaimed. 'Everyone must see Israel at least once. It is the perfect example of a Democracy!'

"Not only did she urge me to go," Gerhard Karplus recalled, "but she gave us so many introductions in Israel that we met a lot of wonderful people and had an unforgettable vacation.

"After this, Mrs. Roosevelt expressed her desire to meet my wife and invited us for tea. Of course we expected a large party and never dreamed that she would take the time to just see the two of us. But this is just what she did. She greeted my wife cordially, calling her 'my child,' and she served us tea and cookies.

The only trouble was that the cookies were still covered by a cellophane wrap and when she urged us to take some we were too embarrassed to draw her attention to it. So we just said, 'No—thank you very much.'

" 'Well, if you don't like cookies,' Mrs. Roosevelt finally said, 'I'll just make us some cinnamon toast, that is really what I like the best. And she got up, went to the kitchen and made cinnamon toast for all three of us.

"The next time we saw Mrs. Roosevelt," said Gerhard Karplus, "was when she invited us to a New Year's Day reception. There were a great many people and Mrs. Roosevelt stood at the head of the staircase greeting everyone. Although she had seen my wife only once before and very briefly, she instantly held out her hand to her and said, 'So kind of you to come, Mrs. Karplus.' "

Many draftsmen are working today in Gerhard Karplus's bright offices, the pictures on the walls show large modern factories and buildings which he designed in all parts of the United States and Europe.

"It was the greatest experience of my life," he said, "that I, who had come to the United States with nothing, had the honor and the privilege of doing the home of Eleanor Roosevelt."

At a meeting of The National Council of Women at the Colony Club in New York, I was introduced to the Honorable Dr. Marion Mill Preminger, World President of the Albert Schweitzer Circle, Consul General of Gabon.

Dr. Preminger is a tall, attractive woman with long blonde hair. She asked me about my work and I told her that I was writing a book on Eleanor Roosevelt.

Dark pensive eyes focused on me. "I loved Mrs. Roosevelt very much," Marion Preminger said. "I often sat with Eleanor Roosevelt at various functions on the dais and she always smiled at me when she saw me. My teacher, Dr. Albert Schweitzer, thought very highly of her."

Some years before this meeting with Marion Preminger I had read her autobiography, *All I Want Is Everything*. From this enchanting book I had learned that Marion Mill Preminger had voluntarily given up her glamour life in Hollywood to work for

Dr. Albert Schweitzer at the leper colony of his hospital at Lamba-rene.

"Would you tell me about your memories of Mrs. Roosevelt sometime?" I asked.

"Just phone me," she said.

"When?" I asked.

"Any time," she replied.

It was December, the coldest and wettest day of the year, with an icy rain coming down in sheets, when I went to visit Dr. Preminger in her museum-apartment on Park Avenue. A uni-formed maid opened the door for me and it seemed as if I stepped into the warmth of Africa. Marion Mill Preminger's house is a museum. It houses one of the best African art collections in New York. The walls are covered with black hand-carved masks and figures, the mirror-bright floors serve as a background for Aubus-son carpets. In the foyer, I quickly removed my overshoes and dripping coat. "Would you like a drink to warm yourself?" the maid asked and showed me Mrs. Preminger's famous *Kitchen Salon*, the only one in New York. Three rock crystal chandeliers provide the lighting and the walls are hung with eighteenth-century food paintings. On display is a six-hundred-piece set of dishes that was given to Marion Mill Preminger's Hungarian great-grandfather by the Sultan of Turkey. The lion and pigeon design, the family crest, is in the border.

The warmth of the place suddenly intensified: Dr. Preminger had stepped into the room. The only ornament on her plain black dress was the flame ribbon of the French Legion of Honor. "I am so glad you came," she said and kissed me.

We went into the living room with its priceless Gobelins and paintings, the library with a very rare eighteenth-century bed with original velvet cushions on which Napoleon used to sleep, and a rosewood inlaid desk that had been used by Talleyrand.

"Come," said Dr. Preminger, "I want to show you the most cherished of my possessions." She led me to a glass case. It con-tained a pair of shoes turned upside down; the soles were full of holes.

"These are Dr. Albert Schweitzer's famous thirty-two-year-old shoes," Dr. Preminger told me, her voice very gentle. "I asked for them when I won a bet. You see, I spent the last seventeen birthdays of Dr. Albert Schweitzer's life with him. On his eightieth birthday he told me that he did not expect to live much longer. I replied that I was willing to make a bet he would be around for his ninetieth birthday and he was. Here—" she motioned to a wooden bench—"I engraved the date of his birthday here every year. We used to sit on it together . . ." Her voice trembled a little.

"On his ninetieth birthday," she continued after a moment, "Dr. Schweitzer remembered our bet and asked how it was to be paid. The only thing I wanted were these shoes I had always seen him wear, at first to play the organ, later on the hospital compound, and finally in the muddy earth when we built the new leper village." Displayed in the case with the shoes was a black pastor's tie that also looked very well worn. "Dr. Schweitzer only wore it for funerals and insisted that it was practically new," Marion Mill Preminger said. "I told him that in America there were men who own a hundred ties. He replied amazed, 'For one neck?' "

"For Mrs. Roosevelt's last birthday I sent her a bust of Dr. Albert Schweitzer," Marion Mill Preminger told me. "I thought she would like that. I often felt that Mrs. Roosevelt could have been the model for Dr. Albert Schweitzer's innumerable quotations: 'Man belongs to man—man has rights on man, more— man has claims on man.' 'Example is not the main thing in influencing others—it is the only thing.'

"Eleanor Roosevelt understood," said Dr. Preminger, "that in 'Human Rights' the word 'Human' must be larger than 'Rights.' It was Mrs. Roosevelt who taught me that brotherly love is the only positive promise for the limitless future. And the only sure investment is to invest in people, rich or poor, ugly or beautiful, passionate or cold, young or old, educated or illiterate. People, however they differ. 'But,' Mrs. Roosevelt asked, 'do they really differ? Birth and Death, Love and Hate, Hunger and Thirst, Children and Lovers, and millions of other things are making us equal. Our similarities are greater than our differences. They always have been, they always will be.'

"Albert Schweitzer said there are only two classes of people in this world: 'helpers and nonhelpers.' Mrs. Roosevelt was a helper," Dr. Preminger said. "For her there were no prejudice barriers. She was a dreamer, and for her nothing that she set out to do was impossible. 'We must open closed doors, closed minds, closed hearts.' Mrs. Roosevelt said to me. 'We are the architects of the future of mankind. If today's problems are too much for us, how will we have the courage to meet the problems of tomorrow—tomorrow, which is already here?'

"There is an old Hungarian saga and I believe in it," Dr. Preminger said. "It says that Christ is on earth, but not in one person, in hundred of millions of people is one atom of Christ. And you can recognize these people. Mrs. Roosevelt was one of them. And yet I am sure that Eleanor Roosevelt did not know how much courage she had, as I am sure that Saints do not know that they are saints in their lifetimes, as a giant palm tree in Africa does not know how high it towers above all the other palm trees. But I felt Mrs. Roosevelt's influence when I worked for seventeen years in the leper colony in Africa and when I adopted seventeen children who call me Mother."

Marion Mill Preminger fell silent and I thought of her autobiography.

I asked, "Did you find in Africa all that you wanted? Everything?"

Dr. Preminger's dark eyes turned pensive again.

"Yes," she said after a moment's deliberation. "Everything that money cannot buy. Charity, friendship, love. This too I have learned from Mrs. Roosevelt, to discipline my own heart, to turn constructive worrying into active compassion, to swear disobedience to conformity and blind obedience to love."

Dr. Harry D. Gideonse, Chancellor of The New School in New York, is also President of Freedom House. He remembered a meeting with Mrs. Roosevelt in 1940, when he was President of Brooklyn College.

"Because I spoke up against the Nazis then," he recalled, "I was branded by some of our students as a 'warmonger.' In order to annoy me, they got a restaurant workers' union to picket a small place across the campus where I used to take my meals. I ignored the matter and it went on for several weeks, even months. One day I got Mrs. Eleanor Roosevelt to give a speech at Brooklyn College. In order to embarrass me, the union threw a picket line around the College, convinced that *Mrs. Roosevelt* would never cross a picket line.

"I myself picked up Mrs. Roosevelt at her apartment on Washington Square and escorted her to Brooklyn College. The protesters were marching around the school when we arrived. Eleanor Roosevelt marched right up to them, 'Now, gentlemen, what is all this about?' she inquired in her courteous but firm way. She listened carefully to the protesters' grievances against *me*," said Dr. Gideonse. "Then she motioned at the picket signs of the restaurant workers' union. 'If I understand you correctly,' she declared, 'this protest has nothing at all to do with the restaurant. The workers there are being treated all right and *they* have no complaints. I do not respect a picket line unless I respect what it stands for.' And with these words," Dr. Gideonse concluded his story, "Mrs. Roosevelt walked right through the crowd of protesting students."

Mr. Alger Hiss is a former State Department aide who now lives in New York's Greenwich Village. One day in June 1968, I had lunch with him in a small Italian restaurant. He was to tell me a memory about Mrs. Eleanor Roosevelt.

Mr. Hiss, about sixty, is a tall, slender man. He is very courteous, cultured, and soft spoken. His features, I thought, were rather tense.

"What I remember about Eleanor Roosevelt is not a big story really," he said, as he neatly wound his spaghetti around a spoon. "It probably will be of no use to you. It all happened in London, in January or February of 1946. The United States Mission had gone to England for the first organizing meeting of the United Nations. Mrs. Roosevelt was a United States delegate and I myself was someone they called 'liaison official.' One day a young staff member of the Belgian Mission came to me with a problem. He told me that he planned a surprise birthday party for M. Paul-Henri Spaak, the Belgian Foreign Minister and head of the Belgian Delegation. The young staff member had approached Mme. Spaak, trying to find out whether there was anything very special that M. Spaak would enjoy as a present. Mme. Spaak replied that she could not think of a single thing that her husband would need or want. 'Except,' she added as an afterthought, "Mrs. Eleanor Roosevelt as a guest at the party.'

"Would it be at all possible for me to approach Mrs. Roosevelt on this delicate matter, the Belgian staff member asked me rather timidly." Mr. Hiss continued his story. "I promised that I would try. When I went to Mrs. Roosevelt and told her about the invitation, she responded with almost girlish delight." Mr. Hiss's eyes had softened as they gazed into the past and his features had relaxed. "Really, she appeared quite flattered," he said. "Oh, of course I will be delighted to go to M. Spaak's birthday party," she said, then added, 'but if I go to a ball, I will, of course need an escort! Tell the Belgian young man that I only can attend if you can come with me.'

"And so it was arranged that way," Mr. Hiss said with a soft chuckle. "We went in Mrs. Roosevelt's official car in which she would have gone anyway, and certainly she did not need me to escort her. However, it was a magnificent affair and I shall never forget," Mr. Hiss concluded, "that night in London when I escorted Eleanor Roosevelt to a ball."

Chapter Twenty-One

The United Nations

and Human Rights

"I HAVE ON MANY STATE OCCASIONS and in my writings paid tribute to Mrs. Eleanor Roosevelt, for her devotion and dedication to the solution of the many problems that afflict human beings throughout the world," wrote President Harry S Truman in a personal letter to me on June 19, 1968. He concluded his letter with these words: "I have, as you know, officially proclaimed her the 'First Lady of the World.'"

In December of 1945, President Truman sent a message to Mrs. Eleanor Roosevelt; he reminded her that the first meeting of the United Nations General Assembly would be held in London, in January 1946. He asked her to serve as a member of the United Nations delegation. Mrs. Roosevelt accepted. She believed the United Nations to be the one hope for a peaceful world.

In the spring of 1946, President Truman nominated Eleanor Roosevelt as the United States representative to the Human Rights Commission. She was elected the first chairman of the Commission and was instrumental in drawing up the International Covenants on Human Rights.

It was in recognition of the indissoluble link between respect for human rights and human survival itself, that the United Nations Nations took upon itself the formulation of mankind's first Universal Declaration of Human Rights as a common standard of achievement for all peoples and for all nations, large and small. This Declaration was adopted without dissenting vote on December 10, 1948.

In a speech she delivered at the first anniversary celebration of the Universal Declaration of Human Rights by the United Nations, Mrs. Roosevelt said: "In every land, the people must accept and respect these rights and freedoms in their own communities and in their own lives and by so doing, create countries, and in time, a world where such freedoms are a reality."

It was Mrs. Roosevelt's conviction that only through a determination on the part of the United States to make a reality, within America and everywhere else, of the Universal Declaration of Human Rights, could there be any possibility of achieving a peaceful world order. The fundamental provision of the Declaration, Mrs. Roosevelt felt, was the right to education, for, as we are rapidly discovering in our own country, without the right to education there can be very little hope for gaining any other rights.

For Eleanor Roosevelt herself, the Universal Declaration of Human Rights was an expression of something that she had practiced all her life. In her introduction to Henry Viscardi's book *Give Us the Tools*, Eleanor Roosevelt said, "In my travels throughout the United States and in many other nations, I have been concerned with many things, but the underlying factor which is basic to all these concerns is human rights. Human rights and all that this phrase implies is based on the value of human worth and of personal dignity."

Epilogue

How do you call a halt to a book like this? There are so many more people from all over the world who have written to me about their brief meetings with Eleanor Roosevelt. I did not have the room for all of them, I sadly realize. And then, of course, there must be all those people in every part of the world who also met her but whom I did not reach with my appeal. I suppose it could go on and on without ever ending. Unhappily, I have to face the fact that there are many more Eleanor Roosevelt stories, which never will be recounted. And yet each story will live in each individual who has experienced it. It will be passed on to the next generation and the next, and Eleanor Roosevelt will continue reaching out her hand to touch many more lives everywhere.

Index

Abilities, Inc. (Human Resources and Training Institute), 91
Academy Award, 153
Addams, Jane, 170
Advance, The, 181
AFL, 179
Albert Einstein College of Medicine. *See* Einstein College of Medicine
Allen, Gracie, 147
Altman Foundation, 23
American Christian Palestine Committee, 127
American Friends Service Committee, 41, 170, 191
American Jewish Archives, 114
American Newspaper Guild, 192
American Youth for World Youth, 24
Amsterdam News, 162, 164, 166
Andersen, Hans Christian, 109
Anderson, Marian, 156, 157
Asaf Harofe Hospital, 133
Ascali, Cardinal (Archbishop of Naples), 85

Asch, Scholem, 136
Atkins, Dr. Henry A., 128
Atwood, Albert W., 232
Aufbau (Reconstruction), 34

Bach, Jean, 153
Baker, Russell, 63
Ball, Ambassador George, 196
Baruch, Bernard, 100, 101
BBC Orchestra, 108
Beersheba Youth Center, 130, 131
Belafonte, Harry, 157, 221
Bellamy, Ralph, 71
Ben-Gurion, David, 132, 133
Benny, Jack, 19, 146–48
Benton, Sidney, 182
Berlin, Irving, 136
Berlin Philharmonic, 108
Bernstein, Charles, 228–29
Bert, Ellis L., 190
Black, Algernon D., 171–75
Black, Justice and Mrs. Hugo, 156
Blair, Joseph S., 232

Blue, Effie L., 164
Borelli, Father Mario, 84–88
Boston Globe, The, 191
Boy Scouts of America, 21
Boyer, Charles, 53
Brandeis, Louis, 136
Brandeis University, 158
Brandt, Harry, 20–22, 140
Breitbach, Mrs. Emmie, 234–35
Brooklyn College, 245
Broughton, Julia, 229
Brown, Claude, 25, 32
Brownell, Attorney General Herbert, 236
Buchwald, Art, 63
Bullitt, Ambassador William C., 169–70
Burlington Mills, 99

Cahn, Rabbi Judah, 231–32
Camp Grayville, 229
Camphill Special School, 206
Cannon, Poppy, 162, 164
Cantor, Eddie, 69, 129
Cardozo, Benjamin, 136
Carson, Mrs. Gerald, 75
Carter, Claremont, 105
Cerebral Palsy Fund, 21
Chatfield, Don, 68
Child and Youth Project Department, 24
Children's Aid Society, 24
Christian Science Monitor, The, 68
Churchill, Winston, 39
Chyet, Dr. Stanley F., 114, 120
CIO, 179
Citizens Committee for Children, 180
City College of New York, 232
Civil Rights, 14
Civilian Conservation Corps, 170
Clark. Senator Bennett Champ, 156
Clark School, 101
Colitt, Jerry. *See* Old Denmark
Columbia University, 42
Columbus, Christopher, 135
Coolidge, Calvin, 55

Corr, Maureen, 115, 131, 196–200
Curnan, Archie (Tubby), 218–21
Curnan, Charles, 19, 210–11, 212, 215
Curnan, Mrs. Charles, 211, 213
Curnan, Helen, 218, 219

Daly, John, 153
Daughters of the American Revolution, 15, 156, 192
Dewey, Thomas, 75
Deyo, Jerome V., 205–6
Diller, Phyllis, 145
Displaced Persons Camps, 124
Divine, Father, 226
Dorsch, George, 96
Drewry, Dr. Elizabeth, 203–5, 208
Drogan, Abe, 51
Dubinsky, David, 136, 177–79

Ebony, 158
Einstein, Professor Albert, 131, 136
Einstein College of Medicine, 21
Eisenhower, Dwight D., 15, 72, 211
Eisenhower, Mamie, 211
Eisner, Robert, 34–36
Eleanor Roosevelt Cancer Fund, 20
Eleanor Roosevelt Foundation, 200
Elson, Hilbert, 181
Emerson, Faye, 139
Encampment for Citizenship, 171–72
Entrup, Barbara, 210
Entrup, Garret, 216–17
Entrup, Lester, 214–17
Entrup, Marge, 214
Ernst, Joan, 102
Ernst, Lily, 43
Ernst, Margaret, 101, 185
Ernst, Morris L., 101, 185

Fala, 74
Farley, Sergeant Harold, 208–9, 224–25
FBI, 187
Feldman, Rabbi Abraham J., 137
Fickett, Mary, 71

Field, Marshall, 23
Fieldston School, 172
Fisher, Dorothy, 92
Francis, Arlene, 153
Frankfurter, Felix, 136
Franklin D. Roosevelt Library, 192, 201, 203, 224
Franklin D. Roosevelt Museum, 203
Fromkin, Selma, 17–18
Fuchs, Dr. Lawrence H., 116–18
Funt, Allen, 142

General Motors, 100
Gershwin, George, 136
Gideonse, Dr. Harry D., 244
Gildzen, Alex, 63
Ginott, Dr. Haim, 132
Glazier, Sidney, 152–53
Goldberg, Arthur, 196
Golden, Harry, 72
Golden, Paulina, 213, 218–21
Goodman, Benny, 136
Gordon, Jack L., 185
Granat, Harvey, 153
Grant, Cary, 19, 153–54
Gross, Charlotte, 140–41
Guadalcanal, 142

Hadassah, 130
Haile, Rebecca Susan, 237
Halpern, Dr. E., 133
Hammerstein, Oscar, 136
Harriman, Averell, 205
Harrison, Irving, 227–28
Hayes, Helen, 147
Hearst, William Randolph, 193
Heckscher, Mrs. M. D., 84
Heifetz, Jascha, 136
Hellman, Lillian, 136
Hello, World!, 106
Helm, Admiral, 229
Helm, Mrs. Edith, 229
Hess, Dr. Albert A., 81
Hesselbarth, Suzanne, 206–8
Hessler, Carl, 236
Hillegas, Frederic, 66–68

Hillman, Sidney, 181–82
Hiroshima, 69, 70, 71
Hiss, Alger, 245–46
Hitler, Adolf, 33, 43, 186
Hoover, Herbert, 55
Hope, Bob, 142–43
Hospital for Deformities and Joint Diseases, 94
Howe, Louis, 56
Hughes, Chief Justice and Mrs. Charles, 156
Hull, Secretary of State Cordell, 41
Human Resources and Training Institute. *See* Abilities, Inc.
Human Resources Center, 90, 91
Human Rights, Commission of, 102, 116, 247
Humphrey, Mrs. Hubert, 92
Hyde Park, 21, 25, 79, 100, 106, 118, 121, 126, 127, 131, 134, 157, 158, 180, 192, 195, 206, 212, 235, 239

IBM, 100
Independent Film Journal, The, 140
India, 77
Inheritance, The, 181
Institute for Retired Professionals, 53
International Ladies Garment Workers Union, 176, 177, 202
Israel, 19, 124, 240
Israel, Bob, 111
Israel, Bonds for, 65, 236
Israel Digest, The, 133

Jenkins, Dan, 149–52
Jerusalem Post, The, 129, 131–33
J.O.B. (Just One Break), 100
Joel E. Spingarn Medal, 157
Johnson, Calvin, 162–64
Jonas, Franz, 79–80
Juliana, Queen, 73
Just One Break. *See* J.O.B.

Karplus, Gerhard E., 237–41
Karplus, Gertrude, 238–41
Katz, Leon, 49

Kaye, Danny, 148–52
Kelley, Florence, 177
Kennedy, John F., 21, 73, 191, 211, 215
Kennedy, Senator Robert F., 143, 144
Kent State University, 63
Khrushchev, Nikita S., 52, 113, 117, 190, 191, 205
Kidd, Mrs. Claire, 127–28
Kidd, Reverend Gordon L., 126–28
Kilpatrick, Dr. William H., 25
Kingdon, Dr. Frank, 169
Kleinfeld, Senator Philip M., 137
Knowland, Senator William, 47
Koch, Mrs. Reinhart W., 232
Kol, Moshe, 129–31
Kopolov, Connie, 180–81
Koussevitzky, Serge, 136

La Guardia, Fiorello, 21, 156, 182
Ladies' Home Journal, The, 162
Lattanzi, Claudio, 194–95
Lavine, Samuel R., 82
Lawrence, Gwendolyn, 167
League of Women Voters, 16
Lehman, Governor Herbert H., 99, 109, 182
Lehman, Orin, 99–100
Lendman, Rita, 235–36
Lerner, Max, 121–22
Levy, Marcia, 65–66
Lima News, The, 189
Lincoln, Abraham, 11, 55, 139, 140
Little Orchestra Society, 107
London Symphony, 108
Loretan, Dr., 104
Lyons, Ateemese, 165

MacArthur, General Douglas, 82
McCall's, 141
McCarthy, Joseph, 236, 237
McGovern, Senator George, 144
MacLeish, Archibald, 152
McNary, Senator Charles, 156
Maktos, John, 236
Malamud, Dr. Daniel I., 11

Mandelbaum, Samuel, 137
March of Dimes, 21, 151
Mark, Flip, 111
Mark Cross, 51–52
Marshall, Joseph, 203–5
Martha, Princess, 223
Maslow, Will, 166
Masons, 224
Mayer, Martha C., 81–82
Mayer, William, 109–10, 113
Mead, Dr. Margaret, 28, 186
Menschel, Freeda, 170, 171
Midtown Supper Club, 102
Milgram, Morris, 160–62
Milgrim's, 178
Miller, Arthur, 143
Miller, Mrs. Laura, 234
Monroe, Marilyn, 11
Morehead, Agnes, 145
Morgenthau, Henry, Jr., 57
Morgenthau, Mrs. Henry, Jr., 124
Morocco, Sultan of, 203
Murray, Dr. Pauli, 158–59
Murray, the Outlaw of Fala Hill, 74
Mutual Real Estate Investment Trust, 160, 161

NAACP, 162, 231
Nagasaki, 70
National Conference of Christians and Jews, 21
National Recovery Act, 182
Nehru, Prime Minister Jawaharlal, 198
Netherlands Radio, 69
Neuman, Janet, 44–45
New Deal, 139, 168
New School for Social Research, 17–18, 38, 48, 53, 105, 160, 166, 231
New York Herald Tribune, 228
New York Journal, 153
New York Post, 12, 18, 72, 143
New York Times, The, 133, 138, 156
New York University, 17, 75, 176
New York University–Bellevue Medical Center, 99

Newcomb, Professor Theodore W., 193

Norris, Val, 87

Oberlin College, 232
O'Brian, Jack, 68–69
Ochs, Adolph, 136
Old Denmark, 82–83
Orchestre de la Suisse Romande, 108
O'Reilly, James, 76
l'Organisation de Santé, 24
Otto, Susan, 110–13

Papanek, Dr. Ernst, 23–32, 80
Papanek, Dr. Helene, 32
Pasternak, Boris, 189
Patterson, Floyd, 30–31
Peabody award, 108
Peace Corps, 105, 117
Pearl Harbor, 41, 71, 96, 193
Pegler, Westbrook, 192–93
Pelswick, Rose, 153
Person, Bernard, 69
Philadelphia Orchestra, 109
Picasso, Pablo, 57
Pickett, Clarence E., 42
Pirk, Robert, S., 71
Planned Communities, Inc., 160
Pleasures in Learning, 17
Polenz, Anna, 195–96
Polier, Judge Justine Wise, 22, 123, 193
Pollick, Mrs. A. I., 169
Pollitzer, Alice K., 171–75
Potofsky, Jacob, 136, 179–80
Poulson, Norris, 46
Powell, Adam Clayton, 117
Preminger, Dr. Marion Mill, 241–44
Priester, Elena, 45–47
Priester, Helen, 45–47
Pulitzer, Joseph, 136
Quanza, 39–41
Queens College, 23

Ranis, Dr. Gustav, 119–21
Red Cross, 21, 97, 163

Reynalds, Gerald H., 229–30
Reynaud, Premier Paul, 39
Right to Work Law, 187
Robinson, Edward G., 143
Robinson, Major, 97
Robison, Dr. Sophia M., 41–42, 48, 165–66
Rodgers, Richard, 136, 143
Rogers, Kathi, 231
Rogers, Will, 222
Roosevelt, Anna, 56, 212, 225
Roosevelt, Eleanor, Cancer Fund, 20
Roosevelt, Eleanor, Foundation, 200
Roosevelt, Franklin D., 21, 33, 43, 51, 56, 71, 74, 75, 117, 132, 137, 139, 141, 168, 177, 179, 185, 186, 201, 202, 212, 216, 222, 223, 224, 225, 226, 229, 230, 233, 239
    Library, 192, 201, 203, 224
    Museum, 203
Roosevelt, Mrs. James, 56, 212, 225
Roosevelt, John A., 188, 212, 223, 235, 239
Roosevelt, Mrs. Sarah Delano, 203, 225
Roosevelt Home Club, 204, 222, 223
Rosen, Herb, 27
Rosenstein, Julia, 37–38
Rosenthal, Phyllis, 111
Rossmore, Barbara, 233–34
Rowan, Carl T., 191
Rusk, Dr. Howard, 97, 98, 99

Sachar, Dr. Abram, 62, 114–16, 119
Salk Vaccine, 21
Sarnoff, David, 136
Scarborough School, 100
Scherman, Thomas, 107–9
Schwartz, Sol, 52
Schweitzer, Dr. Albert, 241–44
Secret Service, 216
Seletski, Mollie, 106
Selkowe, Gertrude, 104–5, 134–35
Selznick, David, 136
Shein, Barbara, 214
Sinatra, Frank, 19, 141

Skidmore College, 83
Smith, Arthur E., 208, 221
Smith, Florence Pritchet, 73
Smith, Margaret Chase, 60
Smith, Moses, 222
Social Security, 217
Society for Ethical Culture, 171
Sokolsky, George E., 177
Solomon, Bernard and Susanne, 76
Sondheimer, Elizabeth, 186–89
Spaak, M. Paul-Henri, 245
Spaak, Mme. Paul-Henri, 245
Springarn, Joel E., Medal, 157
Spota, George R., 138–40, 185
Spota, George-Ann, 140
State of Israel Bonds, 59
Stein, Gertrude, 136
Sterling, Shephard, 22–23
Sternberg, Martin L. A., 103
Stevenson, Adlai, 66, 72, 155, 205
Stiefel, Erica, 134
Stiefel, Fred, 134
Strong, Mrs. Hope, 189
Sturgen, Peter, 167
Suckley, Margaret, 74
Suleiman, Sheik, 134
Sulzberger, C. L., 133
Suyin, Han, 153
Swain, Robert L., Jr., 102

Taft, Senator Robert A., 156
Taxi Drivers Union, 48
Theresienstadt, 81
Thompson, Malvina, 97, 197, 198, 229
Thompson, Roy, 72
Triangle Fire, 176
Truman, Harry, S, 21, 43, 47, 69, 70,
    82, 211, 228, 229, 247

UNICEF, 38, 107, 200
Unitarian Service Committee, 24
United Jewish Appeal, 124, 126, 218
United Nations, 71, 105, 124, 180, 198

United Nations General Assembly,
    116, 247
University of Michigan, 193
U.S. Mission to the United Nations,
    196

Val-Kill, 19, 79, 80, 106, 121, 158,
    208, 209, 210, 211, 235, 239
Vardon, Beth, 206
Vargas, President Getulio and Sen-
    hora, 192, 203
Vermes, Mrs. M., 76–77
Vienna, University of, 23
Vienna Chamber Orchestra, 108
Villager, The, 104
Viscardi, Henry, Jr., 90–101
Viscardi, Lucille, 99

Wagner, Senator Robert, 156
Wakefield, Mrs., 176
Walter Reed Hospital, 97
Warm Springs, Georgia, 233
Warm Springs Foundation, 21
Washington, George, 11
Waterhouse, Helen, 68
Wechsler, James A., 18
West, Morris, 84
West Virginia, 13, 127, 169, 185
White, Walter, 162
White Citizens Council, 162
Wilson, Earl, 143
Wiltwyck School for Boys, 21, 213
Winchell, Walter, 136
Windsor, Duke and Duchess, 39
Wise, Rabbi Stephen S., 22, 123, 136
Women's Trade Union League, 177
Work Camps for Democracy, 171
WPA, 165, 170

Yanover, Dr. Robert, 90, 95, 99
YMCA, 232
Youngman, Henry, 69
Youth Aliyah, 128–30